AF840969

A Radical Bargain for Europe

A Radical Bargain for Europe

Progressive Visions of a European Basic Income

Dominic Afscharian, Viktoriia Muliavka,
Marius S. Ostrowski, and Lukáš Siegel

ROWMAN & LITTLEFIELD
Lanham • Boulder • New York • London

Rowman & Littlefield
Bloomsbury Publishing Inc, 1359 Broadway, New York, NY 10018, USA
Bloomsbury Publishing Plc, 50 Bedford Square, London, WC1B 3DP, UK
Bloomsbury Publishing Ireland, 29 Earlsfort Terrace, Dublin 2, D02 AY28, Ireland
www.bloomsbury.com

Copyright © 2024 by The Rowman & Littlefield Publishing Group, Inc.

All rights reserved. No part of this publication may be: i) reproduced or transmitted in any form, electronic or mechanical, including photocopying, recording or by means of any information storage or retrieval system without prior permission in writing from the publishers; or ii) used or reproduced in any way for the training, development or operation of artificial intelligence (AI) technologies, including generative AI technologies. The rights holders expressly reserve this publication from the text and data mining exception as per Article 4(3) of the Digital Single Market Directive (EU) 2019/790.

British Library Cataloguing in Publication Information Available

Library of Congress Cataloging-in-Publication Data

Names: Afscharian, Dominic, author.
Title: A radical bargain for Europe : progressive visions of a European basic income / Dominic Afscharian, Viktoriia Muliavka, Marius S. Ostrowski, and Lukáš Siegel
Description: Lanham, Maryland : Rowman & Littlefield, 2024. | Includes bibliographical references and index.
Identifiers: LCCN 2024015512 (print) | LCCN 2024015513 (ebook) | ISBN 9781538167922 (cloth) | ISBN 9781538167939 (epub)
Subjects: LCSH: Basic income—Political aspects—European Union countries. | Basic income—Government policy—Europe Union countries.
Classification: LCC HC240.9.I5 A3 2024 (print) | LCC HC240.9.I5 (ebook) | DDC 331.2/36094—dc23/eng/20240416
LC record available at https://lccn.loc.gov/2024015512
LC ebook record available at https://lccn.loc.gov/2024015513

For product safety related questions contact productsafety@bloomsbury.com.

Contents

Acknowledgments

This book is the culmination of a research project that began in 2020, when we each decided to confront the epochal horror and existential isolation visited upon the world by the COVID-19 pandemic by joining the virtual community of the Foundation for European Progressive Studies' Young Academics Network (FEPS YAN). Spurred on by the hope and dynamism that FEPS YAN brought into our lives, we converted our shared interest in better understanding the idea of a Universal Basic Income into a deep, granular engagement with every conceivable side of the UBI debate—albeit through the as-yet untried prism of the European tier of policymaking. One policy report, several articles, many presentations, and more Google Meet calls than we could dare to count later, we can say with some degree of justification that we have given the idea of a European UBI substantial attention within social policy discourse. We would like to express our considerable gratitude to Elena Gil, Céline Guedes, Ania Skrzypek, and Angelika Striedinger for first giving us the opportunity to join forces as a collaborative group, and to our colleagues at all our respective institutions for their advice, guidance, and support, which has proved to be of immeasurable benefit in the development of the arguments we outline in this book.

For a progressive Europe!

Dominic Afscharian
Viktoriia Muliavka
Marius S. Ostrowski
Lukáš Siegel

Introduction

For decades, and in various precursor forms even for centuries, the idea of a Universal Basic Income (UBI) has captured the imagination of thinkers, activists, and politicians alike. However, its implementation still seems to lie far outside the realm of current possibility. Politicians of all partisan stripes suspect the idea of being a plot or a scam concocted by their ideological opponents with the worst conceivable intentions. UBI has been framed as everything from a 'neoliberal' assault on the welfare state to a way of introducing communism through the back door, a defeatist entrenchment of the motive logic of capitalism or its destabilisation and rejection. This has left the idea of a UBI cast, often and determinedly, in negative terms: as an ideological foil, a shibboleth, even a demonic spectre, that encapsulates everything supporters of a given ideology rail against, and represents the direct antithesis of everything they stand for. The task of making a positive case for UBI is left to a handful of advocates scattered asymmetrically across the groups, movements, and parties that make up the European ideological spectrum—typically in relative ideological isolation but more occasionally in tentative alliances forged across ideological lines.

In this book, we develop this collaborative tendency to push back against the suspicions that surround much ideological discourse around UBI. Instead, we ask how different ideologies—activist groups, movements, and parties—might design a UBI in line with their preferences. Specifically, we ask how they might construct a UBI designed and implemented not at the level of the nation-state, but at the European institutional tier, as a specific development of the pro-European tendencies that these ideologies generally share. We embark on a journey through the worlds of five progressive political ideologies and the ideal varieties of a European UBI they might favour. Finally, we explore where they overlap and diverge—and what kind of European UBI they might rally around as a consensus position.

A LAYERED DILEMMA

As the twenty-first century advances, Europe's democracies face a fundamental dilemma. One of their abiding strengths is their ability to give representation to diverging views in their societies. At the same time, protracted and unresolved disagreements can block crucial policy progress. The European Union (EU) reproduces a very similar dynamic in its attempt to bring together very different states—however partially or gradually—in an 'ever closer union' (Belgium et al. 1957, 2) that is 'united in diversity' (European Union 2022). As authoritarian movements and Eurosceptics become ever more daring in leveraging prominent examples of lengthy decision-processes to frame democracies and the EU itself as inherently dysfunctional (Condruz-Băcescu 2014), the future of Europe as a united, democratic entity on the geopolitical stage is increasingly at stake (Afscharian and Ostrowski 2022). Political actors urgently need to find ways to achieve policy progress more effectively, while maintaining adequate space for controversial debates within democratic processes and institutions. Considering the rising tensions over inequality and social precarity as well as anti-democratic actors' tendencies to politicise them, the need to resolve this dilemma is becoming particularly pressing in the realm of social policy.

However, in attempting to achieve substantial reforms, democratic political movements face yet another challenge. As electorates become increasingly diverse across the EU and within its member states, it becomes proportionally more difficult to rally large societal groups around a common cause. This development is particularly distinct for parties on the political left and, more generally, 'progressives' who want to push forward meaningful change within and beyond their societies. While European social democrats in particular mobilised strong workers' movements in the nineteenth century, and later united workers and key fractions of the middle class behind shared goals in the twentieth century, electoral interests have become too individualised—or rather, collective claims for support have become too diverse and cross-cutting—for such unified progressive projects to still hold up in contemporary politics. Institutional arrangements in countries like the United States and (to a lesser extent) the UK have remedied some effects of this development, but they can only superficially conceal structural developments that become clearer within the EU: for the last several decades, many European democracies have experienced increasing electoral atomisation. This has been reflected in long-term developments within their various respective party systems. While certain countries, such as Belgium and the Netherlands, already had highly pluralistic systems characterised by many political parties, countries like Austria, Germany, Italy, and Spain have seen an increasing atomisation of their party systems as well, with far-right, far-left, and green parties gaining ground.

The effect of this has been to make it increasingly difficult to form working, stable majority governments. As a result, progressive as well as conservative parties in countries such as Austria, Germany, and the Netherlands have pursued a strategy of forming coalitions built on the lowest common denominator between their members. This can have a strong impact on progress in policy fields that are particularly contested between the member parties in the government, as agreements on substantial reforms become harder to achieve. Social policy is a prime example of this, as it constitutes the main traditional line of division between the political left and right: Should the state intervene and redistribute resources, or should free markets be left to their own devices? Thanks to these fundamental cleavages, deadlocks can easily emerge. These, in turn, can prevent necessary changes in one of the policy fields that can most easily be leveraged by authoritarian movements to dismantle democracies if reforms are stalled—as well as the EU from within.

SEEKING REMEDIES

To resolve such deadlocks in social policy and beyond, one strategy—at least in theory—is to attempt to form coherently progressive coalitions (Ostrowski 2020). However, such coalitions often do not materialise in practice due to the sheer diversity of their various members' electoral and policy demands. Different parties might agree on a broad outline of culturally progressive visions of a cosmopolitan future, while disagreeing vehemently on their preferred socioeconomic policies—or indeed *vice versa* (Zürn and De Wilde 2016). In such cases, fundamental disagreement on one ideological dimension could overshadow in-principle agreement on another, thus precisely reinforcing the deadlocks these coalitions are intended to solve. This puts progressives on an uneven playing field with conservatives, as these deadlock conditions inherently favour the preservation of the *status quo*, while explicitly hindering any kind of progress. Again, this risks playing into authoritarian narratives about the supposed dysfunction of the EU and its member democracies when it comes to far-reaching social reforms.

In this book, we explore how progressive democratic actors across Europe might be able to overcome this issue in the realm of social policy. Considering the complexity of the matters at stake, we do not claim to offer a one-size-fits-all solution that can single-handedly resolve such democratic deadlocks altogether. Rather, we propose one specific, carefully defined building-block that has the potential to underpin what would need to become a much broader strategy of fostering democratic resilience.

More concretely, we argue that progressive democrats can pursue one pathway of political action more systematically than is currently the case in many European democracies: intra-parliamentary 'agenda coalitions'. Rather than having to agree on every policy in all imaginable policy fields in the form of a coalition agreement, parties in an 'agenda coalition' could try to achieve shared goals in a specific area by forming temporary coalitions around a single policy (or a small number of policies). Crucially, such a policy would have to be innovative enough to bridge (some of) the divides that prevented cooperation between the various actors involved up to this point. If disagreement on traditional policy approaches is so fundamental that it blocks any social policy progress at all, specific innovative policy options could potentially be embraced and deployed by agenda coalitions in parliament if the actors involved share sufficiently compatible idealistic goals. For instance, social democrats and liberals might share the ideal of emancipating individuals and fostering open societies but disagree on whether this would be better achieved by expanding the roster of civic rights or by directly redistributing money to those in material need.

AN IDEAL POLICY?

Finding concrete examples for innovative policies that could enable intra-parliamentary 'agenda coalitions' in the social realm while also fostering meaningful change is far from a trivial task. While many reform options come to mind that might fit an individual party's preferences, there is no policy—especially no *social* policy with the potential of fostering fundamental societal change—that is without its critics. This becomes even more complex if we widen our gaze to consider not only the (shifting and expanding) ideological spectrum within any single member state, but also the 'higher-level' spectrum in place across the EU at large. After all, if the goal is to find social policy reforms that not only stabilise European democracies, but also shore up European unity, they must deliver a clear vision of a 'social Europe' as well.

All things considered, this might seem an impossible task. Crucially, however, the social policies that would make appropriate candidates for these progressive agenda coalitions do not need to command universal support. Rather, they only need to capture sufficiently large numbers of actors within a sufficient number of political groups to add up to a majority on aggregate. The empirics of how many individual politicians within a party support a policy depend on a vast number of factors such as individual conviction, vote-seeking, or office-seeking (Strom 1990). However, the theoretical compatibility between policy ideas and political parties can be examined using ideology as a proxy. By implication, in order to establish whether a policy idea carries the potential of rallying agenda coalitions around it, said idea must be scrutinised through the lenses of various political ideologies. If these ideologies—at least in theory—share a common denominator of support for a basic policy idea, its associated concrete policy design can be adjusted to deliver on these areas of common ground while avoiding ideologically rooted conflicts. In the case of progressive social policy reform across the EU, this implies comparing a policy idea that reflects, or aligns with, the essential concepts of those dominant political ideologies in Europe that retain considerable potential for progressive thinking. Against this background, a theoretically ideal social policy for the approach we propose is one that enjoys *some* support across the political spectrum, and one where the cleavages over it (*for* and *against*) cut across party lines. Otherwise, if cleavages ran strictly and uniformly between parties, the vote shares of these parties would perfectly represent wider social support for the associated policy in parliament. This, in turn, would render cross-partisan agenda coalitions impossible and the political strategies associated with them ineffective and irrelevant.

But which policy ideas might theoretically be suitable for these kinds of agenda coalitions in the future? One option for such a policy has dominated social policy debates for years like few others: UBI. Putting aside the separate question of whether or not one agrees with the idea of a UBI, it offers an ideal example for illustrating the concepts we develop in this book. This is not *despite,* but precisely *because* the policy tends to evoke strong opinions among a diverse array of political ideologies—including the passionate opposition we alluded to before. Unlike many other social policies, supporters and opponents of UBI can be found across party lines—albeit for often very different reasons. Among the sceptics, there is a shared tendency towards mutual distrust. On the one hand, socioeconomically left-leaning actors accuse UBI of being a 'neoliberal' project that aims to erode the welfare state and save capitalism from its timely demise (Lombardozzi and Pitts 2020; Mathers 2020). On the other hand, socioeconomically right-leaning actors are afraid that a UBI would be used by the left to provide welfare for the 'lazy' and 'undeserving' and would act as a negative work incentive (Hamilton and Martin-West 2019; Zelleke 2008; Bick, Fuchs-Schündeln, and Lagakos 2018; Midões 2019).

Interestingly, these ideologically very different critiques of the same basic policy idea echo a similar fundamental distrust: A policy that is presented by the 'other side' as a tool for emancipating people and for fostering a more open society is actually allegedly intended by said 'other side' to achieve the exact opposite. By logical implication, however, there are also other members of the same ideological movements *on both sides* who speak out in support of UBI. Critics of UBI are extremely keen to point out the voices of UBI supporters among their ideological opponents, but far less willing to acknowledge the same voices among their ideological allies. In all of this, it is impossible to find one political ideology that takes a clear lead on either supporting or rejecting UBI. This lack of any clear ideological 'belonging' makes UBI more-or-less unique among contemporary social policy proposals that are both highly salient and contested in political and public discourse. It also makes the idea of a European UBI (EUBI) particularly interesting as an option for giving the EU a concrete social dimension that is not clearly associated with a single ideology. Thus, UBI is a prime example for an idea that could in principle unite actors from different affiliations across Europe under a single common agenda coalition.

TOWARDS A UNIFIED UBI?

Although an (E)UBI presents an ideal case to explore the options for agenda coalitions in Europe, such coalitions are yet to be formed in practice. The mutual distrust among ideological movements towards each other's conceptions of UBI up to now has essentially stymied the emergence of a united progressive vision for a UBI. This is particularly puzzling as UBI holds considerable untapped electoral potential. According to public opinion research, the policy enjoys 'overwhelming' public support (Roosma and Van Oorschot 2020, 203) across many European countries (Bartha et al. 2020, 67–69; Baute and Meuleman 2020). In addition, UBI is far from being an esoteric or niche proposition, as its salience is high in public, political, and academic debates alike (Afscharian et al. 2021, 1–2). In short, UBI is a well-known, popular proposal with considerable capacity to solve a fundamental problem for many parties. This only makes it more surprising, however, that it has not yet been more widely embraced.

In this book, we address this puzzle and explore the theoretical potential for agenda coalitions around a EUBI. We reveal the scope for potential agreement between ideologies that might enable the formation of agenda coalitions over a UBI, as well as the disagreements that might prevent such coalitions from taking shape. We approach this task from an interdisciplinary perspective, incorporating insights from policy analysis, political theory, history, and philosophy.

As a first step, we define the key policy concepts of this book. In doing so, we elaborate on what a UBI generally is (and what it is not), what could constitute a 'European UBI', and to what extent there can be divergences in how the policy is concretely conceptualised. Second, we discuss potential arguments for UBI viewed through the lenses of different political ideologies. Our focus on the arguments in favour of UBI should not be mistaken as an insouciant negation of the many important arguments against the policy that exist and circulate in the debates on various ideological sides. However, since our conceptual starting point consists in a desire to better understand the potential appeal of UBI from different theoretical perspectives, we have decided on an economy of resources and space that allows us to conduct a deeper engagement with the reasons why different ideological groups, movements, or parties may be positively interested in UBI. For readers interested in overviews of arguments that include critiques of UBI, we recommend our previous research in this space, where we offer an at-a-glance map of the debates on UBI, both *for* and *against* (Afscharian et al. 2021, 2022b).

From the arguments we identify as key to different ideologies' theoretical interest in UBI, we derive several characteristics and priorities for policy design. In our choice of political ideologies, we focus on those which we categorise under a very broad interpretation of the label of 'progressivism'. These ideologies are social democracy, the far left (in its many and varied permutations), green ideology, liberalism, and—perhaps counterintuitively to some—Christian democracy. For each ideology, we engage with the key arguments from its internal debates on UBI and examine which facets of and positions on UBI appeal to the core constitutive elements of different political ideologies. In line with this, we elaborate on the implications that these different arguments have for concrete policy design, seen through the ideal-typical lenses for each ideology. This means that we propose one very rough policy design for each ideology that would adjust key elements of UBI to deliver on the respective ideology's priorities. The result is a group of five distinct progressive visions of UBI with some overlaps and some areas of disagreement. Following this, we elaborate our concept of intra-parliamentary agenda coalitions in greater detail. We then reflect on the commonalities and differences between the five ideal-typical, broadly progressive visions of UBI and propose agenda coalitions that might be formed around each of these policy designs.

Through these steps, this book makes several key contributions. From a theoretical perspective, it scrutinises the widespread empirical claim that UBI appeals to various political ideologies. It substantiates this claim in concrete terms by providing an overview of where the overlaps and divides between the ideologies we examine lie. From the perspective of policy development, our work demonstrates how a UBI could be designed in practice to strike an optimal balance between achieving its professed goals and avoiding potential pitfalls. Finally, considering the political dimension, our results give progressive stakeholders a clearer sense of where compromises need to be made in order to form new coalitions, and to achieve substantial social policy progress in a time of diversified electorates and partisan deadlocks.

This book is positioned at the intersection of academic and policy research, between social science and social activism. It is neither purely an empirical analysis, nor an advocacy piece for or against UBI. Rather, it is intended as a specific theoretical reflection on ways to build bridges between policy ideas and political practice. As such, the arguments presented throughout this book reflect theoretical considerations for how those who are drawn to UBI might argue for the scheme if they base their arguments on the core concepts of different political ideologies. Accordingly, we invite readers to critically reflect on the arguments we present here through the lens of their respective political preferences. Although we present concrete proposals for policy design, the ultimate point of this book is not to develop a ready-made UBI that only needs to be implemented. Rather, we want to sensitise those participating in UBI debates to a crucial yet often overlooked fact: UBI is not the 'simple solution' as which it is often framed. Just like any other policy, UBI has dials and parameters that can be adjusted to achieve fundamentally different outcomes (Aerts, Marx, and Verbist 2023). As a result, public debates on UBI that demand to know whether one is 'for or against UBI' are misleading. There is not just one UBI, but rather there are many possible UBIs. Ultimately, whether we choose to support or reject UBI as a social policy scheme is thus also a matter of how well a particular UBI policy design matches our ideological preferences. Answering this question is, in turn, in the hands of anyone who chooses to participate in the UBI debates circulating in society today.

Chapter 1

The Fundamental Concept of a European UBI

If we acknowledge that there is not just 'one UBI' but many possible versions of it, this still raises an important question: If many policies can be labelled a 'UBI', what does this label actually stand for? Generally, the more diverse the policy ideas that are subsumed under the same conceptual umbrella, the higher the potential for their overarching concept to become semantically overstretched. If this process is taken to its extremes, this can lead to UBI losing its meaning entirely and becoming terminologically vacuous and arbitrary—a 'catch-all' term that does nothing to advance progress in the social policy sphere. In this chapter, we therefore turn to clarify what we mean by the concept of UBI, and in particular its European version.

Concept stretching is no purely theoretical risk. Contemporary public debates regularly blur the lines between minimum income schemes and UBI (e.g., Thorwarth 2022; Lyman 2019). Such tendencies could dilute the ambitions of UBI, causing theoretical ideas to become increasingly detached from political discourse. As 'UBI' is a popular term with wide public recognition, politicians may be tempted to use it when referring to less disruptive policies (e.g., Giugliano 2019). In turn, this may numb the public to the core principles of UBI and thus deprive the initial idea of its singular appeal. For instance, needs-tested social assistance schemes may end up being rhetorically framed as universal policies by eliding them with UBI, subsumed under the vague label of 'basic income'. However, both approaches build on fundamentally different understandings of social justice. Hence, overly broad interpretations of the term 'UBI' may do a disservice to proponents of both universal and needs-tested welfarist schemes.

We explicitly acknowledge that such risks are something of an occupational hazard of working with the broad interpretations of UBI we have chosen to explore here. However, overly narrow UBI definitions are no remedy for all the conceptual issues with UBI either. For instance, a narrow definition of UBI may conflict with the ideas of justice inherent to various political ideologies—which often treat questions of 'fairness' and 'due' from a whole-population perspective. Meanwhile, an understanding of UBI that requires strong redistributive efforts may contradict market-liberal ideas. Even so, liberal actors may still sympathise with the general idea of a UBI—although they might prefer one that is constructed a little differently. Overly narrow definitions can thus lead to conceptual confusion within the debate as a whole if different actors with incompatible ideas of UBI try to claim sole ownership over the issue.

It is certainly useful to have a clear understanding of what UBI entails and what it excludes. However, in this book, we refer to UBI in a deliberately broad sense both for normative and pragmatic reasons. First, academic scholarship is increasingly producing research on public opinion on UBI (Laenen 2023) that is starting to feature prominently within the broader debate (e.g., Bartha et al. 2020; Baute and Meuleman 2020; Parolin and Siöland 2020; Roosma and Van Oorschot 2020). Yet survey respondents might fundamentally disagree on what UBI should precisely entail. Thus, much of the existing research already builds on an understanding of UBI that is open to interpretation, at least to a certain extent. Using an overly narrow interpretation of UBI would therefore risk introducing a subtle but significant disconnect with the findings that research has produced up to now.

Second, leaving sufficient room for interpretation is an inevitable feature of any salient debate on policies that do not yet exist in practice. If many people discuss an idea without a universally agreed-upon point of reference, it is fairly inevitable that diverging interpretations of this idea will arise. Such a point of reference could conceivably consist in a policy that has already been implemented in practice. But this is clearly not yet the case for UBI, which exists in practice so far only in the form of isolated trials (Afscharian et al. 2022a). Accordingly, any contribution that speaks about UBI in general terms must account for a certain degree of ambiguity in the debate. Simply ignoring this ambiguity is a viable option only for purely theoretical work. However, since the aim of our book is to sketch out relatively concrete political scenarios, we attempt to factor in a certain degree of conceptual breadth to our analysis.

Third, the idea of UBI has a long history throughout which the term has been used in various ways—referring, among other things, to endowments, dividends from holding a stake in the overarching economy, an income guarantee, and proposals that best resemble existing systems of pensions or employment benefits. This implies that several valid interpretations of UBI exist, simply due to long-lasting path dependencies in the theoretical hinterland from which they originally emerged.

Fourth, from a normative perspective, a broad interpretation of UBI quite simply allows for a more inclusive debate. This is key, given that if a UBI is implemented, it may have major impacts on large parts of societies that today are (as often as not) extensively democratically organised. We therefore consider the inclusion of diverging views and interpretations of UBI as an essential ingredient of a UBI that is palatable to the democratic systems and institutions that predominantly make up European political space.

Finally, this book attempts to illustrate the large variety of possible (E)UBI policy designs against the background of different progressive political ideologies. An overly narrow definition of UBI would, by construction, exclude some or even most of the wide range of parallel visions of UBI these ideologies have to offer—which would defeat the purpose of our analysis.

All these considerations lead us to one clear conclusion: before discussing the idea of an EUBI through different ideological lenses, we need to clarify the basic concept of UBI without falling into this trap of overly narrow definitions. In the following sections, we engage with what UBI means, first and foremost in general terms. Within the scope of the resulting basic definition, we systematise the various lines that give different types of UBI their unique character, and their capacity to respond to different ideological preferences. Finally, based on these considerations, we outline what we mean when we refer to the basic idea of an EUBI.

UNIVERSAL BASIC INCOME

Given the considerations above, it can be challenging to find a definition of UBI that is both delimited enough to avoid conceptual confusion, yet also has enough scope to do justice to the diversity of a debate on a policy that as yet exists largely in theoretical form. As a starting point, we use one of the most prominent definitions of UBI, provided by the Basic Income Earth Network (BIEN), which contains many of the key elements necessary to understand what a UBI can entail. As one of the world's most prominent associations of UBI advocates, BIEN has considerable influence on the debate, and its definition shares many of the key characteristics of how the term 'UBI' is used in literature and public discourse. BIEN defines UBI as 'a periodic cash payment unconditionally delivered to all on an individual basis, without means-test or work requirement' (Basic Income Earth Network 2021). BIEN further specifies that UBI should be paid out in regular intervals in 'an appropriate medium of exchange' to enable individual spending choices. This explicitly precludes vouchers and in-kind options such as services, and since it is paid directly and automatically to individuals, it eliminates any conditional components related to other sources of wealth and income or employment status.

This definition offers a practical common ground for various interpretations of UBI. However, it precludes a number of policy attributes that could result in arrangements that closely approximate the idea of UBI. For instance, rejecting any role for means-testing may also exclude policies based on the idea of 'nudging'. Policymakers might, for instance, opt to make default payments conditional on means while maintaining the right for everyone to actively claim their payments if they wish to. This design would violate the strict absence of means-testing—but it would be hard to argue that it would not constitute a form of UBI. The strict condition of making payments on an individual basis further precludes a potentially important leeway in cases where designated caretakers would need access to the respective funds allotted to another individual—such as parents on behalf of children, family members with power of attorney, and other similar 'caregiving' scenarios. Overall, however, the BIEN conception offers a practical working definition of UBI that lays important groundwork for the analysis below.

These limitations of BIEN's definition can become problematic when discussing a variety of possible approaches to designing a UBI. Since there is high potential for such UBI policy designs to differ substantially from each other, we consider it a more productive approach to think of UBI in terms of a number of spectrums of policy design. For such an approach, De Wispelaere and Stirton (2004) suggest a list of dimensions to systematise attributes of different UBI proposals, covering universality, individuality, conditionality, uniformity, frequency, duration, modality, adequacy, and the fuzziness of policy design. In addition, we suggest that funding can be justified as its own dimension for the purposes of our later discussions. This list stands in contradiction to some elements of the BIEN definition. After all, the BIEN definition considers certain elements of UBI to be fixed, which De Wispelaere and Stirton instead discuss as potential dimensions of variation. It is worth outlining in greater detail what this can imply for policy design.

The dimension of *universality* describes the 'extent of the population that is covered by a given policy' (De Wispelaere and Stirton 2004, 267). Simply put, this implies the question: Who should receive the money? Purists might respond that this dimension of variation undercuts one of the most central elements of UBI. A universal monetary payout, so the argument goes, would simply need to be paid out to everyone *tout court*. However, a consistent application of this line of reasoning would necessitate that every single individual across the globe would need to be included in a truly universal UBI scheme. Any attempt to limit it to the citizens of one nation, to insert borders and boundaries into the definition of 'universality', would imply limiting the 'universe' within which UBI is intended to operate. Once this option for policy design is enabled, other definitions of UBI's 'universe' may also be considered legitimate. UBI could, for instance, also be limited to every (permanent) resident or as a partial basic income to every child or pensioner. Thus, what appears initially as the simple and straightforward idea of UBI being paid out unconditionally to 'all' turns out on closer inspection to be anything but trivial.

The matter of universality is closely tied to the understanding of legitimacy in state-building. Thus, variation between UBI proposals is likely to correlate with different ideas of 'belonging' and 'community'. This is particularly apparent when discussing the prospects for an EUBI. The EU as an 'ever closer union' (Belgium et al. 1957, 2) that is 'united in diversity' (European Union 2022) leaves a significant degree of room for controversies over who 'belongs'—what the 'extensity' of the EU should be, with what intensity its existence should be affirmed, and what the procedures and timescales are for its formation (Ostrowski 2023b). Such controversies include the question of whether and when migrants from outside the EU should get access to an EUBI scheme. They may also look inwards and, for instance, limit access to the EU member states who are also part of the Eurozone—that is, EUBI as a marker of 'fully committed' economic integration. Further, universal access to a social policy scheme tends to be linked to particular notions of solidarity, which means that UBI debates in the EU have to confront disputes over the appropriate level at which a UBI scheme should be implemented. Some advocates might argue that 'true' solidarity can only be shown locally, whereas others might regard the nation-state as the intuitively correct level for implementing a UBI. By contrast, other voices might push for implementation at the EU level, perhaps even to develop a stronger sense of European solidarity. We will discuss these considerations on the involvement of the EU in further detail below. For now, the key takeaway is that different ideas of UBI can diverge greatly where their target group is concerned.

A closely linked but less obviously controversial locus of variation is the dimension of *individuality*, defined as the 'standard unit at which a policy is directed' (De Wispelaere and Stirton 2004, 267). Again, the question that follows from this is, quite simply, who should receive the money that UBI awards. However, individuality is not concerned with the overall target group (i.e., UBI's 'universe') as such but rather defines who receives the respective payments *within* this target group. As we briefly suggested above, a UBI could be paid—among other possible 'targets'—to individuals, households, or caretakers. In any of these scenarios, the per capita payouts would be equivalent. What changes is whether they are pooled and received by a single individual who then further distributes them, or whether every individual in society directly and personally receives their payout from the state.

Again, a purist approach would reject this dimension of variation, on the basis that such pooled payouts harbour potentially paternalistic implications. Precisely on these grounds, the basic definition of UBI presented above aims to standardise matters by limiting the scheme to individuals themselves. However, this artificially narrows the scope of possible policies and, thus, the compatibility between UBI and some of the more communitarian-minded political ideologies. More importantly, the implication would be that a fully unconditional regular payment of money to every household would no longer be considered a UBI. Yet such a scheme could hardly usefully be categorised as anything else except a UBI—and it is entirely plausible that public discourse would perceive any push to introduce such a policy as self-evidently a move towards UBI. Further, such a policy could, depending on precisely how it is designed, deliver on most—if not all—the goals associated with UBI. This is especially true in societies in which most individuals are free to choose whether to live in their own households or to share them with others. Similar considerations also apply in the case of caretakers. There are plausible cases in which an individual would not gain much freedom if they were to receive a UBI themselves as opposed to a caretaker receiving it on their behalf—children, the elderly, or individuals living with severe health conditions might well struggle to make use of a UBI that is paid out on a strictly individual basis. Thus, the dimension of individuality must also be regarded as an option for variation within UBI proposals, especially when considering the various directions in which political ideologies can take the concept.

A similar logic applies to the dimension of *conditionality*, the 'extent of conditions built into a policy that may restrict a person's eligibility for a service' (De Wispelaere and Stirton 2004, 268). This dimension asks: What does a person have to do to receive payouts? At first sight, any conditionality built into a nominally universal policy seems counterintuitive. As we have already seen, the labelling of conditional minimum income schemes as a 'UBI' can quickly cause conceptual confusion and undercut what makes UBI as an idea unique and distinct. Nonetheless, there are specific cases in which some conditionality may be introduced while leaving the key pillars of UBI intact. For instance, policymakers might want to temporarily withhold payments in case a person commits a crime, or to enforce pending fees or penalties with reduced bureaucratic effort.

There are good arguments against such an approach. For example, it is easy to see how opening up the possibility of such cases might run the risk of starting down a slippery slope of increasingly egregious contingency. Once some conditionality is introduced, this might gradually grow to undermine the basic idea of UBI, ultimately leading to a *de facto* conditional scheme tied to arbitrary criteria justifying state intervention. However, as long as such cases occurred only in rare and clearly specified instances, it would still be difficult to make the case that the associated scheme would not represent a kind of UBI at its core. After all, it would remain a regular monetary payment to all members of society that fundamentally does not come with any strings attached. In this scenario, payments are only partially withheld if an individual were liable to pay an equivalent fine anyway, which would result in the same net transfers as a (bureaucratically more convoluted) scheme that did not withhold payments but instead demanded them back via fines.

Other limitations to conditionality might be introduced through the mode of accessing payments. For instance, money could be paid out only upon active application, though without any option for the state to refuse payments. This would still imply a universal right to basic income, albeit one with a built-in nudge to avoid the wealthiest members of society claiming their money. While this approach certainly operates at the limits of what would still be considered a UBI, some minimal conditionality is inherent to any UBI design. As monetary payments have to be transferred through some channel such as a bank account, any payment is in principle at least conditional on the availability (and effective operation) of the requisite infrastructure. While this point might seem trivial at first glance, it can pose serious challenges for implementation, especially at the EU level. Thus, the ways in which an (E)UBI would attempt to overcome these challenges *de facto* defines parts of the scheme's element of conditionality.

A potentially less controversial dimension of variation between UBI designs concerns their *uniformity*, which refers to the 'extent to which all those who are eligible receive a similar level of benefit' (De Wispelaere and Stirton 2004, 269). Here, the question for policy design is whether every recipient of UBI should receive the same amount of money or if some should receive more than others. Again, it is easy to see how critiques of this might form fairly intuitively based on considerations around the scope of social justice. One might argue that a universalistic idea of justice should imply that everyone has to be treated equally—otherwise, especially if pushed to its extremes, variation in uniformity could open the floodgates to concept stretching. For instance, politicians might claim the label of 'UBI' to introduce a means-tested minimum income scheme where only a few receive sizeable, amounts of money, with everyone else only receiving a symbolic payment such as €0.01. Such a scheme would still technically be delivering on the basic mechanisms of UBI but use variation in uniformity to undercut the substance of the underlying policy idea.

While critiques along these lines are entirely valid, even a purist perspective is likely to concede that variation in uniformity might need to happen to some degree. As the cost of living varies significantly between different regions—depending on the nature and level of industrial development, population density, infrastructure availability, and many other factors—UBI schemes would need to respond to these differences, at least to some extent. If they did not do so, UBI would provide those living in low-cost regions with a considerable income, even while it is reduced to little more than a *de facto* symbolic payment in high-cost areas. Thus, the same logic used to critique variation in uniformity becomes a justification for non-uniform payments as soon as cost of living is factored in. Varying on the dimension of uniformity, UBI levels could be fully tied to the cost of living, to regional purchasing power levels, to median income levels, or to no indicator at all.

Besides the indicators themselves, the size and character of the regional entity that acts as the barometer to measure these indicators is key for policy design. For example, UBI levels might be varied between states, regions, or even cities. This implies a trade-off in policy design: a more 'jurisdictional' approach would broadly increase UBI's capabilities of reducing poverty in a granular—even targeted—way but at the cost of a significant uptick in bureaucratic complexity. However, this dimension of variation can also be used as a lever to compensate economically weaker regions. Thus, adjusting UBI to local standards of living becomes not only a way of making the scheme appropriate for high-cost areas but also a dial that can be adjusted to achieve more nuanced economic effects. In turn, the lack of practical experience with large-scale UBI schemes implies that such decisions could also be prone to high risks, which simply means that any implementation along these lines would need to be monitored extremely closely.

Besides this regional dimension, two temporal elements of UBI policy design can exert considerable additional impact on the scheme's real-world implications. *Frequency* and *duration* ask how often payments are made and for how long a recipient can expect to receive them. These dimensions of variation are among the least controversial. This is especially true for frequency. Within the parameters of the BIEN definition, this could in principle be set in any way except for a single one-off payment, which would properly be seen as a 'windfall' endowment. Typical examples for frequency are weekly, monthly, or yearly payments—in line with the familiar frequencies of wage slips, salary payments, and tax returns. Again, any concrete policy design for UBI faces some trade-offs here. Short payment intervals would emphasise the aim of UBI as providing a minimum of monetary means, designed to avoid dependency. For instance, weekly payments would imply that no individual could lose their UBI beyond the threshold of seven days due to risky spending decisions. However, this would also limit individual independence concerning large, one-off consumption or investment choices.

Conversely, such expenditure would become possible if UBI were to be paid out in larger sums at longer intervals. Choosing the beginning of each year as the point of payout would further enable annual consumption smoothing. An individual may face different levels of monthly costs at different times of the year—such as fluctuating financial burdens due to increased energy costs during cold seasons or higher expenditure on leisure during typical vacation times. Here, a yearly one-off payment could maximise individual flexibility to adjust spending appropriately. Proponents of more regular payments might object that recipients of UBI could also simply save up their weekly or monthly payments for hard times. However, this would counteract the main argument for regular payments, which assumes individual spending behaviour is too short-run-oriented to guarantee long-term security. Both of these preferences thus have reasonable arguments on their side, and policy design must ultimately follow political priorities.

In terms of duration, the purist view on UBI is somewhat clearer. Viewed through this lens, the simplest proposal would be a UBI paid over the course of an entire life. Such a policy design would consistently deliver on the principles that guide UBI debates, since it maximises the aim that everyone should receive a regular income, with no strings attached. By the same token, proponents of this approach might reject proposals like a UBI only for pensioners or those in social care (see, e.g., Sargeant et al. 2022) as insufficient partial basic incomes. However, real-life policy design faces constraints that can easily be ignored in a purely theoretical scenario. For instance, fiscal constraints might lead to a trade-off between adequacy and duration. Policymakers may have to make decisions between covering everyone at a lower income level or covering only some parts of society at a higher level.

These issues would further intersect with justice considerations and perceptions of 'deservingness' (van Oorschot 2000), as some might find it easier to support a basic income for those who are not of working age. It would be a valid objection to argue that this would effectively limit UBI to a universal basic pension scheme, which goes against the hopes that UBI might be used to emancipate individuals from the social pressure to work. However, this underestimates the dependencies that can come about as a consequence of purely contributory pension schemes and assumes the absence of any other constraints. The dimension of duration becomes even more complicated if we consider applying it to young children rather than pensioners as UBI recipients. Here, conflicts might arise with strict interpretations of individuality. Young children may benefit less from independently having a regular income at their disposal than adults. By contrast, their caretakers could use this income to provide for them quite effectively. While this seems trivial at certain lower ages (neonatals, toddlers, pre-teens), matters become more complicated when defining a cut-off point: should individuality only become effective once someone becomes an adult by law? If a younger age should apply, at what point exactly would this be appropriate—and why? While there are no objectively 'correct' answers to these questions, they underline the general point that duration is far less trivial than the simple approach of individually paying UBI throughout an entire lifecycle might suggest. Either way, temporal dimensions are a key consideration when concretely spelling out what the abstract idea of a UBI could look like in practice.

The dimension of *modality*, which describes the 'particular shape that a universal transfer takes' (De Wispelaere and Stirton 2004, 270), can be another point of contention between UBI designs. This dimension asks: What precisely should a recipient of UBI get? This is not so much a question about the generosity of a UBI scheme, but rather to the *form* that its payouts take—for instance, as cash or in the form of an alternative currency. Contrary to the BIEN definition, UBI proponents might also propose vouchers with a certain degree of flexibility, such as flexible consumption vouchers which are restricted to the local economy, defined as falling within a certain place-based boundary.

One reason for why this might be appropriate consists in an unclear blending of alternative currencies. With the rise of online consumption and cryptocurrencies, there is good reason to assume that alternatives to simple cash payments could still be considered a UBI. Crucially, payouts would need to maintain sufficient flexibility to allow UBI recipients to fully exercise their consumption preferences. But many alternative currencies are not universally usable, meaning that the line between them and specific forms of consumption vouchers becomes extensively blurred. This does not mean there is no difference between UBI and universal basic vouchers—after all, in their extreme forms, vouchers would counteract the ideas of individual flexibility inherent to UBI. However, more flexible vouchers and alternative currencies might be considered as an optional addition to policy design that adds differentiation between concrete UBI proposals. For instance, vouchers could be used to top-up a partial UBI. Alternatively, one might introduce a component of individual choice. Citizens could be given the opportunity to voluntarily choose vouchers with a higher net worth than the monetary UBI they might otherwise receive. These vouchers could then be tied to various forms of consumption, such as targeted support for the local economy or sustainable consumption.

Another option might be to partially grant UBI to members of society in the form of shares in funds or public companies. This could be used to address the issue with individuality and duration raised above for models of UBI that include young children. Before turning of age, individuals' UBI might be paid into a fund, with shares made available once a person is legally considered an adult. It is possible to envisage many similar schemes, which serves to illustrate the point that modality is one of the most fundamental dimensions of UBI policy design, albeit one that can quickly spiral in complexity.

Tied to modality and uniformity in particular is the dimension of *adequacy*, which refers to the 'capacity to satisfy recipients' basic needs' (De Wispelaere and Stirton 2004, 271). In the simplest terms, this is the question of how generous a UBI scheme should be. Answering this question brings us to the enormous variety of fundamentally different ideas of what UBI could be. At the lower end, UBI could be entirely bound to the fluctuating number of available resources, for instance through a sovereign wealth fund. In such a design, adequacy as defined by De Wispelaere and Stirton would not be an independent goal in and of itself but would instead be interpreted based on resource availability, such as how closely UBI tracks the state of the economy as a whole. This approach would be linked to some obvious trade-offs. On the one hand, it would likely resolve many concerns about the fiscal feasibility of UBI and would effectively transform the scheme into a simple mechanism to translate societal revenue into private income. The latter would be fully dependent on the factors influencing revenue, such as market performance and political decisions on tax policy. One advantage for such an approach could be that citizens would feel the positive effects from economic growth directly. A key negative implication would be that this pro-cyclical approach would not be able to act as an automatic stabiliser in times of crisis, and in fact crisis effects on the economy might become more severe due to increased consumption differentials over time. Unlike this input-driven approach, more problem-oriented policy designs might aim to cover an absolute poverty threshold, a nationally defined at-risk-of-poverty level, or even higher levels depending on how ambitiously policymakers were prepared to set their sights for social outcomes.

The definitions of adequacy associated with each of these models can broadly be grouped into three categories. First, designs geared towards complementing existing schemes would contribute some amount of money to a system that has otherwise already been established. Here, the UBI level itself would not be sufficient to achieve a set goal such as poverty reduction, but could address existing gaps in the overall system. Second, designs geared towards preventing monetary poverty would provide an amount of money that, by itself, should be high enough to cover a defined poverty threshold. This does not necessarily imply abolishing the welfare state, as many in-kind services, public goods, and needs-based transfers might still be needed. Third, emancipatory approaches might go above and beyond poverty thresholds, with the aim of enabling individuals to be truly independent from income through labour. Within these categories, there are infinite imaginable specific policy designs, depending on the underlying definition of individual needs.

Alongside all these dimensions, we propose including *funding* as a key element of UBI policy design. Of course, this is not to suggest that previous categorisations of UBI gave insufficient consideration to funding as a distinct concern. Rather, we believe that it is crucial to more explicitly lift it to the same analytical level as the other output-oriented elements of policy design. The first—arguably less important—reason for this is quite simply its salience, since questions of funding play a consistent major role in debates on the feasibility of UBI (e.g., Joseph Rowntree Foundation 2021; Greenwell 2022), which means that any concrete policy design championed in political debates will also have to prominently address this issue. Even if several politicians or activists, or the parties and groups with which they are affiliated, were to support the idea of UBI at the same time, their proposals may vary considerably regarding how their UBI scheme ought to be funded.

The second, more important reason for making funding a prominent feature of UBI design concerns the likely outcomes of the scheme. These theoretically hinge on funding, perhaps even more than on the often over-emphasised aspect of UBI payments. We can consider an extreme example to illustrate this quite effectively: irrespective of how high UBI levels are, they become meaningless if they were entirely funded by a 100 percent tax on the same UBI payments. Or to take a case more relevant to the structure of actual policy proposals, a UBI largely funded through taxes on high wealth levels would have very different distributional implications from one funded through high but flat taxes on all income from work. As we have already discussed, there are also intersections with other dimensions involved for funding. Perhaps most powerfully, funding would fully define the level of UBI in any design in which adequacy is entirely linked to revenue sources. This means that funding defines the distributional implications of UBI, its potential adequacy, implicitly its relationship to other welfare schemes, and its sustainability. While UBI debates tend to focus on the 'output' side of the equation—that is, the money that is transferred to recipients—we take the view that inputs are equally as important for successful policy design.

While it is entirely possible to conceive of other dimensions of policy design, this list represents a fairly comprehensive overview of the key elements that apply in the case of an effective UBI. Yet this does not mean that every policy proposal addresses all of these points. As De Wispelaere and Stirton (2004, 272–73) point out, some proposals are more concrete whereas others remain more on the 'fuzzy' side. This *fuzziness in policy design* is a key asset in enabling coalitions to form in support of UBI from a variety of competing perspectives. As some proposals remain broad, they can serve as umbrellas for other more detailed ideas that adhere to similar principles. Such broad 'families' of UBI designs can then also serve as a basis for agenda coalitions (see chapter 8). For instance, policy designs might vary slightly in terms of their frequency or their individuality. However, if they are all geared towards preventing poverty among the elderly, they could still be considered to form part of a common family of proposals. Considering that the basic definition by BIEN limits how far UBI proposals can vary along some of the dimensions we have outlined, this definition itself has the potential to act as an example for such UBI families.

Over the course of the following chapters, we develop this concept of 'UBI families' and link it to insights from political theory. We identify families of UBI policy design based on ideal-typical attributes of five political ideologies. In doing so, we focus on the policy settings that these different political ideologies might be likely to favour if they were to embrace the idea of a European basic income. We discuss different ideal-typical policy designs that could be part of such families in each respective chapter. In order to effectively link these political ideologies to different types of an EUBI, we first elaborate what sets an EUBI apart from its national counterparts.

THE EUROPEAN BASIC INCOME

Just as the basic idea of a UBI can take different concrete shapes whose implications are heavily dependent on policy design, an EUBI can be set up in several fundamentally different ways. The dimensions of UBI policy design apply equally to an EUBI—some in slightly more complex forms—and are ultimately dependent on political preferences. These preferences, in turn, are likely to be rooted in more general political preferences associated with different ideologies. After all, when approaching debates on an EUBI, actors do not do so with anything close to a 'clean political slate'. Instead, they hold a range of preexisting political views through which they approach new ideas, including that of an EUBI.

While we engage with these views in greater detail throughout this book, it is necessary to outline some of the bare bones of the idea of an EUBI here to help frame and systematise the later discussion. Irrespective of the nuances of different ideological preferences, any conception of an EUBI would entail some form of basic income paid to everyone in a specific group across Europe. Against this background, all the dimensions of differentiation mentioned above also apply and could substantially influence the shape that the concrete EUBI proposal takes. Throughout our later presentation of EUBI ideal-types linked to different ideologies, these dimensions of differentiation can serve as a guiding framework.

The European dimension adds a crucial layer of complexity, as further considerations must be taken into account when developing a concrete policy proposal. Most obviously, the definition of what 'Europe' entails has important implications (Ostrowski 2023b). These concern not only the people covered by the scheme, but also the polities it can be 'nested' in. Intuitively, 'Europe' could refer to the continent in general or the EU in particular. In order to simplify the later stages of our analysis, we limit our approach to the EU. This choice is a prime example of the influence that the definition of the 'universe' within which UBI is treated as 'universal' can have in practice. We fully acknowledge that this choice might enhance inequalities between the EU and its neighbours within and beyond the European continent. While considering an EUBI beyond the borders of the EU might be compelling when seen through the cosmopolitan lens that is often applied in UBI debates, there are good reasons to limit the scheme to the EU. Functionally speaking, focusing on the EU would allow the EUBI to be attached to a well-established set of institutions and policies. While Treaty changes might be necessary for such a proposal (for opposing arguments, see Denuit 2019; Milevska 2014), they would likely be far less complicated than setting up an entirely new, Europe-wide institutional framework within which an EUBI could be embedded. From an intra-EU perspective, an EUBI could also be an effective tool to tangibly deliver on the otherwise abstract promise of a 'social Europe', and effectively strengthen the material meaning of EU citizenship. This is not to say that there are no valid arguments for a continent-wide or even a global UBI. However, as our analysis of potential agenda coalitions around concrete EUBI designs presupposes an established political framework within which an EUBI could be developed, the EU offers the most suitable basis.

In theory, an EUBI limited to the EU could be implemented through various policy mechanisms. In its most disruptive form, it might be designed in a centralised fashion, meaning it would be implemented and provided by the EU directly. This approach would face the biggest obstacles, ranging from the Treaties, over member state resistance in the Council of the EU, to the lack of any previously established policy infrastructure that could be used to implement the scheme. However, this approach would also be the most effective one if the goal is to emphasise the European character of the policy. Direct transfers from the EU are likelier to actually be recognised by citizens as a social benefit of the EU, while an EU-wide scheme has the potential to mitigate allegations of 'welfare migration' (Milevska 2014; Van Parijs and Vanderborght 2017, 218–19). If implemented nationally, such arguments are to be expected irrespective of the empirical plausibility of welfare magnetism, which could both undermine support for UBI and—in a worrying case of collateral damage—for intra-EU free movement as well. An implementation of a UBI at EU level would mitigate this risk, as EU citizens would be able to access the scheme from anywhere.

Alternatively, a basic income Directive could enforce the existence of a UBI all over the EU. Crucially, the specific details and processes of implementation would be left up to the member states themselves in this scenario. This approach would solve some of the issues with the centralised approach, most prominently the lack of an effective policy infrastructure for actually carrying out these transfers. It would also allow for some additional flexibility to adjust to national peculiarities, assuming that the Directive is formulated in the necessary way. However, this would come at the cost of an increased risk that the scheme will be implemented unevenly: the higher the flexibility to adjust the EUBI to national contexts, the lower the likelihood that the EUBI will actually guarantee an equal quality of life across the EU. Furthermore, the advantage of a directly palpable social dimension of the EU itself would be extensively undermined. Since each UBI would ultimately be implemented and thus transferred by national authorities, citizens would hardly be aware in their everyday lives what role the EU played in setting up the scheme. Of course, this would mainly be an issue for those who favour an EUBI primarily to foster support for the EU, rather than to first and foremost emancipate individuals.

These trade-offs become increasingly clear when considering even less centralised systems of implementation. In a softer form, an EUBI could be proposed by the EU to its member states through a nonbinding Recommendation. Such a step might potentially enhance the likelihood that member states will pursue their respective national schemes. After all, a Recommendation would give proponents of UBI schemes a significant measure of soft power in political discourse, allowing them to refer to the EU's stated preferences when pushing for implementation. Furthermore, a Recommendation might normalise the idea of UBI across the EU, moving it from occasionally fringe ends of political debates to the centre of a well-established political institution. As a Recommendation would not necessarily presuppose changing the Treaties, this approach increases the chances of an EUBI actually being pursued under favourable political conditions. However, it would also heavily reduce the EUBI's value as a European social policy. Furthermore, it would most likely imply a rise in anti-European sentiment if allegations of welfare magnetism increase in reaction to a partial or asymmetric introduction of UBI in only a few states, and not in others.

Finally, an EUBI could also *de facto* develop without such EU-level action by developing independent national schemes. In this scenario, national political debates would converge, for instance due to dominant ideas in public discourse that transcend national borders. As a result, various national schemes would emerge, creating a European space of basic incomes. Crucially, this is a scenario where the EU level itself has little direct or active involvement. There are only a few 'soft' pathways that could foster convergence here, with UBI proposals potentially being communicated through systems similar to the Open Method of Coordination (European Parliament 2014). Furthermore, EU-wide media outlets and networks could report on national experiences in other states, potentially nudging national publics to demand similar policies in their respective states as well. This approach would minimise the institutional hurdles to introducing an EUBI but also maximise the familiar problems associated with national implementation.

Taking all these considerations into account, we argue that although an EUBI would be undoubtedly and irreducibly European as a policy measure, it could still be developed, implemented, and administered nationally. As the debate on 'Social Europe' and a 'European Social Union' (Vandenbroucke 2015) suggests, there is a tendency in the literature to argue that a 'European' social policy could also be one that just features a minimal layer of genuine EU action. By implication, the term 'European' can remain vague and open for contestation even after it is decided whether it should refer to the continent or the EU. Along similar lines, any policy design for an EUBI must clarify the exact nature of its relationship to national welfare states. The intention might well be to (partially) replace these by a UBI that could be proposed, designed, and implemented either nationally or at the EU level—or, instead, the aim might be to find ways of making the two seamlessly compatible.

Other elements that are important for designing an EUBI are more technical. For instance, the distribution of funding is more complex than in a purely national context, as financial infrastructures might vary between member states. In this regard, the EU might aim to pay the money directly to individuals or, alternatively, pay it to member states' administrations with the responsibility of then distributing it to their citizens accordingly. Funding would further be linked to the question of the EU's own resources. This matter is generally still in motion, and the EU currently faces much stronger fiscal limitations than its member states. Thus, the question of an EUBI goes directly to the heart of the fundamental question of the preferred degree of overall EU integration.

An EUBI would also not exist in a policy vacuum. Even if some actors are in principle in favour of the idea of an EUBI, the scheme would likely be very costly (Coote and Yaziki 2019; Kearney and Mogstad 2019; Afscharian et al. 2021) and would necessarily have to compete with other potentially desirable schemes for a limited portfolio of newly introduced EU fiscal resources. While this is a secondary concern for a purely ideal-typical discussion of policy designs, it would absolutely have to be factored in when transposing this theory into practice.

Further, the institutional hurdles to an EUBI—such as the Treaties and the Council of the EU—imply some difficult questions for precisely how an EUBI is to be introduced. For instance, one could debate introducing it slowly and carefully in order to be able to pass veto points. This would come at the cost of sacrificing a radical emancipatory impact from one day to the next. Similarly, one might aim to design an EUBI primarily as an economic policy intended as an automatic fiscal stabiliser, similar to the way that other ideas for European social policy have been framed in the past, as with a European unemployment insurance (Dullien 2013; in't Veld, Larch, and Vandeweyer 2012; Spath 2016). Such a framing for an EUBI may potentially enhance its feasibility, as it could broaden the basis of support to include primarily economically minded politicians, and might also reduce resistance from economic actors such as businesses and financial institutions. However, it would likely reduce the social benefits of the scheme since policy design decisions would follow economic imperatives and potentially limit its redistributive effects.

The additional complexities involved in such an EU-wide introduction raise an important question: Why should anyone opt for an EUBI over a national UBI in the first place? Arguments for an EUBI can follow two basic lines: one that is primarily pro-EU, and one that is primarily pro-UBI (Afscharian 2023). From a primarily pro-EU perspective, an EUBI might be a tool to foster EU integration and stability, with the central hope in this regard being that an EUBI might prove an effective tool to combat Euroscepticism. Giving the EU a strong, palpable social dimension would allow it to counteract any associations between EU integration and welfare retrenchment, thus eroding the basis of political support for anti-EU forces. Yet there is a major risk involved in this strategy. The effect of an EUBI on EU support could easily switch to the opposite direction if it turned out that welfare states were systematically eroded with explicit reference to the EUBI. Thus, the scheme would need to be designed in such a way that it would stabilise and supplement national welfare states rather than replacing them. After all, an EUBI would be one of the very few EU-level social policies that are strongly palpable to EU citizens while not competing with any equivalent policies at the national level.

Since UBI does not yet exist in any member state but would have a strong direct impact on citizens' lives in all of them, it strikes a rare balance that few other policies would be able to deliver. However, it is worth noting that the precise opposite could be argued as well. Many UBI proposals play with the idea of abolishing the welfare state and the monetary transfer schemes that already exist in member states. Thus, an EUBI might, in fact, be perceived as a direct piece of legislative competition to long-established systems of social justice. While good arguments for both positions exist, their ultimate arbiter is likely to be how they are variously perceived in practice. If actors see an EUBI as a threat, they will almost certainly oppose the scheme. *Vice versa*, if they regard it as a solution for a sizeable proportion of the problems they face, they will be inclined to voice support. Further benefits of an EUBI might derive from its probable effect as an automatic stabiliser for the Economic and Monetary Union, as well as its potential to act as a basic security scheme for mobile EU citizens. As responsibility for the latter group is currently being pushed back and forth between various levels of governance (Schmidt

2019), a regulatory social policy gap has emerged that an EUBI might be able to (partially) close.

Intra-EU freedom of movement is also key for the primarily pro-UBI perspective, since for pro-European supporters of a UBI the European dimension is almost a necessity. So far, this necessity is often overlooked in UBI debates across the EU. However, thinking through the national implementation of UBI in the EU gives rise to a very specific dilemma. Due to the nondiscrimination rules (Ellis and Watson 2012) that apply in the realm of universalistic social policies across the EU, a UBI introduced at the national level by any member state would likely have to be made available to mobile EU citizens as well. This, in turn, could quickly lead to a ratcheting-up of anti-European discourse: although empirically unlikely (Ellis and Miller 2000; Martinsen and Werner 2019; Giulietti 2014), accusations of welfare magnetism are already prominent in relation to the appreciably less generous welfare schemes that currently exist in the EU (Martinsen and Werner 2019). The introduction of a national UBI within an EU with free movement would most likely trigger a much higher incidence of harshly anti-migrant narratives, which in turn could undermine free movement and the EU itself. Referring to abstract fears of 'welfare migration', Eurosceptics could hijack nationally implemented UBI schemes to justify demands for European *dis*integration. Conversely, such narratives could also be used to oppose introducing a national UBI *in the first place*, rendering this pathway more complex than might initially appear. Besides this seemingly insurmountable issue, a national UBI within the EU further faces issues around the internal coherence and implications of its underlying principles. Earlier on, we hinted that a purist interpretation of UBI would favour including the largest possible group of recipients, as it builds on values of universalism and cosmopolitanism. This would imply introducing it at the highest level of governance that is able to make wide-ranging authoritative decisions and provides formal citizenship. Thus, an EUBI would be both logically and politically more promising than a national UBI within the EU. This does not *per se* render the previous arguments in favour of narrower definitions of universality invalid. However, an EU-level UBI would minimise the theoretical frictions associated with trying to place a UBI scheme on the soundest possible conceptual foundations.

FROM FUZZY TO CONCRETE DESIGNS

While all these considerations help structure and systematise the development of an EUBI policy design, they continue to be somewhat high-level and generic as long as the many questions we have raised remain unanswered. In a nutshell, we have listed different dimensions of policy design that must be considered, but it is still very much an open question how precisely an EUBI should respond to them. In theory, the upshot of our analysis thus far is that an EUBI scheme could take an almost infinite number of possible guises. Each of the policy design elements we have discussed can be implemented in a countless number of possible ways, each adding to the total number of possible policy design combinations. This underlines the point that there is not one EUBI but many to choose from, and that different policy designs have a decisive role to play in addressing some of the reservations against the basic concept of an EUBI. However, it also implies that matters must be simplified somewhat in order to make the idea of an EUBI more tangible.

To pare down the smörgåsbord of different EUBI designs we have presented here, we draw on the concept of (E)UBI 'families' introduced above. While countless different policy proposals for an EUBI might diverge from one another in their respective granular details, many of them can be united by a series of common traits. However, to systematically order these potential policy designs into families that make sense theoretically and have practical relevance, we need to deploy an effective heuristic. We argue that political ideologies are an example of a heuristic that is particularly well-suited to organising different types of EUBIs. At the same time, they are useful theoretical proxies for the different political parties, activist groups, and advocacy movements who would have a stake in campaigning for the introduction of an EUBI. As this book began by stating the aim of exploring the potential for agenda coalitions, ideologies are the ideal middle ground for identifying UBI families that are potentially practically relevant to implementing EUBI schemes. Ideologies have the advantage of being well-established in political research and practice, thoroughly grounded in social and political theory, and offering empirically tested ways to map the commonalities and differences in individual and collective political preferences (Festenstein and Kenny 2005; Freeden, Sargent, and Stears 2013; Heywood 2021; Ostrowski 2022a). Throughout the following chapters, we therefore use political ideologies as the guiding tools to develop our understanding of the main EUBI 'families'.

As political ideologies are still a rather broad differentiator, we apply further limitations to the scope of this book. More concretely, we limit the ideologies we take into account by applying a broad understanding of progressivism and subsequently focusing on political ideologies that match this criterion. We further define what exactly we mean by progressivism in the following chapter. Based on this, we will discuss the different ideologies that fall under our interpretation of progressivism throughout the remainder of the book, while paying special attention to those attributes that can later help us define ideologically specific ideal-types for the EUBI families in operation today.

Chapter 2

Progressivism

To understand how a UBI can be placed in service of the aspiration to build a progressive Europe, we need to engage first and foremost with what the concept of 'progressive' means. Certainly, 'progressivism' as an ideological position—or more precisely, as a description of a particular 'family resemblance' (Freeden 1996) shared by several ideological positions—relates in its most essential form to a *support for societal progress*. Yet that is such a general and at times even nebulous term that it simply shifts the burden of explication one concept further down the line.

To get a firmer grasp on how we should characterise progress and progressivism in detail, we must break these terms up into a number of constitutive concepts—the 'basket' of essential meanings that they gather together, and the 'penumbra' of additional connotations they imply. There are two levels for how to think about this. First, we need to look at what progressivism connotes *lexically*: which ideas and meanings *the word itself* conjures, from its interchangeable synonyms and its regular 'companion' concepts to terms that occupy the same semantic space or are used in a similar sense in social discourse. Then, second, we also have to examine what progressivism means *contextually*: which objectives, values, processes, policies, and so on, it is associated with in society today, 'right here, right now', for which the term 'progressive' often functions as an encapsulating placeholder.

We can start with the straightforward observation that progressivism does not exist in a vacuum. Certainly, it has an absolute meaning, derived as an aggregate from the concepts that it comprises. But progressivism also has a relative meaning because it exists in direct contrast to (at least) one other ideology: conservatism. These two, progressivism and conservatism, are both fundamentally claims about the direction of society, and they stand in contrast to what we can describe as a 'middle' position of 'path-dependency', of carrying on with things just the way they are right now. In a sense, progressivism and conservatism agree that things *cannot* continue the way they have been going. They agree in their diagnosis that there is something bad about society's overarching direction, that left to its own devices society will keep drifting off down a problematic road. But they disagree on what precise course-correction is needed to get society 'back on track'. As ideologies, they form an approximate binary, engaged in processes of 'essential contestation' and 'essential cooption' (Ostrowski 2022a) to decide the meanings that shape and drive society in the direction they would prefer to see.

This binary is approximate in the sense that their mutual relationship is not one of pure 'A vs ¬A' negation, where progressivism and conservatism exist as absolute logical antitheses. Crucially, there are some lexical and contextual concepts on which progressivism and conservatism overlap. Even if they may not mean the same thing by these concepts, they engage with each other by jostling for 'ownership claims' over them in 'turf wars' over which of them gets to 'set the agenda' and assert its version of each concept within society. On other concepts, of course, they stand in literal diametric contrast. They mean the exact and deliberate opposite of each other, and their engagement with each other takes the form of far more pervasive and destructive struggle aimed at achieving total dominance for their own concepts and total eradication of the other's. The currency of this engagement, as it is for more-or-less any ideological struggle, is claims of 'good versus evil', 'right versus wrong', attributed not just to the lexical and contextual concepts themselves, or even to their specific ideological combination 'into' progressivism and conservatism, but also to those who hold and disseminate them within society.

With this key distinction between progressivism and conservatism (and the path-dependent 'middle') in mind, we can start to unpack their absolute and relative lexical connotations (Ostrowski 2023a). At the core of progressivism's dual relationship with conservatism is its relative stance towards two subtly but vitally different forms of ideological moderation. In one case, its stance and that of conservatism are inveterate opposites—whereas in the other, they are strongly aligned. Progressivism is associated with a pronounced tendency towards radicalism, towards a proactive, assertive, 'root-and-branch' and 'all-or-nothing' stance on questions of societal change. Conservatism, meanwhile, brings an equivalent reactionary lean, a default position of defensive waiting, primed to respond—and respond negatively—to whatever society happens to come up with next. Both are, in their own way, extreme positions: 'strong yes' and 'strong no' to societal change, with limited patience for half-measures, partial solutions, or other shades of nuance in between.

One of the most fundamental dimensions of progressive distinction lies in its embrace of novelty, in a way that explicitly departs from—or breaks with—the societal *status quo*. In this respect, it stands opposite both conservatism *and* the path-dependent 'middle', in the sense that 'staying on the current path' is precisely one of the core ways that conservatism tries to maintain this *status quo*. Progressivism consists to a large part in an embrace of heterodoxy, of 'marginal' thinking, 'countervailing' logic, and 'minority reports', in the face of societal orthodoxy—the safe, pedestrian views of the 'middle-of-the-road' majority, which conservatism tries studiously to observe and preserve. In turn, progressive heterodoxy is geared specifically towards provoking the (real or perceived) majority that makes up this middle–conservative alliance into embracing change and subverting the comfortable onward march of its shared conventions as the rules by which society must abide. By definition, progressivism raises the need, and viability, of societal innovation as the substantive goal and lodestone of its views. It is not trying to be edgy simply for its own sake but is specifically trying to unsettle the received traditions that keep society locked into the 'same old, same old' ways of doing things—which conservatism is determined to protect more-or-less as an intrinsic good, regardless of any flaws or limitations they might reveal.

But progressivism's passion for novelty is not limited to putting forward an alternative option for how society should proceed and creating a 'fork in the road' for it to go down. Instead, it offers a far more categorical replacement, a rejection of the current course. By much the same token, conservatism is interested not just in maintaining but also in strengthening this course, 'leaning into' it, and bringing along a few things (ideas, practices, and so on) that society may have left by the wayside previously. Progressivism is an essentially anti-establishment ideology, seeking to 'bring down' and disassemble precisely those prevailing social institutions, rules, and frames that 'middle' path-dependency is happy to support—and which conservatism wants to reinforce by re-establishing a whole host more that society has previously managed to dismantle. It is also a dissenter position, an ideology that registers protest and voices disagreement against the blind conformism of the 'middle ground', and which dismisses the stance of conservatives as laughably quaint and old-fashioned. Together with its subversive, innovative streak, this all gives progressivism a highly experimental flavour: a determination to 'try what nobody has tried before' and 'go where nobody has gone before', to help society 'snap out' of its familiar patterns and avoid the siren-call of conservatism's gauchely dated suggestions.

Here, in turn, lies another way in which progressivism and conservatism are curiously similar. Both are equally sure of their sense of what society *is not* and what it *should be*, even if their respective diagnoses would take it in very different substantive directions. Progressivism offers society an alternative that is premised on the need for something new, on an orientation to the future. Conservatism's alternative, meanwhile, rests on the appeal of the old and is just as firmly rooted in the past. Both lie outside the mainstream, and both to some extent embrace the 'outsider' status that this gives them, as both a marker of internal solidarity and external distinction. Both, meanwhile, are equally committed to their ideological positions. It may be that progressive commitment manifests more as social agitation, while conservative commitment expresses itself more as social loyalty. But neither is content with the slightly vapid neutrality that comes of cleaving to the 'middle' path.

Both progressivism and conservatism have a tendency towards a programmatic, platforming treatment of their constitutive ideas. They imbue them with an internal coherence, regarding them as complete (i.e., closed systems that fully explain reality without any 'remainders'), comprehensive (i.e., macroscopic, ambitious, even totalising aims for reality), and correct (i.e., uniquely insightful about reality to the exclusion of alternative representations). Progressivism in this guise can develop a slightly dogmatic tendency, producing an ever-expanding series of manifestos and declarations with a bewildering array of 'correct positions' that adherents are—often explicitly and fanatically—expected to abide by. Conservatism, meanwhile, mirrors this with a narrow-minded reluctance to deviate from 'the faith', which often expresses itself in a dry, convoluted formalism and sticklerish rule-worship that leaves its adherents barely any room for manoeuvre. Neither lends itself easily to reasonable compromise. But they would respond, at least they stand for something, rather than succumbing to the empty fence-sitting and 'both-sides' vacillation of a more ideologically 'middling' position.

Yet that is where their similarities end, and their remaining lexical connotations are marked by major points of difference. For one, progressivism takes the approach that society can always go further, do more, to enact necessary change, while conservatism holds the view that society could just as often do with pulling back, doing less, keeping more necessary things the same. There is a permissiveness to progressive ideology, a willingness to allow and even foster nonstandard thinking and behaviour *simply because it is nonstandard*, that conservatism sees as unconscionably generous towards forms of deviancy it would never dream of tolerating. Here, the 'middle road' tends to favour the more progressive approach, in the form of a broad, modest accommodation—even if the precise parameters of what it 'rules in' and 'rules out' are not fully clear. But where the 'middle' position sees itself as striking a sensible balance, a 'golden mean' of sorts, it regards the progressive version as simply excessive, a 'bridge too far', and the conservative equivalent as much too intransigent.

Progressivism also distinguishes itself from conservatism in the strident way it presents, or expresses, its societal recommendations and initiatives—and if it has a direction in mind, in the torrential, havoc-wreaking way it pursues it (and signals that it is doing so)—compared to conservatism's mulishly immobile withdrawal. What progressivism sees as a willingness to be a little bit inflammatory, to shock or jolt society into changing tack because, after all, *sometimes things just need to be set on fire*, conservatism criticises as a rabid wildness inherent to its social character. Conversely, conservatism's evident pride in its ability to 'stay the course' come hell or high water renders it impossibly stuffy and obdurate from a progressive perspective. In much the same way, what progressivism prizes as a fluid, malleable flexibility can come across as unpredictable suddenness; while conservatism's statuesque poise is easy to read as total ossification. Neither lays much weight on being measured, gradual, or level-headed as a point of principle: if and when they choose to be so, this is more of an exceptional strategy to be deployed when their more comfortable approaches look unlikely to yield results.

These dimensions of lexical overlap and contrast are encapsulated in the two ideological positions' very different approaches to both the goals and methods of societal change. For progressivism, this takes the form of embracing partial changes within the parameters of society's current arrangements that have the potential to metastasise into systemic overhauls. For conservatism, this manifests as avoiding both wherever possible—precisely because of the possibility of this metastasis. If the 'middle road' to societal change is channelled through bit-by-bit stepwise reform, then progressivism is certainly more amenable to this—however reluctantly or less-than-patiently—than conservatism. Progressivism's concern with reform is that it is not making enough of a difference relative to what society needs, whereas from a conservative angle reformism is already *by definition* a step in the wrong direction. Typically, progressivism finds itself embracing a more revolutionary approach to societal change, the route of drastic wholesale system overhaul. This is something the 'middle' ideological position tends not to consider, either as a criterion of process or of outcome, whereas the possibility of revolution is more-or-less exactly what conservatism sets out to oppose and prevent.

PROGRESSIVISM IN CONTEXT

This rich field of lexical connotations for progressivism and conservatism takes a far more specific contextual form, depending on the conditions and circumstances of the society to (or within) which they happen to be applied. In the first instance, in any given context, the substantive commitments of progressivism and conservatism are mapped fairly seamlessly onto the complex constellation of meanings associated with the 'left–centre–right' ideological spectrum. Today, the most familiar way of modelling what this spectrum substantively represents is by drawing an approximate curve in a space defined by two cross-cutting dimensions of ideological value. One is focused on political economy, and covers questions of wealth and income distribution, state- or market-led regulation and investment, and more-or-less complex and expansive fiscal and social welfare policies, typically presented as ranging from interventionism to *laissez-faire*. The other dimension, slightly more loosely held together, reflects social culture, and captures questions of (codified) morality, demography, existential and epistemological diversity, religiosity, the shape and basis of societal order, and (inter)nationality, which we can distill into a rough gauge of ideological monism or pluralism.

This is the 'ideological compass' (Ostrowski 2022a), and the left–centre–right spectrum is essentially a way of connecting combinations of positions in interventionist–*laissez-faire* and monist–pluralist space. We cannot simply reduce progressive–conservative politics to either the political-economic or the sociocultural dimension, nor simply 'split the difference' and draw the left–centre–right spectrum as a diagonal line. Since the 1960s and 1970s, at least in Europe, sociocultural concerns have begun to grow in importance relative to their political-economic counterparts—although this is not evenly true of all parts of the left–centre–right spectrum (Inglehart 1977, 1990, 2018). In 'compass space', it is perhaps best to frame the spectrum, and the progressive–conservative divide, as a curve that is 'turning' away from the political-economic and towards the sociocultural axis (see figure 2.1). What this produces, in combination with the ongoing pulls towards ideological polarisation across Europe, is an emergent pair of ideological clusters: a 'Brahmin left' that embraces a mixture of political-economic interventionism

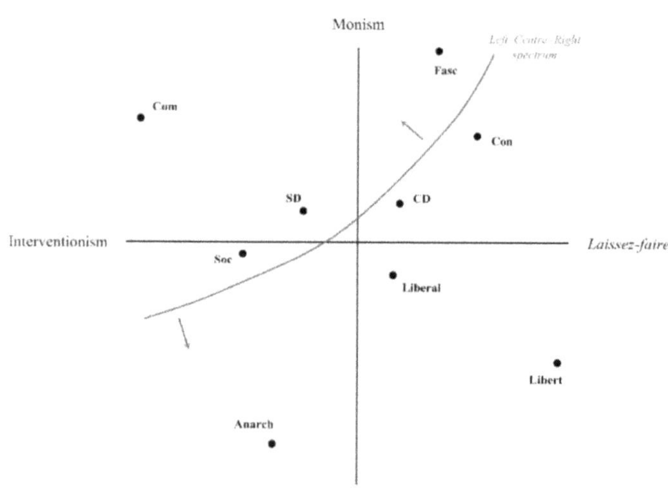

Figure 2.1. The ideological compass
Source: Ostrowski 2022a

and sociocultural pluralism, and a 'Merchant right' that adopts the opposite combination of political-economic *laissez-faire* and sociocultural monism (Kitschelt 2010; Kriesi *et al.* 2008; Piketty 2020, 807–965).

The first level at which the progressivism–conservatism (i.e., left–right) distinction operates is in the way that power-resources are distributed and power-relations are arranged among us as individual members of society, and in the way the structures that make up society are shaped and built (Ostrowski 2020). Progressivism favours empowerment for the broadest cross-section of society's members, with means and resources more-or-less evenly doled out, options and opportunities awarded in a balanced way, and comparable abilities, capacities, and status accessible to all. It aims to achieve parity within and between the various groups to which we all belong and do away with the divisions and stratifications between them so nobody is placed in a position of inferiority or obedience. Conservatism, meanwhile, is perfectly content for power to be asymmetrically arranged between members of society, even if this leads to forms of severe oppression of some of them by others, and equally keen to maintain hierarchies of authority and leadership–followership as the default 'currency' of how society works.

At the next level above this, progressivism and conservatism have deep overarching effects on the social attitudes that predispose how we approach, read, or confront our experiences of society, and the norms and habits of social behaviour that decide how we navigate society and steer it according to our purposes. Progressivism emphasises the importance of recognition as the fundamental currency of how we should receive the sheer quality and quantity of difference with which society and its members present us, and encourages us to take a welcoming, celebratory approach towards novelty and diversity. Along the same lines, it portrays society and social interaction as a shared project, operating as a form of mutual partnership, whose members help one another in a friendly, fraternal way to achieve goals that benefit all of them as a whole. Conservatism is more comfortable with various shades of intolerance and insistence on the significance of our own views, up to and including the point of discrimination, and is more inclined to see society as a competitive fighting-pit of acquisitive rivals and self-interested enemies, who seek to flourish and win at any cost, even if it means destroying everyone else around them.

Yet at the heart of the conceptual maps of progressivism and conservatism, and of how we familiarly think of them as ideological positions, are the signal political values that underpin, and are manifested by, their respective approaches to power, societal structures, social behaviour, and social attitudes. For a number of these, progressivism and conservatism exhibit both a lexical and a contextual overlap, defending rival meanings of the same concepts. Freedom, one of the central values of all social and political thinking, refers to emancipation from forcible control, opportunities for conscious choice, and absence of arbitrary constraints or coercion. Progressivism ties this to democratic citizenship, social rights, and economic self-management, while conservatism instead attaches it to private property, private enterprise, and unrestricted free speech. Both share a commitment to justice, in the sense of giving people fair, adequate, and correct treatment—although progressivism typically thinks of this in terms of social and welfare provision, where conservatism turns this more towards legal and criminal due process. And the two ideologies acknowledge the importance of solidarity in the form of reciprocal bonds, shared purposes, mutual duties, and common interest. Precisely what scale, scope, and intensity of group feeling this inculcates in people, however, is a source of major progressive (e.g., class, world) and conservative (e.g., nation, state) difference.

But for a number of their other values, progressivism and conservatism lie in a profound lexical and contextual contrast, embracing rival concepts with directly opposite meanings. To name perhaps the most significant example: whereas progressivism embraces equality, in the hope of placing people on the same or similar level in key respects or by particular criteria, conservatism is more interested in inequality insofar as this preserves important differences between people, often tied to a particular sense of stable order. Altogether, this constellation of concepts steers progressivism towards a complex sense of individual and group pluralism, heterogeneity, and incommensurability, while conservatism tends to entrench around a specific interpretation of monism, usually but not always tied to an enhanced social role for faith. It is a conceptual map that supports progressivism's contextual pursuit of the forward movement of society, just as conservatism's conceptual map underpins its efforts to stop this movement in its tracks or put it into reverse.

PROGRESSIVISM IN GLOBAL POLITICAL ECONOMY

Evaluating the prospects for an EUBI means zeroing in on a particular subset of the cleavages between progressive and conservative political-economic and sociocultural commitments. The cleavages in question have emerged in response to several fundamental changes to society that have unfolded particularly prominently in the latter half of the twentieth century and the first decades of the twenty-first century. International competition, the lowering of barriers to trade, and the increasingly free movement of goods and people across ever growing territorial expanses have recently put the traditional approach to the welfare state under pressure. Some parts of society—often referred to as the 'losers of globalisation'—have become increasingly dependent on social protection for survival (Dancygier and Walter 2015; Walter

2010; Zohlnhöfer 2015). The nation as the 'home' of the welfare state has also become increasingly challenged by globalisation, with debates growing around feared or expected functional risks, such as a 'race to the bottom' in the reduction of state welfarist obligations and capacity (Swank 1998; Walter 2019). Furthermore, the legitimacy of nationality as a means of determining access to social support has come under increasing criticism in political philosophy, especially in relation to growing commitments around foreign aid, human rights enforcement, and states in the 'global North' reckoning with their imperial and colonial legacies (Wagner and Zimmermann 2004).

These developments have steadily raised the salience of questions of global political economy in the formation of ideologies along the progressive–conservative spectrum. Alongside the evident continuity of these questions with established debates around interventionism and *laissez-faire*, one of the many categorisations within the overarching monism–pluralism divide that captures the essential difference between progressive and conservative positions on the global dimension of these questions is the division between cosmopolitanism and communitarianism. These categories have a long tradition in political theory and have recently enjoyed increased attention in research beyond this realm as well (Helbling and Teney 2015, 447). Generally, cosmopolitanism describes the idea of 'seeing oneself as a citizen of the world and appreciating other human beings irrespective of their national origin' (Kuhn, Solaz, and van Elsas 2018, 1762; Vertovec and Cohen 2002). For the development of formal political institutions, cosmopolitanism thus 'entails the legitimisation of supranational authority and the awareness of the increased interconnectedness of political communities' (Kuhn, Solaz, and van Elsas 2018, 1762; Held 2002). As we engage with the idea of a social policy beyond national borders in this book, the broad idea of cosmopolitanism paired with the political-economic interventionism–*laissez-faire* divide is particularly well-suited to understanding the versions of a progressive EUBI outlined in the later chapters. In what follows, we summarise some key literature on cosmopolitanism and communitarianism. We then derive a unified framework which we use to define how we will evaluate the expected positions of the political ideologies we focus on throughout the analysis.

Cosmopolitanism and communitarianism represent the extreme points of a new societal cleavage that has begun to gain increasing relevance in the twenty-first century. Cosmopolitanism, in the first instance, is a commitment to the idea that all humans belong to one moral community (Kleingeld 1997, 334–35), and that this human unity and attachment to humanity as a whole carries moral primacy in social thinking (Kurasawa 2011, 301–2). From this flows a certain worldliness, a rejection of parochialism and nativism, especially in the form of arbitrary limits or prejudices (Lu 2000, 245), which manifests both as an idea of shared or common moral duties towards others and as the idea that a transnational global order should be established to which all humans should belong as citizens with equal rights and duties. Cosmopolitanism defined in these terms is the 'class conscience of frequent travellers', which says 'yes to open borders, yes to global authorities, yes to individualism and yes to individual rights as primary frame of justice' (Zürn and De Wilde 2016, 293). In contrast, communitarianism is the 'class conscience of friends of the homeland', which stresses the importance of human ties to contexts of place and experience, to particular ties of association and interaction, and to the moral relevance of existing sites and institutions of social power to say, in turn, 'yes to meaningful borders, yes to upholding state or group sovereignty, yes to community life and yes to collective needs and self-determination as primary frame of justice'.

We can understand the divide between cosmopolitanism and communitarianism by breaking it down into two parallel debates between statism and globalism on the one hand, and between contextualism and universalism on the other. Universalism is characterised by the ideal that all principles of morality, including equality, freedom, justice, and solidarity, apply to all human beings regardless of what relations they share (Zürn and De Wilde 2016, 285). Against this, contextualism argues that obligations are bound and owed to communities restricted above all by internal ties and external boundaries of space, but also of culture, history, language, and shared modes of interaction (Zürn and De Wilde 2016, 286). According to globalism, there is only one relevant relation, which applies generally and equally between all human beings in virtue of there being a global order—so that equality, freedom, justice, and solidarity need to be thought of in global terms. Statism, on the other hand, considers the relation between members of a state as a national political community as the only one that carries moral relevance. This implies that equality, freedom, justice, and solidarity remain firmly within state structures. These four ideological groups lead to cosmopolitanism (globalism combined with universalism) and communitarianism (statism combined with contextualism) (Lacewell and Merkel 2013, 78) (see figure 2.2).

The differentiation between cosmopolitanism and communitarianism offers a promising theoretical framework to evaluate solidarity and cooperation in a globalised world. This is the case not least because the concept of cosmopolitanism addresses issues concerning the interaction of people both within and beyond national borders. Within these borders, it can capture a wide range of the dominant issues that constitute the sociocultural monism–pluralism spectrum, where cosmopolitan ideas place considerable emphasis on values towards the pluralist pole, including tolerance and diversity. Beyond the same borders, cosmopolitanism addresses institutional and political issues in an interconnected world by pushing for increased global integration. In this respect, the differentiation between cosmopolitanism and communitarianism

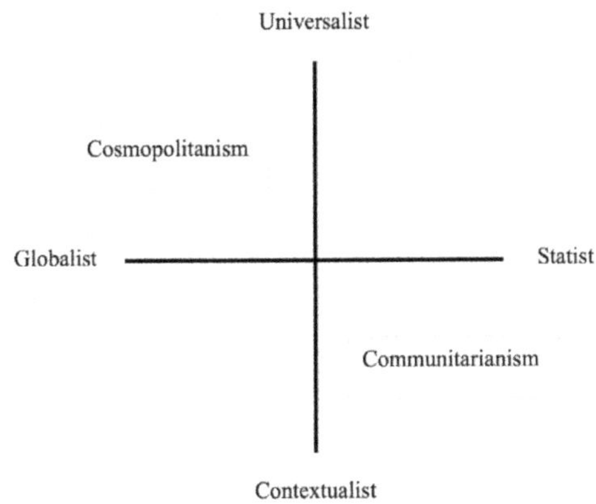

Figure 2.2. An ideological spectrum constituting cosmopolitanism and communitarianism

offers a sound basis for categorising actors as 'progressive' or 'conservative' when it comes to the new challenges of global political economy in the late twentieth and early twenty-first centuries—as long, of course, as this does not entirely crowd out the more traditional view of progressivism as a set of redistributive and interventionist economic positions. Cosmopolitans do not necessarily favour redistribution in general (Kuhn, Solaz, and van Elsas 2018, 1763; Gerhards et al. 2020, 242–43). After all, the universal and global nature of rights frameworks and their enforcement does not currently offer much to suggest that these rights are particularly strong. For instance, from a liberal perspective, one might easily argue that everyone should have equal access to social assistance, but that this social assistance should be kept to a minimal level to reward individual market participation.

To combine these 'new' and 'old' cleavages, we can present four ideal-typical positions: right-wing (i.e., *laissez-faire*, neoliberal) communitarianism, right-wing cosmopolitanism, left-wing (i.e., interventionist, pro-welfare) communitarianism, and left-wing cosmopolitanism (Biskamp 2019; Gerhards et al. 2020, 241–43). The latter term, or its close equivalent 'welfare cosmopolitanism', already carries currency as ways to describe the modernisation of European welfare states, which are undergoing processes of individualising rights for the purposes of cosmopolitan integration (Prandini 2018, 3; Van Gerven and Ossewaarde 2012, 51). This fits within a wider series of debates, where the contrast between cosmopolitanism and communitarianism has also started to emerge as a new label to describe the dominant cleavages in the context of European integration (Gerhards et al. 2020, 241–43).

In this analysis, we build on these approaches to categorise political ideologies as 'progressive' or 'conservative' based on (1) the extent to which they 'buy into' the lexical and contextual connotations towards either pole of the progressive–conservative spectrum, including their commitment to political-economic *laissez-faire* or interventionism, and sociocultural monism or pluralism, and (2) their position towards the integrated concept of welfarist cosmopolitanism (versus neoliberal communitarianism and the other integrated concepts). This framework can best be explained using individual attitudes. A person could be called a welfarist cosmopolitan if they fulfil three criteria. The first two are that the individual in question is both universalist and globalist in their preferences on welfare provision. This means they support universal access to welfare for everyone within the entity that provides it, which in particular implies an absence of welfare chauvinism. Furthermore, they would prefer this entity of provision to be supranational, and ideally global. As the world is primarily organised into nation-states today, the transfer of welfare provision to any entity above the nation-state (e.g., the EU) could be seen as a preliminary form of globalised welfare rights, albeit one that does not entirely fulfil the ideals of globalism (Gerhards et al. 2020, 27; Kuhn, Solaz, and van Elsas 2018, 1762). The third criterion concerns pro-welfare attitudes on the traditional political-economic interventionist–*laissez-faire* axis, whereby the individual in question would tend more to support redistributive policies as well as an active role for state institutions in promoting growth and strategic investment, raising or reducing employment, wage, and price levels, managing the money supply and interest rates, and other ways to correct market failures.

In contrast, welfarist communitarians would be (1) statists and (2) contextualists with regards to welfare provision, while (3) also favouring redistribution and state activism. Welfarist communitarians thus prefer welfare provision and the legitimate provision of justice to remain in the hands of the nation-state. They further consider welfare obligations to be bound to restricted communities and groups, including prioritising welfare entitlements for some but not all members of a national population based on criteria of (e.g.) residency or other demographic status—which implies attitudes of welfare chauvinism (see figure 2.3).

PROGRESSIVISM AND POLITICAL IDEOLOGIES

So, considering this, which specific ideologies fit into the 'progressive' camp? In the first instance, we can answer this by returning to the core principle of progressivism and characterise the 'castlist' of progressive 'family members' in terms of traditions of social thought that hold different ideological views of human and societal progress. Here, there are essentially two approaches to choose from: a *kleinprogressiv* (exclusive, 'smaller progressive') or

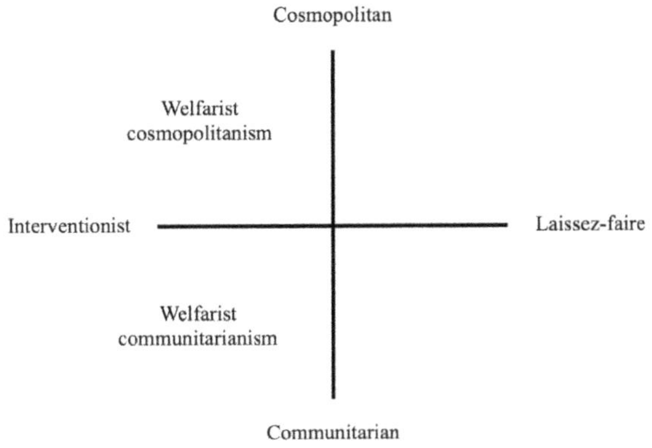

Figure 2.3. An ideological spectrum combining 'old' and 'new' cleavages

großprogressiv (inclusive, 'greater progressive') way to populate the progressive coalition. The difference between these two approaches essentially tracks the long-standing and constantly evolving debates over how far specific ideological *familles spirituelles* ('spiritual families') (von Beyme 1985) that share any number of other 'family resemblances' in their lexical and contextual core concepts can also be classed as belonging unambiguously to the 'progressive' side of the 'progressive–conservative' binary.

We can refine this framework by integrating the specific distinction between welfarist (as opposed to neoliberal) cosmopolitanism versus communitarianism to create a categorisation comprising three groups of political actors. The first group consists of actors that we consider to be 'consistently progressive', who take a progressive stance on both the political-economic and cosmopolitan–communitarian (as a subset of the broader sociocultural) axes of the spectrum we have outlined. As welfarist cosmopolitans, they are situated on the interventionist side of the traditional political-economic axis and tend to lean more cosmopolitan (*qua* pluralist) than communitarian (*qua* monist). Second, we also take into consideration 'semi-progressive' actors that position themselves as progressive on only one of the two axes and as conservative on the other, which could mean that an actor is generally cosmopolitan but economically favours free markets and fiscal restraint or is generally communitarian but still favours state activism and redistribution. Finally, 'consistently conservative' actors are political-economic *laissez-faire* communitarians, whom we exclude from our analysis for the remainder of this book.

These categories broadly correspond with different political ideologies. As our analysis focuses on the EU, as a specific political, economic, and cultural entity within the European segment of the 'global North', we apply our framework to those ideologies that are most prevalent in the contemporary institutions of the EU. While there might be disagreement on the precise way these political ideologies should be differentiated from one another, we find the following list to offer a fairly comprehensive representation of the ideological landscape in contemporary Europe: Christian democrats, social democrats, liberals, greens, conservatives, the far right, and the far left (Freeden 1996; Ostrowski 2022a; von Beyme 1985).

As most conservatives and far-right political actors are not—and do not claim to be—progressive in either a lexical or contextual sense, and specifically do not fit into the progressive characterisation on either of our two analytical axes, we do not take them into account any further in the following chapters. Certainly, we concede that a few far-right parties have recently adopted support for the welfare state into their political demands (de Cabanes 2017). However, their overall stance towards cosmopolitanism and towards sociocultural pluralism in general tends to be so extremely hostile that categorising them as even remotely progressive would fail to reflect the more general ideas of progressivism outlined at the start of this chapter.

Some political ideologies belong fairly unambiguously to the left 'end' of the familiar left–centre–right ideological spectrum, embracing a range of lexical and contextual connotations that resolutely echo progressive approaches to societal change, as well as the welfare cosmopolitan category in particular. Although they vary in the degree of their progressive preferences, we consider social democracy, green ideology, and the far left to be generally situated in the realm of consistently progressive ideological positions. Social democracy is squarely rooted in a critique of both what has happened in the past and how it affects what is still happening in the present, and is oriented towards making tangible changes in society today. It is under no illusions that these changes will inevitably come about by themselves, but instead sees them as the product of painstaking, gradual victories eked out one at a time. Green ideology aligns with social democracy in its support for reformism, albeit as much through passive resistance towards societal threats as actively fighting to surmount them, and adds a particular future-oriented focus on long-term sustainability, including objectives such as degrowth and comprehensive dietary shifts. Lastly, the 'far left' (a collective term for the various socialisms, communisms, and anarchisms that intermingle in the space 'beyond' social democracy) is similarly, if anything more vehemently, critical of society's past and present. However, its sights are set typically more towards the future, with considerable hope and positivity about how far societal change might eventually go. It is preoccupied by questions over the process of change: how predictable it is, how far governed by historical laws, and what form of human agency can best deliver it, whether freewheeling spontaneity or assiduous management.

Then, there are two ideologies that sit more towards the centre of the left–centre–right spectrum, which in both lexical and contextual forms find themselves prone to aligning with both 'middle' and conservative claims about society's direction, and which embrace some but by no means all the welfare cosmopolitan positions. Liberalism adopts a fairly open-ended understanding of the direction society ought to move in, placing its weight mostly on the idea of human flourishing and humanitarian mutual treatment between all of society's members. Its concern is above all to protect and improve the situation of individuals, set against the backdrop of a quasi-evolutionary struggle for survival, which liberalism alternately rejects and embraces. Many liberals also have a tendency towards some key facets of cosmopolitanism, while often remaining committed to political-economic positions that fall more towards the *laissez-faire* end of the spectrum. Christian democracy, meanwhile, is deeply unconvinced of experimental breaks with tradition, and endorses societal change only where it takes a demonstrably anti- or at least non-revolutionary form. If society is to take on a new direction, Christian democracy is determined that it should be one that it can grow into naturally, through an accumulation of the willed developments pursued by its individual members. At the same time, Christian democrats occasionally show preferences for a welfare state while tending to embrace culturally conservative and thus often extensively communitarian sociocultural positions. By implication, the progressive characteristics of Christian democracy are heavily residual, but not entirely absent.

In this book, we choose to take the more inclusive, *großprogressiv* road to defining who is and is not a 'progressive', for many reasons. Above all, it is important for progressives and for social scientists to acknowledge that no single ideology has a cast-iron universally defensible claim to lead, let alone fully define, progressivism as a school of thought or social movement. In the same vein, we must accept that every one of these ideologies has the potential to manifest in not only progressive but also conservative forms—and in several cases, carries a demonstrable history of defending profoundly conservative actions and outcomes beneath a veneer of progressive principles. Lastly, we endorse the view that fundamentally it will (and of right ought to) take the concerted forces of all strands of progressivism to achieve meaningful, lasting societal change. On those grounds, we argue that social-democratic, green, far-left, liberal, and Christian-democratic ideology all have characteristics that could broadly be considered 'progressive'—albeit, of course, to radically different degrees.

IDEOLOGICAL IDEAL-TYPES AS AN ANALYTICAL APPROACH

At the core of the argument we outline in this book lies the claim that holding this sort of progressive 'change coalition' together requires choosing a carefully delineated and carefully reasoned 'cast list' of central aims and principles for progressives of all stripes to mobilise around. The particular combination of a 'progressive Europe' and a UBI—the one realised by means of the other—is just such an aim. Specifically, it is an aim that has the potential to bring out the progressive impetus in all these ideologies and allow those of their advocates and defenders who prefer to take them in a progressive direction to 'steal a march' on those who would rather see them unfold their conservative identity. This is perhaps not uniquely true of a European UBI. But the roster of alternative candidates for this role urgently needs to be populated further and can find in the idea of a European UBI a standard around which they can rally and build in future.

In the following sections, we take a closer look at each of these five ideologies and their guiding principles. We then examine how far these principles could lead actors who broadly subscribe to each of these respective ideologies to accept, and develop, a compelling case in favour of a UBI. We enumerate and discuss the most important arguments for UBI from the perspective of each ideology and derive implications from these arguments for policy design. Within each chapter, we assess the different dimensions outlined in chapter 1 for each of the UBI designs, along with the particular features we have identified that would need to be satisfied by any feasible model of a European UBI. We then reflect on the key principles and preferences of each ideology and put forward a series of concrete mechanisms and tweaks within the general EUBI model that could respond to these principles. This results in a set of simplified, ideal-typical policy proposals for what a 'pure' EUBI would look like if it were to be introduced in a way that fully responded to the foci and preferences of each progressive ideological strand.

Throughout the examination of ideologies and the development of policy proposals, we use an analytical lens of ideal-types to simplify what would otherwise rapidly become overly complex issues. This allows us to develop EUBI families for various ideologies that are in practice highly internally diverse. We acknowledge that this reduction of nuance can bring its own problems—but it is a conscious decision made to accommodate the unavoidable trade-offs between detail and breadth in the design of a policy that has been as widely debated as a UBI. Going into more granular detail and conducting empirical studies of each political ideology's current stance on UBI would have made the broad overview and comparison we are aiming for impossible. Furthermore, aiming to incorporate limitless theoretical details into our approach would have risked running into 'nuance traps', particularly by inhibiting the capacity for this analysis to deliver high-level abstract conceptions of what an EUBI can do for society in macroscopic terms (Healy 2017). Thus, we have chosen to apply an ideal-typical perspective while explicitly encouraging researchers and participants in political discourse to critically scrutinise our proposals.

But what does an approach rooted in ideal-types imply in concrete terms? In welfare state research, the terms 'typology' and 'ideal-type' are often confused despite substantial differences in their meaning. In a typology, every empirical case must be clearly organised or organisable under one category (Van Kersbergen and Vis 2015)—a typology in this sense proposes 'real-types' rather than 'ideal-types'. This analytical approach is therefore particularly well-suited to mapping, or 'coding', empirical cases—but is often not practically applicable and can even be misleading. By contrast, ideal-type approaches do not imply that each empirical case clearly matches one type. Rather, they propose purely hypothetical manifestations of the issue at stake—here, an EUBI—to illustrate how it *might* look like in practice if one entirely and exclusively followed a given underlying theoretical line of reasoning to its ultimate conclusions. Hence, ideal-types are less suited to unambiguously mapping empirical cases but are a practical way of sketching out theoretical lines of division and simplifying complex realities.

For example, a typology of EUBI designs would aim to unambiguously categorise any proposal that actually exists into one type *and one only*. By contrast, an ideal-type approach to evaluating EUBIs would develop theoretically plausible EUBI proposals that maximise the scheme's capacity to deliver on the ideals of different political ideologies. However, this does not mean that if, for instance, green politicians or activists proposed a particular model of EUBI, it would have to entirely and solely match the theoretical ideal-type of a green EUBI. After all, internal partisan struggles, ideological inconsistencies, or political limitations may all nudge the proposal away from what green ideology might suggest on paper. On the other hand, theories on green ideology may simply be off in their assessment of what green parties should prefer. Since in our study we do not aim to map empirical cases—which, after all, are so far fairly few and far between, since both UBI and especially EUBI are still emerging ideas—but instead want to illustrate theoretically plausible policy designs and the often-stark differences between them, we pursue an ideal-type approach. Given the huge variety of political positions in the EU, it is likely that the political preferences of pro-(E)UBI actors will only partly rather than wholly match several of the ideal-types we propose. In other words, 'mixed' or 'hybrid' EUBI types are much more likely to occur in practice than any of the ideal-typical UBI designs *as such*.

A key implication of our ideal-type approach is that the policy designs we present here are not intended to completely define the horizon of possibility for 'what count as' the only respectively appropriate designs under each progressive ideology. Rather, they serve the purpose of illustrating how different theoretical ideological preferences can in principle influence how a UBI might be designed. For every argument we provide, alternative concrete policy realisations are also entirely possible. This implies that even though the following policies are more concrete versions of a broader policy family, they themselves also constitute fuzzy policy families under which various even narrower policies and more tightly defined policy mechanisms could be subsumed, which can be further specified and vary between even more fine-grained proposals.

As we turn to the arguments that different ideologies may deploy to argue for an EUBI, it is worth reiterating three admonitory caveats. First, political, economic, and cultural actors are often not necessarily ideal-typically linked to only one ideology (Ostrowski 2024). Even political parties that claim an affinity, or affiliation, to a discrete ideological label tend to diverge from the ideology they 'officially' subscribe to in practice, sacrificing their own policies or coopting others in response to strategic imperatives. Thus, using only the arguments of individual actors as a basis for identifying the ideal-typical policy designs for each ideology would not deliver its intended outcome, if this were to be based on a primarily empirically driven approach. Second, many political parties and ideologically affiliated civil society groups have so far engaged with UBI sporadically at most. Thus, while there is by now a prodigious number of arguments 'out there' for and against UBI (Afscharian et al. 2021, 2022b), they often cut across the 'clean' ideological lines we use in this analysis. Third, and rooted in the first two reasons, there is still much theoretical work to be done on distinctively attributing different conceptual arguments in favour of UBI to different ideologies in a typological as well as ideal-typical sense. We aim to contribute to this task in the remainder of this analysis.

Chapter 3

Social Democracy

Social democracy—the political ideology perhaps the most automatically synonymous with progressivism on the European continent—can be characterised as a centre-left ideology of compromise (Freeden 1996, 2003; Ostrowski 2022a; Jackson 2013). Rooted in the European workers' movements and rich varieties of socialist traditions that arose over the course of the nineteenth century, social democracy is currently represented at the EU level by the Party of European Socialists and the European Parliament group of the Progressive Alliance of Socialists and Democrats. Initially sceptical of European integration and its market-making tendencies, social democrats today largely belong to the most resolute pro-European voices in the political arena (Marks and Wilson 2000; Wolkenstein 2020). Social democracy to this day tends to forge a syncretic, compatibilising path: in its global commitments, it falls in between cosmopolitanism and communitarianism, while at the same time it supports the welfare state but also, in principle, the existence of free markets.

Today, social democrats resolve the tension between welfare and free markets through the idea of a regulated or coordinated social market economy. Here, the state provides certain 'guardrails', such as infrastructure, social services, and security, to protect workers from the depredations of pure market pressures (see, e.g., Joerges and Rödl 2004). This means that social democrats operate in an ideological field of tension between capitalism and anti-capitalism, where on the one hand they decisively reject the 'radical extremes' of communism (e.g., Kelly 1999) as well as economic liberalism (Crouch 2017). The result is a form of 'managed competition' and a society that effectively reflects a cooperative arrangement between producers and consumers. Strong trade unions, paired with redistributive and interventionist state action, are intended to enable workers to live a 'good life'. Labour and its capacity for productivity are key guidelines for any and all situations in which questions arise around 'who should get what'. However, social democrats also promote ideals of anti-poverty, above all by rejecting the logic of mere 'survival of the fittest'. Yet there is no contradiction as such for social democrats in linking work to ideas of 'deservingness' (van Oorschot 2000, 2006), not least since social democracy ultimately strives for a society marked by full employment (Jackson 2013). As the state is seen as a key actor in resolving redistributive struggles, taxation is an ever-present important part of social democrats' policy toolbox (Jackson 2013, 354).

As a legacy of its roots in the workers' movement (Jackson 2013, 349), social democracy tends to use both the rhetoric and ideas of class struggle (Bernstein 1922). It is firmly committed to the view that hierarchies in society, democracy, and the economy should be overcome. However, this approach must not be mistaken for radical collectivism. Instead, social democracy holds high the idea of aligning liberty and individuality with equality (Kastning 2013): to be free, individuals must receive equal opportunities (to be, to act, and so on). Building on these basic equalities, individuals should be emancipated to freely express their personal identities and creativity.

When it comes to cosmopolitanism and communitarianism, social democrats' ideals are less easily resolved into a single compromise position. Fundamentally, social democrats have promoted both ideas of nationality and internationalism over the course of their extended history (Kuisma 2007). Their support for the latter is rooted in general left-wing conceptions of international workers' movements, and today translates into the avowed cosmopolitan positions adopted by some parties and party factions. Nationality, on the other hand, is seen by many social democrats as an essential basis of social solidarity. Citizenship is a central concept in this respect. On the one hand, it implies social citizenship (Marshall 1950), in the specific sense that citizens are seen as having an entitlement to fundamental social rights. On the other hand, this implication can also lead correlatively to an exclusionary conception of society, where those who are not citizens lack certain rights. To this day, this leads to clear tendencies towards welfare chauvinism among certain social democrats, who have been key drivers of excluding EU citizens from other member states from receiving social assistance (Afscharian, Bruzelius, and Seeleib-Kaiser 2024). Ultimately, social democrats thus fall on a fairly sizeable spectrum of different positions between cosmopolitanism and communitarianism.

In line with these tendencies of intra-ideological compromise, social-democratic parties have demonstrated tendencies more readily associated with political 'centrism' (Keman 2010), albeit clothed in a left-wing garb. The ideology embraces ideas of gradualism and reformism (Jackson 2013, 351), meaning that it rejects radical revolutionary tendencies that would overthrow the (by assumption, democratic) system. Within these democratic institutions, it favours parliamentarism and representative approaches to giving a voice to the wider public (Przeworski 1985, 15). Building on a strong constitution, a 'social-democratic' democracy should thus feature various political parties that compete for votes but do not infringe on citizens' basic rights irrespective of electoral outcomes. Social democrats—at least on paper—thereby embrace cross-party collaboration. Since the policies that should then be pursued are reforms rather than revolutionary disruptions, the paths forward into the future are seen as relatively 'open' (Ostrowski 2022b). As an outgrowth of the revisionist strain of Marxism, social democracy thus rejects any suggestion of 'inevitable' developments such as those promoted by more orthodox Marxist traditions (Berman 2002, 121). Rather than aiming for a grand promise of a different world, social democrats struggle for real-time improvements to workers' lives in the 'here and now'.

BALANCING WORK WITH MEETING SOCIAL NEEDS: SOCIAL DEMOCRACY AND UBI

Concerning the idea of a UBI, social democrats have typically erred on the side of healthy scepticism. No major social-democratic party in the EU has so far made the policy a priority, and in fact, it is far more common to hear social democrats reject the idea as inherently neoliberal (Van Parijs 2016; Kenworthy 2019). Social-democratic critiques of UBI are also closely linked to trade unions' scepticism about the policy as 'anti-labour' (Vanderborght 2006)—ultimately unsurprising, given the strong historical links between trade unions and the social-democratic movement. But despite this well-developed strand of scepticism towards UBI, this is not to say that there are *no* significant groups of social democrats who support UBI, nor that social democracy as an ideology is incompatible with the scheme. From a theoretical perspective, social-democratic ideology embraces many principles that lend themselves strongly to support for a specific type of UBI. In the following sections, we go through each of these principles in turn and identify some key arguments in favour of UBI that social-democratic proponents of the policy might find particularly convincing.

Sociality

The first set of arguments for UBI derive from the 'social' part of social democracy. Within the ideology, social justice has often previously been associated with ideas of national belonging. This was less rooted in the ethno-nationalist notions prominent among far-right movements, but more in the idea of solidarity within a community (Berman 2006). Social democrats consider social rights a key element of what makes belonging to a national group meaningful, as they aim to give solidarity within a community a material dimension (Tilton 1991, 125–44). Without such a material dimension, belonging to a group such as a nation can be abstract and difficult to grasp for its individual members. Much like other social policies, UBI could be leveraged to make the material dimension of communal solidarity immediately tangible at an individual level. In the context of increasingly polarised debates over questions of identity, this can also help social democrats resolve a progressive dilemma concerning the idea of the nation itself. On the one hand, social democracy has evolved out of a context in which national unification in countries such as Germany or Italy was, in some ways, considered an example of societal 'progress'. In turn, many of the state-centred preferences within social-democratic policymaking remain closely linked to the institutional structures and processes of national government. On the other hand, social democracy's relationship with the nation has been highly fraught in post-WW2 Europe, given the continent's brutally horrific experiences of extreme nationalism and fascist rule. National identity is often linked to questions of (monistic or pluralistic) nationality built on language, culture, religion, or ethnicity. This runs the risk of creating exclusionary and oppressive dynamics rooted in negative distinction rather than positive solidarity.

A strong set of universal social rights that accrue to members of the community in question can foster a more progressive definition of belonging. In line with this goal, UBI adds a unique layer and character of affiliation to membership of a national community. Its universal character is key, as this avoids creating further stratifications between members of the community—at least in terms of financial payouts. This can distinguish the community from those at a higher or lower geographical scale such as the supranational, the continental, the international, or the global, as well as subnational scales such as the regional and local level. Further, the universality of UBI allows the policy to unite groups beyond lines of segmentation within a national population, including, for instance, demographic divides such as age and gender. UBI can make national affiliation an attractive choice that is universal to everyone, providing a material 'return on investment' in national participation. While often well-earning or wealthy individuals with low rootedness and high cross-border mobility can more easily reap the benefits of global integration, a UBI would add a core element to 'group membership' even for those who choose not to move. This argument is particularly relevant for social democrats who position themselves slightly more towards the pole of welfare communitarians.

It is important to note that this national perspective on UBI exists in a field of tension with some more contemporary ideas of progressivism and social democracy, which emphasise another key element of the ideology: its commitment to internationalism (Zielonka 2023), which is a characteristic priority for welfare cosmopolitans. Depending on how much weight social democrats choose to attribute to either internationalism or national community, the resulting UBI design associated with either position would change significantly. An internationalist emphasis would intuitively lend itself to a supranational UBI (Van Parijs and Vanderborght 2015). Again, UBI would be a way to generate a layer of unique material ties of membership to a community—albeit a supranational rather than a national one—along with the earlier logics regarding how this can set the community in question apart from other communities as well. A supranational UBI could further enable the creation of a well-developed 'multilevel' social policy system. Since social democracy aims to strike a balance between national and international action, a supranational UBI paired with national welfare states would be a way of enabling them to pursue material dimensions for both social identities simultaneously. Such a scheme could then build bridges between welfare cosmopolitan and welfare communitarian social democrats—with the added benefit of acting as a backstop that safeguards people financially from the worst impacts of rapid changes in national welfare systems.

Whether nationally or internationally, another element of social-democratic ideology concerns the relationship between members of society viewed as both producers and consumers (Ostrowski 2022a). In the social-democratic conception of an ideal community, society and the institutions that structure it are seen as large-scale cooperative enterprises—of mutual reliance and support, reciprocal interaction and exchange. This approach is one key element that makes social-democratic political-economic orders theoretically distinct from its 'purer' communist and capitalist equivalents. It lends itself particularly well to the idea of UBI: the policy could be considered an institutionalised system and a material expression of a 'solidaristic baseline' between all members of society. Regarding consumption, UBI would be a collective way of ensuring a minimum level of subsistence that is available to all. From the perspective of production, UBI could be considered a social dividend, which expresses a recognition of the contributions that all members of society ultimately make to the (re)production of societal wealth and its material basis. Both the production and consumption side tie intimately into one another here. After all, the enterprises that provide the goods and services that generate aggregate societal wealth ultimately benefit from consumers whose social needs are adequately covered. This logic is not fundamentally different from the ideas of a 'social market economy' found in Christian-democratic ideology as well. However, when coupled with further elements that are particular to social democracy, this can still have unique implications for policy design, as we elaborate further below.

One key player for social democrats in mediating the producer-consumer structures of social cooperation are trade unions. Traditionally, their relationship with UBI has been conflicted, not least due to fears of state-guaranteed social minima crowding out collective bargaining (Henderson and Quiggin 2019; Vanderborght 2006). However, if designed properly, UBI could act as a buffer for the contemporary expressions of workers' interests by providing a kind of prophylactic 'strike fund' that ultimately has the potential to strengthen their collective bargaining power. It could give trade unions an upper hand in labour disputes and materially enable workers to be more assertive in their demands—after all, the whole workforce across society would be less dependent on income paid by the very employers they are striking against. Furthermore, as a UBI paired with a strong welfare state would ensure that the bare necessities of workers are met, trade unions could focus on more ambitious goals in their demands. They might, for instance, demand structural involvement when it comes to business decisions, co-determination, sectoral bargaining, or the strengthening of works councils. Finally, UBI could end up steering states' fiscal policies towards the preferences of labour by institutionalising a universal spending scheme. However, the key determinant here will ultimately be the way that funds for this are generated: if resources are leveraged by taxing capital, UBI has the potential to become an institutionalised, permanent redistribution machine.

Democracy

The second eponymous element of a 'good society' that social democrats endorse consists in a high priority for the structures and procedures of democracy. Crucially, this does not solely refer to the formal rule of the people through a prescribed 'castlist' of political institutions. Rather, social democrats tend to promote specific, far-reaching criteria of reform geared towards democratising *all* facets of society. A key element for this democratisation of society consists in carrying out a careful balancing-act between favouring specific anticapitalist concepts within the overarching framework of a capitalist economy—which they often seek to achieve by managing competition and implementing a particular variant of a social market economy (Kelly 1999; Joerges and Rödl 2004; Crouch 2017).

To strike a balance between their critiques of capitalism and their support for a broadly market-based economy, social democrats might use UBI as a complement to the welfare state. The scheme could be considered a way to empower the large majority of people who would remain powerless in its absence in an otherwise undemocratic economy (Goodhart 2008; Pateman 2004). As capitalist economies tend to be to some extent hierarchical—through relations of employment, business management, dynamics of credit and debt—but do not typically derive these hierarchies from any procedural devices such as democratic elections, they also lack democratic accountability to varying degrees. UBI might thus be used as a form of state intervention through fiscal rather than regulatory means, giving every individual participant in an economy a basic set of resources to empower them financially. As a consequence, people may be less at risk of losing faith in a liberal society structured around markets—because they remain quite literally able to 'buy into it'. Given that many modern social-democratic movements tend to subscribe to free markets in principle more-or-less without hesitation, a UBI paired with the existing roster of welfare states could help them 'build bridges' between democratic ideals and capitalism. The result could be a mutual stabilisation of the core post-WW2 political-economic bargain, in which democratic politics accept free markets, while the key actors of the capitalist economy maintain their faith in democracy.

We have already alluded earlier to the fact that the social-democratic interpretation of a functioning form of capitalism is built on the management of competition (Bandau 2023; Meyer and Hinchman 2007, 107–13). In its essential point, this reduces to a very simple trade-off: while social democrats are willing to tolerate *some* competition in principle, the state should equally have *some* control over its extreme forms. Here, social democrats who favour a UBI might consider the scheme a way to flesh out a reasonable compromise. It allows an administration to assert itself over the interplay between consumption, exchange, and production without setting overly rigid rules. In accordance with this, ideals of consensualism and collectivism take priority over economic competition and individualism—albeit without authoritatively mandating what market participants are or are not allowed to do. Furthermore, a progressive UBI could ensure that at least a part of people's livelihood remains untouched by—and untouchable to—the social forces of competition. While participating in market competition could still allow individuals to strive for improvements in their living conditions, their basic needs are not contingent on whether or not they 'win'. This limits the danger of being 'crowded out' by the threat of interpersonal rivalry over scarce resources. A reason why social democrats might support UBI as a concrete policy to achieve these goals consists in its relatively minor degree of intervention in market activities themselves. It does not directly intervene in business structures and operations but still buffers individuals against the worst risks of failure—including, of course, if they happen to want to start up a competitive enterprise themselves. In an ideal scenario, this might offer a way to lower economically harmful risk aversion within individually safer parameters.

Finally, social democrats might support UBI with an eye on the operations of the social market economy (Meyer and Hinchman 2007, 125–35). Here, they have to strike a balance between two potentially conflicting ideals. On the one hand, social democrats set themselves apart from the far left as they tend to reject anything that resembles a closely planned, prescriptive economy. The hope is that markets may, in principle, give people sufficient leeway to come to their own economic decisions. On the other hand, social democrats reject the purely *laissez-faire* approach of giving market forces free rein. As UBI simply equips people with the financial means to participate in market decisions—and, crucially, to *keep participating* in them, even if something 'goes wrong for them' for any reason—it could be one way of making the abstract idea of a social market economy more meaningful (Straubhaar 2017, 2018). Due to its universality, it could ensure that basic, minimum opportunities are equally spread across the entire population. Finally, the scheme could be framed as an expression of democratic social responsibility. In this conception, democracy has a 'civilising' task, in the sense that it ensures that all members of society mutually protect each other from the painful and destructive aspects with which life often confronts them. UBI could be considered one element in formally institutionalising this ideal.

Liberty and Equality

Beyond its cardinal values of sociality and democracy, social-democratic ideology often appeals to particular interpretations of liberty and equality. These have already partly shone through in the analysis so far, but they are central enough to social democrats' political worldview to warrant closer attention by themselves. Within social-democratic ideology, liberty and equality broadly revolve around four mutually related pillars: citizenship, class, the rejection of hierarchy, and the pursuit of full employment (Meyer and Hinchman 2007).

The reasons why social democrats might consider UBI a way to foster citizenship are closely linked to the arguments we have already outlined concerning communal belonging. By providing a material basis in the form of a direct monetary benefit, the state can make the meaning of citizenship visible to all those who formally hold it. Beyond mere signalling, this could enable all members of society to overcome the material hurdles to participating in society and making use of their legal entitlements. The scheme would represent a minimum bar of 'real freedom' under which no member of society could fall (van Parijs 2016). The formal right to free movement in the EU illustrates this rather well. While all EU citizens have the right to settle anywhere in the EU as long as they can sustain a living, this right is highly unequal in practice as it presupposes ready access to material resources. Even within nation states, where such resources are no legal requirement for mobility, they are a *de facto* necessity—after all, the very act of moving itself requires a certain material basis. Universal schemes such as UBI are one way of addressing this issue. While existing welfare states already contribute to these goals, means-tested schemes in particular create new problems through the lens of citizenship, as they may impose judgmental categorisations that discriminate between citizens along lines of differential 'deservingness'. Universal and automatic schemes can allow social democrats to achieve a minimum of equal treatment without the limiting and asymmetric effects of more targeted policies.

The universalistic ideals of social-democratic citizenship respond to the *de facto* pervasive existence of class and hierarchy in many forms throughout society. For many social democrats, class is primarily determined by the level (or the sheer existence) of income and wealth inequalities—most notably, inequality in assets (Atkinson 2015; Piketty 2014). Social democrats may see UBI as a way of pushing back against these inequalities at the lowest income levels. The regularity of UBI is a crucial element of the policy for social democrats, as class inequalities tend to be stabilised when incomes are irregular or not adequately guaranteed. UBI could then act as a wealth buffer that absorbs temporary shocks to prevent people from sliding into precarity. By covering basic necessities of everyday life such as food, rent, and bills, UBI could further open up nonessential consumption such as higher-quality food and clothing to people in lower-income deciles. Hence, social democrats in favour of UBI may hope to use it as a way to erode the many specific material manifestations of deeper class distinctions.

From this follows a specific series of links between social democracy's anti-hierarchical commitments and the idea of a UBI. To a very basic degree, the policy could place everyone at a similar level of minimum entitlement irrespective of any other social differences, and hence overcome the most extreme forms of societal disprivilege. While these effects would only apply at the lowest end of the income spectrum, they could complement more targeted policies that safeguard individuals against falling through the cracks. The result could be a universal—albeit fairly minimal—political-economic 'safe space' within which every member of society enjoys a measure of freedom from social subordination. An important condition for this to work is UBI's non-preferential and automatic nature. This avoids situations where insufficiently nuanced targeting rules or arbitrary case-specific decisions crowd out a dependent individual from being able to access this kind of 'safe space'.

Traditionally, social democrats have first and foremost aimed to achieve these goals by targeting full employment (Callaghan 2002; Meyer and Hinchman 2007, 152). The notion of UBI being paid, even to those who refuse to work, has thus become a point of prodigious contention among social democrats—with some suggesting that this is the primary reason why such a scheme should never be introduced. However, social-democratic proponents of the policy can frame it as a way of enhancing the liberating effects of work. In this line of argument, UBI frees people from the need to take *just any* opportunity on the labour markets that offers itself to them. Rather, workers can *choose* their opportunities, meaning that they gain the power to refuse exploitative offers. This could further shift bargaining power to workers, thus reducing the social incidence of precarious working conditions (see Henderson and Quiggin 2019, 5012). Among the effects of this development could be the reduction of contingently waged day-labour such as zero-hour contracts and gig work in favour of more permanent contracts. Assuming these effects become reality, this would imply a reduction of the 'reserve army of labour' and thus, ideally, a shift of business practices towards more 'decent jobs'. Finally, social-democratic proponents of UBI may hope for smoother labour market matching due to workers' gaining an increased power of saying 'no'. As workers do not have to take up the first job to them, they have more time to invest in the upskilling and lifelong learning they want and need to pursue, thus eventually finding jobs that are better suited to their interests and skillsets.

Statism

Another element that has come through repeatedly in the previous sections is the particular social-democratic interpretation of the role of the state. The state is a major element of how social democrats aim to (re)structure societies to align more closely with their ideals (Meyer and Hinchman 2007, 66). Two important pillars of social-democratic statism that further sets it apart from ideologies farther to the left consist in its embrace of parliamentarism and reformism (Jackson 2013).

Parliamentarism refers to the broad social-democratic commitment to parliamentary representation for members of any given society within a democratic system (Jackson 2013). In the eyes of many social democrats, improving the position of the worst-off in society is a key purpose of state institutions—which means that social-democratic delegates may try to use UBI as a baseline for exercising their democratic responsibilities. Due to its universal nature, the scheme would avoid showing patrimonial or sectarian favouritism towards certain groups, such as those voters who gave their electoral support to the winning party. While blatant forms of such favouritism may not be especially prominent in many European states, social outcomes with much the same effect can occur more indirectly as well. For instance, social-democratic parties with considerable electoral support among pensioners may be incentivised to one-sidedly focus on pension increases when it comes to rolling out social policies. From their preference for parliamentarism, it follows that social democrats would require UBI to be implemented through primary legislation in order to ensure a maximum of legitimacy and democratic accountability. Direct executive action or technocratic rule, by contrast, would lack any such qualities—and would most likely also circumvent secondary social-democratic ideals such as consultation, scrutiny, and democratic approval. However, if implemented democratically, the scheme would strengthen the welfarist appeal of democracy per se relative to informal measures for the worst-off such as philanthropy and charitable donations. Many of the social-democratic goals outlined so far could then best be achieved if the highest democratically legitimised political authority was responsible for the UBI scheme's implementation.

In stark contrast to communist ideologies, social democrats embrace reformism and anti-revolutionist ideas (Meyer and Hinchman 2007, 69; Thorsen 2021, 6). In line with this, UBI could be seen as a significant reform to the current system that does not cross the line of revolutionary action. Current political-economic arrangements would largely remain in place, fiscal and welfare institutions could also be maintained, and the overall functioning of the democratic state would remain intact. What is more, the policy would be entirely compatible with further introductions of future reforms that are (also) geared towards liberating workers from exploitation, such as complementary schemes for living wage legislation, four-day work weeks at maintained income levels, flexible working, and the right to disconnect. As with both policies such as these and the existing set of welfare institutions, UBI could provide an additional pressure valve that addresses serious flaws in contemporary political economy, without risking a disruptive 'leap of faith' concerning the most fundamental institutions of society. Social democrats might thus plausibly frame UBI as a policy that is simple but not simplistic, and as a promise that does not overpromise.

Individuality and Creativity

While social-democratic ideology emphasises collective solidarity, it tends to do so in service of individual prosperity and creativity (Brandal et al. 2013; Meyer and Hinchman 2007, 102; Jackson 2013). One of the key goals for social democracy is the expression of personal identity in a 'good life' and in productive work. Concerning self-expression, proponents of UBI field arguments that are already quite closely aligned with social-democratic ideas. They reason that the policy would recognise individuals as the irreducible core of society, embedded in a complex network of overlapping relationships with those around them (Mays 2019, 73–74). In this context, UBI anchors an empowered individual as a stable node within these networks by emphasising an individual freedom that is rooted in societal solidarity. Hence, the state is institutionalised as a provider of material support that explicitly respects individual uniqueness. In theory, UBI could provide a buffer for individual vulnerabilities while allowing people to express themselves more freely (Van

Parijs 2016). As the bare necessities of survival are covered, social democrats could then explore a more ambitious framework of additional policies designed to foster human flourishing.

While many of these goals are traditionally supposed to be achieved through labour, social democrats might aim for a UBI design that does not completely replace work. As suggested earlier, their impetus here would be to develop a way of implementing UBI that reduces the prevalence of inadequate working conditions by enhancing workers' bargaining power, thus making UBI compatible with the traditional ideals of workers' movements. As advanced economies in particular are shifting increasingly towards sectors that are less labour-intensive in a traditionally physical sense, such a policy agenda would not need to be an active step towards undermining societal productivity. Rather, by decoupling the financial recognition of individual societal value from labour productivity, new avenues for more meaningful work may open up. Specifically, more creative types of work paired with more time for social interaction may benefit society as a whole. For social democrats, this is a crucial development to pick up on, as their traditional constituencies begin to fade.

Welfare

Contemporary social democracy is closely tied to the development of the welfare state. While institutional arrangements diverge between countries, social democrats across borders tend to support the fight against poverty through taxation, redistribution, and public services (Jackson 2013; Korpi 2008; Merkel and Petring 2007). The fundamental importance of overcoming poverty is one of the most intuitive reasons why social democrats might consider UBI a viable path for the future. Clearly, the most immediate effect of UBI concerns the material components of what it means to be among the 'worst off'. Depending on policy design, the scheme could drastically reduce absolute poverty—but it could also be set at a value relative to other economic indicators to reduce relative poverty. In either scenario, the scheme would effect a decisive break with the extreme downward spirals that mark those falling into income poverty. As each individual case of poverty is different, a monetary scheme would provide people with the most individualised way of addressing their particular needs.

It is essentially inevitable that the process of tackling poverty through a UBI will mean confronting specific questions of taxation and redistribution. For social democrats, this is likely to be more of an advantage than a drawback. As a fixed sum, UBI would have proportionally the greatest financial impact on the lives of those with the lowest prior incomes. As we show later on, these effects can also be turned into 'proper' redistribution by adding certain elements to the policy design. For instance, the automatic receipt of payments could be tapered off based on income levels, forcing those above these levels to actively claim their income if they want to receive it. To perhaps even greater effect, UBI could be used as a redistribution tool simply by financing it primarily through taxes on capital, wealth, or extremely high incomes. As there are unavoidable limitations to these effects, social democrats would need to ensure that UBI is not seen—over-ambitiously and wrongly—as a 'silver bullet' of redistribution. It merely establishes a redistributive baseline but does not preclude additional targeted measures such as pensions, parental support, or disability aid.

This compatibility with other approaches is central for linking social-democratic ideology to UBI (Van Parijs 2016; Pitts et al. 2017, 16). After all, contemporary and historical social democrats have clearly indicated that UBI is not their first preferred path of welfarist social policy to pursue. Instead, social democracy has traditionally fostered the coexistence of in-cash and in-kind benefits (Klitgaard 2007, 180–90). The upshot of this is that a social-democratic UBI would not be intended to *replace* services, but rather aim to *complement* and *enhance* them. For instance, UBI could act as a monetary supplement that would allow individuals to overcome the hurdles that stand in the way of them accessing in-kind services. This is particularly important in the field of education. As even universal basic services could not ensure *de facto* accessibility in all cases, UBI could contribute to making such services a reality. Generally, social democrats might consider UBI more as a form of policy 'grout' to seal gaps in the existing systems, rather than as a viable alternative to in-kind schemes. This way, they can avoid perpetuating an ever-increasing system of complex and bureaucratic needs for state activities in niche areas. This may further alleviate pressure from the state to catch up to the unexpected individual shortcomings of the welfare state.

Human and Social Progress

Alongside its membership of the loose grouping of 'progressive' ideologies we have assembled in this analysis, social democracy also features an explicit commitment to foster human and social progress. While this entails many of the issues we have already examined above, it also stretches beyond them to include specific ideas of progress, gradualism, and anti-inevitability (Thorsen 2021, 6). Concerning progress, social democrats might see in UBI a response to long-standing social issues like poverty and cost of living, but also to more acute challenges concerning interpersonal connectivity and transformations in the nature of work. Part of the appeal of UBI in this context is the fact that it is immediately actionable. As the changes needed for its implementation are at least conceptually speaking 'assessable', UBI could be seen by social democrats as a ready-made pragmatic response to the far-reaching challenges society faces today. It would also be an elegant attempt to fix issues with the institutions that social democrats themselves have built without drawing too much attention to the potential previous mistakes that have subsequently emerged. If, for instance, social democrats find benefits built on insurance models or means-testing to be inadequate policy solutions by themselves, a complementary UBI could allow them to close gaps in these schemes without throwing out all of their prior achievements and starting again entirely from scratch.

In attempting such reforms, social democrats have traditionally embraced gradualism. While UBI would undoubtedly be a major policy reform, it is still conceptually manageable, as it does not aim to bring about a cataclysmic rupture between fundamentally different models of society. It thus reflects the social-democratic view that policy interventions do not have to be presentationally dramatic in order to be substantively radical (Meyer and Hinchman 2007, 69). Furthermore, a social-democratic UBI would likely not be intended to be an endpoint *in and of itself*, but rather a key waymarker along a continuous trajectory of reform. As one step along the path of cushioning people from the most detrimental effects of capitalist labour markets, social democrats could consider UBI as a partial, contingent piece of a much bigger picture. By creating the moral and legal conditions for income that is not tied to economic status but rather to citizenship, UBI could enable future restructurings of society to come about—without necessarily having to embody them wholly by itself.

Crucially, this does not mean that social democrats would consider such developments to be inevitable—which is to say that UBI and any other adjacent reforms would need to be tirelessly fought for. This is particularly important if social democrats want to avoid a policy design that diverges too far from their own preferences. As we discuss further below, such a design would entail universal and regular payments, and would complement rather than replace social services in particular. Throughout the latter parts of this book, we argue that certain other ideologies can be expected to favour fundamentally different policy designs. Even if social democrats were to struggle for and achieve their ideal UBI design, their commitment to anti-inevitability (Berman 2002, 121) would further imply that the policy would not *need* to remain in place indefinitely. Given that social democracy accepts that the future of society is open-ended and uncertain, UBI may also be seen as a transitory tool, a mechanism that moves society towards something entirely different. One reason why UBI could be considered particularly compatible with such views of anti-inevitability is that it does not prescribe what counts as progress. It simply provides the material basis to enable people to individually or collectively pursue what *they*, jointly or severally, consider to be progress. It is thus compatible with various potential future trajectories for societal development. All the same, it may provide a platform to catalyse their emergence.

Political Strategy

While the arguments we have considered so far may matter for social democrats from a more theoretical ideological perspective, UBI also has a strong *political* component attached to it. From this angle, social democrats might seek to pursue it as a policy in order to continue and 'lock in' a preexisting agenda of extending social rights. UBI can be seen as the introduction of a positive right *through which* political rights to noninterference by the state are complemented by economic, social, and cultural rights to state provision. Social democrats could also pursue the formal constitutionalisation of these rights in order to embed an activist role for the state into the legal identity of society. Framing a basic income as a constitutional right would enshrine it in the legal architecture of citizenship and expand the sphere of social rights that are legally untouchable to include an additional economic dimension. This would go beyond the already widespread rights concerning property and labour, as it would set for individuals a consistent 'rate of return' from aggregate societal wealth. Through the earlier logics concerning the effect of UBI on bargaining power, this could implicitly be accompanied by a constitutionalisation of workers' collective economic empowerment.

Finally, as we argue throughout this book, UBI harbours extensive theoretical potential for cross-party collaboration, which may translate into new power options for the parties involved. Some of these benefits in the realm of politics are independent of the various political ideologies, whereas others are unique to social democracy. Generally, the pledge to introduce UBI carries considerable strategic risks, which often reduce the issue to something of an afterthought in party contestation. Only when the policy becomes salient do politicians typically take a more explicit, detailed stance. The dilemma posed by these risks could be circumvented by prominently and proactively committing to a cautious strategy, such as UBI trials or phased roll-outs (Afscharian et al. 2022a). Such approaches would clearly signal support for a minimum social guarantee and may thus galvanise support without alienating risk-averse voters. By committing to the idea in principle while staying cautious on policy substance, progressive actors can further engineer a litmus test to identify which of the actors they are dealing with are inclined to adopt more conservative socioeconomic views in political competition. This is particularly relevant for coalition-building, considering the increasingly complex differentiations between left and right cosmopolitans and communitarians. As social democrats in particular have recently struggled with their role in promoting socioculturally progressive, cosmopolitan agendas (Paster 2008), they could further use a salient and controversial proposal like a UBI to reorient debates towards a socioeconomic focus. Finally, building social and democratic coalitions that support the broader systemic *status quo* is a strategically crucial goal for social democrats if they want to get into power. To achieve this, they need policy proposals that are open to adjustments depending on the preferred coalition partners they are intending to work with. UBI is a highly adaptable idea that can be tailored to various agenda coalitions while starving anti-system movements of a key basis of their support. Accordingly, it is a comparatively simple yet salient 'ask' that social democrats can table as a starting point for the development of cross-ideological compromises.

THE MIDDLE WAY: A SOCIAL-DEMOCRATIC VIEW OF EUBI

As these arguments illustrate, there are substantial overlaps between the theoretical ideals of social democracy and some of the key ambitions that proponents of UBI hope to achieve by implementing the policy. While social-democratic parties have struggled with the idea of UBI in the past (Haagh 2011; Van Parijs 2016), an EUBI thus has great potential to deliver on some of the goals they have as yet failed to achieve. In particular, it could put in place the framework for a united and strong Social Europe, effective in covering the basic necessities of each EU citizen, without directly competing with the established, nationally unique sets of welfare schemes. However, the match between UBI and the theoretical ideals of social democracy hinges on concrete decisions in policy design. Even if we leave the critique of UBI as a concept to one side, the devil is still very much in the detail.

In this section, we sketch out one proposal for a policy design that we consider ideal-typically close to social democracy as an ideology. We follow the different dimensions of variation between UBI families which we introduced in chapter 1: universality, individuality, conditionality, uniformity, frequency, duration, modality, adequacy, and funding. We also add information on the expected role of the EU, as well as on technical issues of EUBI introduction and distribution. Importantly, the concrete proposals we present here are intended as schematic tools for illustrative purposes. They are meant to demonstrate how malleable UBI can be as a policy depending on one's ideological preferences. By implication, they are not intended as a ready-made solution that can be immediately implemented regardless of political context, current socioeconomic developments, or institutional constraints.

Universality

Following the tensions between communitarian and cosmopolitan preferences within social democracy outlined above, the universality of UBI can potentially become a point of controversy for this ideology. One of its elements is simple to resolve: considering that social democrats aim to strengthen social citizenship, an EUBI that would suit social-democratic ideology has to be paid out to all citizens. However, it is unclear here what precisely the concept of citizenship is referring to. After all, there is no real consensus among social democrats about whether to prioritise internationalism or national identity—or, if both need to be taken into account, about what balance to strike between them. Cosmopolitan social democrats would naturally prefer an internationalist focus, meaning that all citizens of the EU rather than of its member states would receive UBI payments. By contrast, communitarian social democrats would push for a UBI that is delivered to each citizen of a specific country (Meyer 2012). However, if one agrees on the aim of making a UBI European, this differentiation loses its practical relevance. As EU citizenship is linked to national citizenship, any citizen of a member state is also automatically an EU citizen and would thus be entitled to the EUBI either way.

The more problematic aspect of the principle of UBI's universality for social democrats is the fact that the payments should be transferred to everyone regardless of class or income levels. Specifically, an EUBI cannot exclude the rich, as means-tests designed to prevent individuals with a higher income from receiving any payments would contradict this principle. Social democrats may take issue with this if they choose to emphasise ideas of distributive, contributory, and needs-based justice. Although there are some measures to limit this issue (see the section on conditionality below), this is likely to remain an unresolved challenge. It would, however, increase the likelihood of EUBI being first introduced only for groups like children who sit outside the employment system (Strengmann-Kuhn 2023), as they are not subject to the same considerations of deservingness-through-work.

Individuality

On the question of whether to pay an EUBI directly to an individual or instead to a household or other collective entity, social-democratic ideology gives certain indicative hints through the way it describes the individual's relationship with society and with the state. As social democrats tend to emphasise collective solidarity (Brandal et al. 2013; Meyer and Hinchman 2007, 41; Jackson 2013), one might suspect they would aim for some form of payments to collective actors such as trade unions. The argument here would be that such actors institutionalise collective solidarity and should accordingly also be responsible for distributing financial means to their members. However, this would be a misleading interpretation, since within social-democratic ideology, collective solidarity usually works as a tool for individual emancipation (Brandal et al. 2013; Jackson 2013). Social democrats' focus on individuality and individual independence from markets and societal hierarchies implies that an EUBI should similarly be a way of making the individual flourish independently. Thus, in an ideal-typical social-democratic EUBI framework, individuals would receive the largest parts of their payments directly themselves.

Another reason for this approach is social democrats' emphasis on providing individuals with immediate social rights. Institutions such as trade unions are rather seen as effective ways of ensuring that individual social rights are maintained (Merkel et al. 2006). Accordingly, individuals may still be encouraged and incentivised to use their income to strengthen trade unions, but they would ultimately be free to choose whether or not they want to pursue this route. There is, however, room for tapered adjustments to this approach. For instance, a small share of each individual's EUBI could be directed to trade unions' budgets by default in order to strengthen workers' bargaining power while earmarking the largest share of payments for direct individual receipt. This partial automatic transfer of an individual's EUBI could further be differentiated by groups. For instance, inspired by parity and social insurance schemes, partial trade union support could be deducted exclusively from payments to every individual of working age. This would also include employers, while excluding the young and the elderly (see sections on modality and duration).

Conditionality

Previously, we pointed out the tension between universalism and ideas of justice rooted in needs, contributions, and distribution. As social democrats prioritise redistribution in particular (Meyer and Hinchman 2007, 81; Merkel and Petring 2007, 136–37), a social-democratic EUBI would have to find a robust way of dealing with scepticism towards transferring money to wealthier members of society. This is a fundamentally challenging task within a scheme that is, at its core, geared towards reducing rather than increasing conditionality in the welfare state. An ideal-typical proposal for a social-democratic EUBI would thus have to include mechanisms of conditionality that are nested in an otherwise universal system. An example of such a mechanism that is in line with social-democratic preferences and the principles of a broadly defined UBI concerns automatic payment. Social democrats could propose an EUBI that is framed as a right rather than an automatic transfer mechanism. This would imply tapering off automatic payouts while giving everyone the right to actively claim their EUBI. Ideally, those who are in need would receive payments without any associated bureaucracy, whereas richer citizens would have to file regular applications to receive their share. If the wealthy forgo claiming a payment, it could be automatically 'donated' in their name to other projects, or 'reinvested' to support the funding of the scheme itself. As a social-democratic EUBI could be paid in the form of vouchers to people of working age (see section on modality), the incentives for the rich to claim their EUBI would be rather low in that age group, especially if vouchers are partly bound to goods rarely consumed by the rich (e.g., public transport). Public databases of who 'donated' their UBI could further encourage the rich to abstain from claiming the payments.

Uniformity

One facet of policy design that is relatively easy to define based on social-democratic ideals is that of EUBI's uniformity—that is, the question of whether and how much payment levels should vary. Given that social democrats support the idea of redistribution (Meyer and Hinchman 2007, 81; Merkel and Petring 2007, 136–37), variation in payment levels could be justified without too much difficulty. In addition, elements of needs-testing in the social policies favoured by social democrats in practice indicate high degrees of sensitivity towards stratified social requirements depending on the target group or region in question (Fosse 2009, 293). Following this logic, EUBI levels in a social-democratic policy design would ideally vary depending on the context in which EUBI payments are due to be received (and ultimately spent). This is particularly important for regional differences. Local or regional costs of living and income levels should be taken into account when calculating the precise amount of an EUBI. However, it is questionable quite how fine-grained such differentiation could be in practice. For instance, this would require statistical knowledge to be relatively up-to-date at all times—and the smaller the entity of differentiation were designed to be, the more complex this statistical work would become. In light of this, especially considering both their ideological links to national community-building and political entrenchment in national welfare state administration, social democrats might opt to first introduce variation in EUBI levels between EU member states. Ideally, this could then be adjusted over time to match more closely *de facto* differences in living standards across provinces, regions, or localities.

Frequency

Concerning the frequency of payouts, we have already mentioned before that social democrats have strong preferences for regular over one-off payments (Skevik 2014). Among other factors, this is linked to the social-democratic ideals of statism, individualism, and liberty, coupled with the goal of preventing destitution and inequality as a result of illiquidity. Large one-off payments would likely be conducive to both capital accumulation as well as risks of overspending. If both phenomena occurred simultaneously in different groups, this could exacerbate inequality rather than remedying it. Furthermore, a social-democratic EUBI would be conceptualised as a right to permanent basic minimum subsistence rather than an investment-oriented basic capital. All the same, this does not necessarily mean that social-democratic ideology implies an extremely short timespan for payments, such as daily transfers. After all, social democrats are keen to balance these preferences with the loftier goal of fostering individual emancipation and freedom (Brandal et al. 2013). In a capitalist economic system in particular, both ideals require a certain degree of freedom to allocate consumption independently. In addition, extremely frequent transfers would be administratively highly cumbersome. While this is less of an ideological issue for social democrats as such, it is an important pragmatic consideration. Given that there is no particularly forceful reason for social democrats to override this pragmatic argument with an ideological concern for daily payments, an ideal-typical social-democratic EUBI might be expected to strike a middle ground. More concretely, the most plausible solution here would be monthly EUBI payments, similar to typical wage or salary receipts. These payments could be timed to be anti-cyclical to income from work in order to stabilise income flows: if, for instance, employers typically transfer wages on the last day of the month, the EUBI could be paid out in the middle of the month. However, as payment days vary between countries and sometimes even employers, this would be likely to entail significant additional administrative complications—so it should remain an entirely optional feature.

Duration

As for the duration for which an EUBI should be paid, the social-democratic ideal-type diverges from many of the publicly salient UBI proposals. Here, it is key that social-democratic ideology tends to link income and ideas of deservingness to work and productivity (Widerquist 2019, 41). In the cooperative relationship between consumption and production, every citizen has a certain role to play in generating societal wealth, and accordingly in providing the basis for the welfare state. This can easily become a source of tension with the idea of UBI, with the fear being that the policy might undermine the prominent role of labour in society. This implies that the social-democratic EUBI would ideally be a scheme that is paid out only during times of life in which income through work is usually not assumed to be the desirable standard—which means that the social-democratic monetary EUBI would be paid out to young people and to the elderly. However, this limitation by itself stands in contradiction to the scheme's scope for conditionality requirements, whereby part of the EUBI received by those of working age could be directly transferred to trade unions. If we take both proposals together, a social-democratic EUBI could consist in monetary payments to the young and the elderly, and in vouchers handed out to those of working age (see modality section). The monetary equivalent of a certain percentage of these vouchers could then go to trade unions. Needs-tested schemes outside of the EUBI would continue to cover individuals with special needs who would otherwise not be appropriately supported under the proposed scheme.

Modality

The idea of including vouchers as part of an EUBI is rooted in a specific dilemma within social-democratic ideology. On the one hand, social democrats embrace the ideal of individual independence. They want to emancipate and empower the individual and provide them with the capacities to make their own decisions (Brandal et al. 2013), which in a market economy—even in one that is regulated and accompanied by a welfare state—also implies allowing individuals to make independent spending decisions. On the other hand, social democrats also promote the idea of linking monetary wealth to labour (Klitgaard 2007, 177–78). This brings the risk that market forces may drive the individual into particular interpersonal or structural dependencies, thus limiting their *de facto* freedom. In UBI debates, social democrats accordingly walk a slightly perilous tightrope between wanting to shield income through labour from competing approaches and wanting to empower individuals financially.

This dilemma is the point of origin for the particular social-democratic proposal on modality. Ideally, a social-democratic EUBI would transfer money to the young and the elderly, as they are not expected to work for income under the social-democratic conception of deservingness. Similar policies such as basic pensions and child benefits are already well-established in many states, especially across Europe—although they are not always universal. In contrast to the young and the elderly, those who are expected to work would instead receive vouchers, which could be used to access services and products that cover a set of basic material and cultural needs. Such needs may include public transport and food on the material side, while also stretching to include, for instance, books or socially engaging activities such as access to theatres and cinemas on the cultural side. In addition, as with the individuality principle earlier, a share of the monetary equivalent of the EUBI received by people of working age as vouchers would be paid to trade unions in order to strengthen the bargaining power of workers both individually and viewed as a collective group.

Adequacy

While the previous considerations are all important for adjusting an EUBI to the ideals of social democracy, one of the policy's most fundamental issues concerns adequacy. The question of how high an EUBI should be is closely linked to its functional goal: what precisely should the scheme achieve? For social democrats, one central response to this question would be poverty relief (Widerquist 2019, 41). Combined with the goal of individual emancipation, social democrats would likely aim for a relatively high level of payouts, as long as the necessary amount of redistributive funding is available (see funding section). Accordingly, the monetary part of a social-democratic EUBI would ideally cover the at-risk-of-poverty threshold at 60 percent of the regional median or 50 percent of the regional mean income—aiming for whichever of these is the respectively higher threshold, in order to ensure that poverty is eradicated as widely as possible.

However, it is worth remembering here that this is a theoretical, ideal-typical goal. Even non-universal social assistance schemes that are explicitly geared towards poverty alleviation and are widely supported by social-democratic parties often fall woefully short of these thresholds in practice (Kuivalainen and Nelson 2010). Already at a theoretical level, additional complications need to be considered when introducing the key element of distributing EUBI in the form of vouchers for those of working age. In principle, these vouchers should enable basic social and cultural participation while covering the most basic physical needs. The social and cultural element in this context is crucial to allow the scheme to live up to social-democratic goals of a 'good life'. However, quantifying these ideals so that they can be used for the calculations associated with this kind of dissemination of vouchers is anything but trivial. This process would likely require the continuous work of a board or even an entire apparatus of experts who use baskets of goods and their associated prices as a baseline and then adjust estimations of current needs to the respective contexts. Layering this with local-level variations in payout levels would be particularly difficult—which underlines that social democrats might well see national-level variation as a well-placed compromise on uniformity. As monetary precarity is common among those of working age as well, needs that cannot be addressed through vouchers would still remain to be covered by other welfare schemes such as conventional social assistance.

Funding

In chapter 1, we argued that funding may be at least as important an adjustment to UBI policy design as payouts. The case of a social-democratic EUBI is a prime example. Carefully designed funding strategies could offset many social-democratic concerns about UBI while maximising its potential. A social-democratic EUBI would first and foremost try to leverage taxes that would result in redistribution from the higher to the lower wealth and income brackets, and from capital to labour. This would entail taxes on essentially any forms of non-EUBI income that is not linked to labour and productivity in a social-democratic understanding of the term. Specifically, this would include taxes on extremely high wealth, inheritances and incomes, financial transactions, and corporate profits, which taken together would form the foundation of EUBI revenue sources.

Even if social democrats failed to achieve their preferred levels of adequacy through these taxes, they could design an EUBI as an automatic redistribution mechanism. As will become clear when we examine this question through the lenses of other ideologies, this would achieve a radically different outcome than, for instance, a liberal EUBI. Broken down into its most fundamental mechanisms, a simple UBI financed through this portfolio of taxes could be considered a funding-centred approach to redistribution. Holding payouts constant across recipients, a means-based differentiation of contributions is used to control the EUBI's distributive effects. Combining these with the payment-side specifications of the social-democratic EUBI would only serve to exacerbate these effects still further. The taxes outlined here would largely remain at the national level, as the policy would be implemented through an EU Directive (see the next section). Nevertheless, EU-level resources could also be used to additionally subsidise the scheme. However, there would be some limits to how this taxation is levied in practice, due to the long-standing social-democratic conflict between being traditionally anti-capitalist while embracing contingent elements of capitalism through reformism and gradualism. Unlike the far left, for instance, social democrats could not simply opt to collectivise productive capital and fully distribute any revenue from it to all citizens.

EU Policy Instruments and Relationship to the National Welfare State

Beyond funding, social-democratic ideology also has implications for the concrete policy instruments chosen to implement an EUBI. However, its leading theoretical arguments create yet another area of tension here. On the one hand, the internationalist tendencies of welfare cosmopolitan social democrats would suggest a clear preference for an EU-level implementation of the scheme. However, these directly clash with welfare communitarian preferences and the longstanding social-democratic support for the national welfare state (Van Gerven and Ossewaarde 2012).

While ultimately a theoretical toss-up, two considerations can clarify policy implications here. First, empirically, social democrats have tended to defend the national welfare state in debates on the Europeanisation of social policy competences (Rhodes 2013). While this tells us something about the likelihood that particular implementations will be the ones that social democrats might opt for, it is less helpful for deriving an ideal-typical policy design. Thus, second, we can turn to the social-democratic ideal of parliamentarism. As we have previously seen, a social-democratic EUBI would aim to increase democratic legitimacy through policy design. Given the trenchant and wide-ranging critiques regarding the democratic deficit at the heart of the EU, this preference could be maximised by pursuing a purely national implementation. As this would, however, fundamentally contradict the internationalist preferences inherent to modern social democracy, the ideal-typical middle ground would instead be an EU Directive. This type of legislation would allow the EU, with the inclusion of the European Parliament, to bindingly require member states to introduce UBI schemes, albeit with a certain degree of flexibility concerning the granular details of implementation. However, the prominence of gradualism and reformism in social-democratic ideology implies that a non-binding EU Recommendation for national schemes may also be an option in non-ideal scenarios. As social democrats have largely worked to set up national welfare states and still embrace the national nature of social policy, preexisting welfare arrangements would not be affected in any binding form through an ideal-typical social-democratic EUBI Directive. The only restraint to national welfare states that might be recommended would be to replace purely monetary schemes that are fully covered by the EUBI and have therefore become redundant, such as basic pensions or child benefits.

Technical Distribution and Introduction

Finally, regarding how an EUBI should be introduced and distributed, the key issues here are the considerations on nationality we have already discussed, along with the chosen instruments of Directives and Recommendations. The social-democratic EUBI would first be distributed by the EU in monetary form to all member states. In a second step, the member states would then use their national systems to implement the scheme in practice. Gradualism and reformism as well as fears of endangering national welfare states would lend further weight to a more gradual implementation process. Starting at an extremely low level, the generosity of the scheme would slowly be levelled up until the ideal goal of the at-risk-of-poverty threshold is eventually achieved. This would also allow political decisionmakers to track the policy's impacts in 'real time', and react promptly to any unforeseen and undesired effects. To increase its (temporary) redistributive effects, the parts of the EUBI that are funded by the EU's own resources would first grow equally across Europe until payment levels reach the first at-risk-of-poverty threshold in the poorest member state. Until this point, all member states would receive equal amounts of money per capita from the EU's own resources. This would allow poorer states to implement schemes that are more generous relative to their respective income levels. Thus, funds would temporarily favour poorer states, leading in principle to a prolonged decrease in EU-wide inequalities. Once EUBI levels hit the at-risk-of-poverty threshold in a given state, they stop increasing there and only keep increasing in states that have not yet achieved their respective goals.

All in all, the proposed scheme for a social-democratic EUBI is a middle-of-the-road design compared to the other proposals which we discuss in the following chapters. This EUBI covers basic social, cultural, and economic needs, but also aims to protect national welfare states and the privileged role of earning income through work. It strikes compromises between preserving national sovereignty and embracing EU integration, between individual independence and collective solidarity, as well as between anti-capitalist ideas and gradualism and reformism. Much like social democracy itself, it is thus a middle way between liberal proposals that embrace the markets, and a far-left EUBI that ultimately aims to overthrow the institutions of capitalism.

Chapter 4

Green Ideology

Green ideology is the 'youngest' of the traditions we discuss in this book, but it features many elements that derive from a much older philosophical and political heritage. As a distinct ideology linked to particular political parties, it began to blossom in the 1970s, and rose to growing prominence during and after the 1980s. Against the background of the anti-war and anti-nuclear movements, green ideology historically enjoyed particularly strong support in Austria, France, and especially Germany. At the EU level, the ideology is represented by the European Green Party, which for many years has formed a joint faction with the regionalist European Free Alliance in the European Parliament and has a strongly pro-European profile (Pearson and Rüdig 2020).

One of the core principles of green ideology is, unsurprisingly, environmentalism (Stavrakakis 1997). Green parties reject ecological degradation and marginalisation on the grounds that they consider humans and societies to be rooted in nature (Dickens 1992), which, in turn, should be conserved as a matter of urgent priority. This can, theoretically, imply a both 'biological' and 'organic' conception of sociality and solidarity. Under this view, society takes the form of a social ecosystem, in which every element plays an important role. Such 'ecosystem thinking' has recently been featured in a range of different social research projects (e.g., Hodgson and Spours 2016; Wang and Altanbulag 2022) and can suggest that the impetus for conservation applies not only to nature, but also to society in the sense of social protection. While this is ordinarily taken to imply social progressivism (Zimmerman 2003), it can also be linked to (sometimes marginal) notions of historical nostalgia, especially in the context of agriculture and older methods of subsistence cultivation (Lubarda 2020). Modern forms of production may be rejected, sometimes vehemently, in favour of supposedly more 'natural' interactions with the land (Cassel-Piccot 2013, 106).

In debates around climate change, the principle of sustainability is key for green discourse, which traditionally rejects the exploitation of resources and favours the use of renewable energy (Sharlamanov 2023, 166). Beyond the realm of climate change, this is also linked to the fight against pollution, as greens similarly reject the excessive production of waste both privately and collectively (Evrard 2012). Such ideals can spill over into support for practices like vegetarianism and veganism, or 'sustainable consumption patterns' in general. At a larger scale, this implies support for degrowth or less radical critiques of economic growth (Gunder 2020, 49), which when combined with sustainability and environmentalism can lead greens to also favour explicit efforts at 'decivilising' and 'rewilding' (Ostrowski 2022a).

Green ideology also features strong links to ideas of social justice (Pepper 1993), via conceptualisations that are deeply influenced by ideas of cosmopolitanism that run throughout the ideology more broadly (Sharlamanov 2023, 86–87). Greens also favour legally enshrined civil rights and liberties, but do not link them as clearly to citizenship as other ideologies do, instead rooting them in a specific understanding of universalism (Boggs 1986, 877). This also applies to other concepts that green ideology shares in particular with social democracy. Greens favour welfarism, aided by fiscal redistribution and state intervention (Talshir 2002, 117). They further support partly free economies that operate within clear limitations, injecting some anti-capitalist overtones into their principles of environmentalism, sustainability, and social justice (Heywood 2021). Beyond the use of more structural interventionist and regulatory approaches, greens may also promote state incentivisation via 'nudging' to push members of society into more 'desirable' forms of behaviour (Ostrowski 2022a).

The local dimension is key to green ideas of democracy (Torgerson 2008), which emphasise individuals' connectedness to their local communities—and thus derives an idea of federalism in which devolved powers are not only acceptable but also often desirable (Talshir 2002, 215). This then translates to a certain style of political engagement. Greens rely both on grassroots mobilisation (Sharlamanov 2023, 187) and mass movements which can be organised 'outside' the state. This can, for instance, mean that local issues are discussed 'on the ground', mobilised through civic engagement, and translated into international movements united by a shared goal such as climate protection.

Finally, green ideology is historically underpinned by principles of nonviolence. The ideology evolved from societies characterised by pacifist movements and anti-militarism, which gave green activists and movements an additional nonviolent layer marked by a widespread embrace of passive resistance (Sharlamanov 2023). Generally averse to ideas of violent overthrow, despite more recent turns to the dramatic in ecological activism, green ideology resembles social democracy in its support for reformism.

BUILDING COMMUNITY IN THE ECOLOGICAL TRANSITION: GREEN IDEOLOGY AND UBI

Of all the ideologies we discuss in this book, green ideology has been among the most consistent and outspoken in favour of UBI. The idea of an ecological UBI has been extensively discussed (e.g., Langridge et al. 2023), and even though greens do not generally deploy the scheme as the centrepiece of their programmes, they have been more open to it in principle than many of their ideological rivals—in particular social democrats (Denuit 2019). This was revealed especially clearly by greens' support for UBI experiments in their most recent European election manifesto as well as their deep intellectual engagement with the idea itself (European Greens 2018, 5–6; Mehrer 2021). This support is not surprising from a theoretical perspective, as green ideology contains various principles that are closely aligned with the ideals of UBI. In the following sections, we discuss green arguments for UBI under the rubric of five guiding themes: environmentalism, sustainability, social justice, democracy, and nonviolence.

Environmentalism

Environmentalism lies at the core of green ideology (Stavrakakis 1997), defined in terms of not only the goal of protecting the environment as such, but also a particular ideological understanding of humankind. Humanity is seen as a part of nature and should accordingly live in harmony with it. In an extreme form of the ecologistic worldview, society itself can be conceptualised as a complex social 'ecosystem' in which every component has its role to play. In this context, green advocates of UBI may consider the policy a tool to preserve a balance between all parts of society (Langridge et al. 2023). By providing a minimum floor, the scheme would protect individuals from disappearing as an active and contributing part of their social context, thus ensuring balance in their overall 'social ecosystem'. This conception plays into basic notions of conservation and control. Following the same principles, greens may also see UBI as an expression of the importance of balancing large-scale intervention with humility about the natural limits to our efforts. While it is likely to generate a measure of policy disruption, a redistributive UBI could cap consumption among the richer members of society. Thus, depending on policy design, it could act as a way to contain environmentally harmful, excessive behaviour (Lawhon and McCreary 2020). As the green transition in general is a long-term process, its social underpinnings need to be addressed as soon as possible, and greens may see UBI as a way to kickstart this aim. Crucially, this argument also speaks to the recognition that the radical societal interventions that may be needed for a green transition can tear the fragile fabric of society, leading to unpredictable outcomes. UBI could be seen as a way of circumventing this risk by intervening within existing frameworks in order to achieve medium-to-long-term transformations.

Closely linked with these ideas of conservation is the goal of preventing ecological degradation and marginalisation. In this regard, green UBI advocates may consider the policy a 'helping hand' to allow people to live in harmony with their environment. Recognising the importance of all human beings having a good relationship with the natural world, UBI may provide some basic preconditions for this to happen in regular people's everyday lives. Depending on funding, UBI may funnel revenue from the exploitation of natural resources to individual citizens, thus underlining the green idea that social prosperity depends on a resourceful environment (Cieplinski et al. 2021). Further, UBI could be a tool to help members of society adapt to times in which such resources are scarce, such as due to crop failures. Green supporters of UBI may hope that the scheme ultimately 'crowds out' income sources associated with ecological damage. An environmentally responsible state could use UBI to provide its citizens with an alternative to employment in resource-intensive, destructive industries. This could allow states to regulate these industries more harshly, knowing that workers have a reliable safety net during times of transition. Such an approach has implications for policy design (see below) as it would imply funding a UBI via fiscal levies that target ecologically harmful industries and businesses. A green UBI could thus function as an 'externality compensation scheme': it redistributes money from those harming the environment to those suffering the consequences.

A theme that runs through all these considerations is the idea that humans are rooted in nature and should thus maintain and foster their own natural capacities. This principle could lead greens to see UBI as an ambitious method to prevent situations that temporarily or permanently strain our human physiology and psychology, for instance as a precaution against damaging working and living conditions. In addition to this 'negative' framing around protection from harm, greens may further emphasise the 'positive' potential of UBI as an encouragement for essential human creativity. By providing citizens with financial freedom, the scheme could enable them to explore and realise their individual 'human nature' through more meaningful occupations. The reduction of social complexification such as bureaucratic burdens and forced obligations could 'declutter' everyday lives and make room for personal fulfilment. This would come in the form of a broader social 'low-complexity' package, compatible with other forms of policy ranging from *laissez-faire* to interventionism—enabling greens to stay open to various political goals beyond environmental protection.

UBI could further be framed as an expression of an 'organic' sociality and solidarity promoted by green ideology, which emphasises the shared 'alikeness' and interdependence of human beings with one another. It reflects the previous idea that society can be conceptualised as a web of interrelationships similar to a 'social ecosystem' that relies on preserving each 'node' in its networks. A green UBI would accordingly be intended to help individuals meet their basic livelihood requirements, which entail access to decent food, shelter, energy, and other resources. While large-scale public infrastructure and services provide this in parts, UBI would act as either a failsafe or a top-up mechanism for these schemes (Hamilton and Martin-West 2019). Besides protecting the 'nodes' of society from collapsing, a green UBI would further aim to dial back interpersonal competition to instantiate the idea that there is more to natural interactions than the competitive 'struggle for survival'.

In such metaphorical notions in particular, another aspect of green ideology's environmentalism shines through especially strongly: its association with agrarianism and historical nostalgia (Lubarda 2020; Cassel-Piccot 2013, 106). These concepts are perhaps more relevant to regionalist and localist greens than the globally minded political actors that emphasise climate protection. However, they do not for that reason necessarily clash with progressivism, since they can also be framed as a critique of capitalism. Greens may see UBI as a way of putting a limit on degrading, exploitative path-dependencies in culture and political economy by resurrecting and financially institutionalising a sense of the value of human beings *as such*. Since the scheme would make income partially independent of the markets, it may contribute to reversing the atomisation and depersonalisation of humans in the modern economy. Materially and intellectually, the scheme would hark back to historical debates about how to ensure that all members of society have a share in the 'wealth of the land'.

Individual independence (Van Parijs 2004) gained through UBI could also allow individuals with strong place-based ties to remain where they are rather than being forced to move for financial reasons. This may further encourage workers to choose employment in strategically and socially necessary but often underpaid sectors around agricultural food production. Individuals who are in principle interested in a life outside of (post-)industrial urban centres may thus relocate, which has the knock-on beneficial effect of limiting urban sprawl. Here, however, green ideology finds itself conflicted between divergent pulls of environmentalism and sustainability (see below), which may often be more feasible to achieve in highly developed urban areas. Still, the capacity of a scheme like UBI to boost agricultural resilience by empowering people to invest in their own small-scale agri-food production is, in principle, close to green ideology. This entails fostering self-sufficiency via individual gardens and small local agri-businesses, leading to reduced dependency on large-scale global producers. In this way, UBI can act as (literal and metaphorical) 'seed funding' for small-scale entrepreneurship, which may encourage domestic production along with the recovery or protection of locally rooted production techniques.

Sustainability

Besides environmentalism, sustainability is another key pillar of green ideology. Here, the starting point for a green argument in favour of UBI is the fundamental recognition that sustaining society, its individual members, and its environmental context is interlinked. Thus, if a green UBI were to be implemented and was intended to last, it would need to ensure the long-term sustainability of its revenue sources, including sustainability in explicitly ecological terms (Birnbaum 2010a). As a consequence, the industries that create societal wealth would need to be reoriented towards a sustainable logic, for instance concerning their energy consumption, product and service development, employment conditions, and capital investment. To reinforce these goals, a green UBI would explicitly link UBI payments to sustainable revenue sources (see policy design). One example for this could be a sovereign wealth fund that invests in 'desirable' assets such as renewable energy stocks or real estate constructed under the aegis of sustainable building practices. Such a fund could be supported by revenues from the export of renewable resources. The specific role of UBI in this kind of system would be one of an individual material reward for sustainable economic practices implemented by society as a whole. This could strengthen the intra- and intergenerational social contract between all members of society by paying a dividend to those who assume responsibility for future sustainability.

While such arguments around renewable resources are key for sustainability, they do not cover the entire spectrum of green arguments in this area. Another element here concerns the familiar green resistance to waste and pollution. Here, UBI may be framed as a way of enabling people to pursue home improvements and household-level changes in the use of technologies and behaviour patterns. For instance, investing in more energy-efficient insulation or heating devices can be a costly endeavour, which many members of society may only be able to embark on with monetary support. In addition, a UBI may empower already environmentally committed people to go beyond what mere state regulations incentivise them to do. For instance, a government may provide subsidies for heat pumps but not for solar panels, and direct monetary payments could close such subsidy gaps for those who want to but cannot afford to invest in green technology. If the scheme is funded via ecological taxes and fines, it yet again expands its capacity as a compensation mechanism for those who suffer from pollution and waste.

Another facet of sustainability concerns a specific consumption pattern, namely vegetarianism and veganism. A major problem with meat alternatives can be their consistently higher prices than meat-based products—despite the best active efforts of the 'meat substitute' industry to make their goods competitive in terms of quality and cost. Green UBI advocates may consider the policy a way to bypass this hurdle without price controls. It could enable consumers to get access to nutritious and healthy diets while also gaining the (literal) capacity to take ethics and sustainability into account. This extends beyond food to areas such as fashion, cosmetics, and pharmaceuticals. If funding for the scheme is further complemented by revenue sources from the production and sale of non-sustainable goods, the scheme would effectively become an indirect subsidy for sustainable producers. All the while, UBI is a far less prescriptive method of achieving these goals than a direct distribution of sustainable goods. This allows individuals to tailor their consumption decisions to their individual needs while maintaining a healthy roster of ecologically beneficial incentives.

Green ideology does, however, go beyond consumption incentives in its sustainability efforts. Degrowth has become a key part of debates among green activists and parties. Here, green advocates of the policy could embed it in an argument around sufficiency akin to recent models of 'doughnut economics' (Raworth 2017). Combined with critiques of established prosperity measures, greens may see UBI as a step towards reorienting the metrics of social success and progress away from narrow criteria of economic growth. Current preoccupations with GDP, capital accumulation, and profit-maximisation may be replaced by a focus on adequate social floors for all. In a nutshell, maximalism for a specific tranche of society would give way to 'maximinimalism' for every member of society. Through UBI, greens may additionally hope to remove pressures around working hours and income through employment, thus limiting the expansion of production, turnover, and profit to a 'sufficient' level. The hope here would be that people gain the material confidence to replace production-oriented work partially with volunteer work and small-scale entrepreneurship, both creating space for alternative understandings of value. This may emphasise social usefulness more and dial down the impetus for economistic value-optimisation. Again, such goals have consequences for policy design, specifically for funding. In this case, taxes would primarily be levelled at profits, specifically those geared towards capital accumulation. Asset and property sales, investments, and rents may be especially targeted by a UBI scheme that is focused specifically on degrowth—and such a scheme may also eye personal and corporate assets themselves above a given threshold.

Finally, green UBI advocates face a potential dilemma concerning sustainability, specifically regarding their preferences for rewilding versus urbanisation. On the one hand, greens may emphasise the benefits for sustainable lifestyles of living in dense urban areas—since, for instance, living in smaller apartments and reducing car dependency could reduce CO_2 footprints. On the other hand, greens focusing on individuals' 'connection to nature' may reject highly urbanised societies as antithetical to what it *really* means to be human at all. Those in favour of urbanisation may consider UBI a way of enabling citizens to move into city centres with otherwise extortionately unaffordable levels of rent. Here, the argument would be that a sustainable urban life comes at a fixed monthly cost that UBI could offset. This would enable individuals to trade quantity for quality, assuming individual preferences were in line with an urbanite life. Consequently, previously inhabited areas in the countryside could be used for rewilding. However, in direct contradiction to this, greens who oppose urban centralisation may hope that UBI would encourage people to move *away* from cities instead. Here, the relevant mechanism would be that individuals become less dependent on inner-city jobs that require them to live within a close commuting distance. As a consequence, land value would be geographically more evenly distributed, which may drive down urban price levels. This, in turn, could disincentivise property developers from 'parking' unused housing in the hope of selling the property at higher prices in the future. This may ultimately foster more efficient land use and reduce the sealing of soils. Citizens who moved away from urban centres may then use the leisure time they could gain through UBI to engage in 'home gardening' or making the most of 'green spaces'. Crucially, such outcomes are not set in stone and would need to be supported by proactive rewilding policy in urban and rural spaces alike. Such policies may range from planning reforms including mandatory minimum 'wild' spaces per development to environmental education.

Social Justice

As indicated above, environmentalism and sustainability in green ideology are not confined to the planet itself but also extend to ideas of society. For instance, civil rights and liberties can be framed from a green perspective as constituting a vital part of a socially sustainable and just society. For green UBI advocates, the scheme may accordingly be a minimum material safeguard of free agency in the face of the repressive and exploitative artificial structures of human societies. Greens may argue that modern capitalist structures impede humans' latitude for authentic choice by forcing actions into the framework of monetary optimisation. To be able to make the most of society's possibilities, particularly concerning social justice, people would require basic independence from these forces. This, so the argument goes, could be enabled through UBI. The policy would give every individual the monetary basis for making claims on their behalf and thus may lead to a more sustainable set of societal arrangements. After all, it would be a way for the state to reinforce individuals' 'positive' right of recognition in society against those that contribute to societal and ecological precarity. Additionally, UBI could be presented as an irreducible material component of membership of a society, as it universalises eligibility for collective support. By being framed as a right, the scheme could be woven into the political constitution of society. In this way, greens may aim to permanently restructure society towards a long-term assurance of just treatment for all, paired with a reliable guarantee and recognition of individual freedom.

Such notions of social justice are closely linked to welfarism and fiscal redistribution. Here, green pro-UBI framings edge closely towards those favoured by social democrats, albeit with some key unique attributes. Generally, UBI would be considered a way of deconcentrating wealth and giving all members of society an irreducible 'stake' in economic prosperity. As green ideology is less clear than social democracy about whether or not additional redistributive schemes should be pursued, UBI represents an effective baseline for welfare. Additionally, it recognises that all members of society are at risk of welfare infringements due to ecological dangers. The immediate effects of the destruction of ecosystems, extreme weather events, or crop failures could be partially mitigated by UBI without invoking lengthy and Byzantine bureaucratic procedures to determine people's eligibility for emergency support. The scheme gives all members of society the basic means to look after themselves, while remaining in principle compatible with additional, more targeted benefits and public services. Finally, as a basic device for social compensation, UBI remains flexible in terms of who carries its costs. For greens, this is a key point, as they can focus revenue sources on those causing environmental damage. As with a number of previous arguments, this could entail individual wealth, income, or corporate profits. By designing a scheme that is redistributive through the decisions governing its intended revenue sources, greens can use UBI to implement a financial accountability mechanism of targeted 'fines' and universal 'awards'. This may increase the societal acceptability of punitive taxation by allowing citizens to reap the benefit from them as a whole.

The consequence of this logic is that greens may consider UBI a vital tool for state-driven behavioural incentivisation. The policy would be an institutionalised recognition that the state carries the responsibility for instantiating clear and simple visions of social justice linked to environmentally desirable behaviour. Additionally, the state can still step in as a 'troubleshooter' for any of the more specific challenges that society faces. This logic of combining universal and targeted policies rests on the assumption that universal state action is an effective yet imprecise 'sledgehammer' that requires complementary schemes to work. In addition to state-driven incentivisation, green ideology also entails particular models of an entrepreneurial state that must actively take investment risks to tackle ecological challenges. With this in mind, greens may use UBI as a protective shield to buffer citizens against the worst fallouts of such risk-taking. At the same time, the policy represents an alternative to strategic subsidies for businesses in growth sectors. Rather, it can be conceived of as an investment in individual human creativity that encourages small-scale entrepreneurship. Both aspects—the incentivising and the investing state—ultimately complement each other. Greens can frame UBI as a deliberately 'open-ended' social investment policy that incentivises individuals to rely on their own capacities for innovation and generate new solutions to social problems. The assumption here is that the state cannot plan for every eventuality—but *can* enable individuals through broader state entrepreneurship to prepare themselves. Again, a green UBI would need to be designed in a way that incentivises both producers and consumers to keep environmental sustainability at the forefront of their minds in all their social activities.

Concerning one of the most fundamental questions of social justice—the question of capitalism—green ideology operates in something of a field of tension. On the one hand, greens vehemently criticise free-market capitalism for upsetting the fragile balance of society and the environment if its rapaciousness is left unchecked. On the other hand, greens are less convinced than socialists that simply shifting to an alternative economic model such as central planning could rectify this by itself. Green UBI advocates may frame the policy as one part of a more complex solution to this situation. UBI is a 'system-neutral' society-wide intervention that could lay the social groundwork for a green transformation while remaining compatible with non-capitalist systems in principle. It could empower individuals to take ownership of and responsibility for how they engage with their environment. At the same time, if financed through sources that distribute money away from polluters, it gives recipients a stake in the survival of the environment, as only those benefit who pollute as little as desired. A green UBI may thus incorporate both individual responsibility and state action. As a consequence, it would aim to empower individuals financially to make the most of the beneficial elements of capitalism while the state steps in to remove or hedge its harmful consequences. For instance, markets may still be used to manage large parts of resource distribution efficiently and allow for consumer choice and entrepreneurship, while commodification, profit-maximisation, and the exploitation of labour and the environment would be placed within severe limits.

Democracy

On the question of democracy, green ideology's emphasis on grassroots mobilisation contains clear points of engagement for UBI advocates. The 'basicness' of UBI allows the scheme to work as a 'bottom-up' approach to solving social problems. Unlike conditional transfers and in-kind benefits, UBI can be wielded to address challenges immediately and unbureaucratically from the individual scale upwards. This, on one reading, represents an inherently democratic approach to social policy. Here, green arguments move somewhat close to liberal ideology—which becomes even clearer when examining the way that UBI may be used economically. As we have seen already, greens may consider the scheme a form of 'seed funding', which treats every member of society as worth 'investing in' to foster their self-development and democratise the accessibility of investment capital. The latter is typically provided by private finance institutions outside of democratic logics such as banks. If such entities were taxed to fund a UBI, investment capital would be redistributed to all citizens and insofar become 'democratised'. Concerning the political sphere, green UBI advocates may further aim to give the disprivileged the financial means and independence to be able to participate in democratic processes. This is key, as many citizens—and by extension their material interests—are currently not adequately represented in the various democracies around Europe. For an often grassroots-centred green view of democracy, such gaps in representation are a major problem. Greens may be additionally attracted to UBI on the grounds that the policy is currently also primarily promoted through grassroots and on-the-ground movements, while being underrepresented in parliamentary debates (Afscharian et al. 2022a).

Tied to these grassroots movements is the green emphasis on localism and federalism, which ties in with the ideal of allowing individuals to live according to their own place-based preferences. For a green UBI, this implies that it should react to local variances in costs of living but remain universal in its fundamental form to assist everyone in their independent choice of residence. In a nutshell, everyone should be able to meet their material needs whenever and wherever they arise, rather than having to relocate to do so. Hence, migration should be a question of choice rather than necessity. Given this flexibility of movement, a green UBI should then kickstart local economic development, weakening the 'drag' effect of areas with few employment opportunities on the overall economic profile of a region. The scheme may achieve this by fostering the dispersal of business branches and independent enterprises: if people's livelihoods depend less on territorially concentrated economic centres, local economies may be able to survive due to a more resilient consumer base in otherwise neglected areas. This effect can be supported and enhanced through dedicated policy design (see the section on 'modality' below).

While the localist and grassroots-oriented ideas of democracy promoted by green ideology might suggest otherwise, greens also have strong links to *mass* movements. Unlike social democracy, these movements have been less concerned with workers' rights and more with ecological aims. For democracy, this implies a preference for shifting the political influence enshrined in capital away from small elites towards the broad mass of the population. As previously discussed, a UBI built on redistributive revenue sources can effectively achieve such an aim. Additionally, rising or falling UBI levels could be linked to (1) democratic decisions and (2) overall economic output, which means that the scheme could democratise redistribution much more directly than more complex and less transparent welfare schemes. What is particularly unique about UBI is that it is one of the very few examples of (fiscal and social) policies that affect every member of society without exception equally at the stage of payouts. This implies that instituting and later altering it becomes an integral component of the wider social contract that binds together the mass of individuals *into* a society. As UBI enjoys high levels of salience and popularity already, greens may further attach themselves to the policy before implementation as one puzzle piece in a larger agenda for green movements. The scheme's intuitive comprehensibility and its widespread appeal make it easy to communicate as a core building-block of a wider agenda for societal transformation.

Nonviolence

The final principle of green ideology we focus on here concerns nonviolence. Emerging from the green movement's early years during the Cold War, this principle features strong elements of pacifism and passive resistance. Green advocates of UBI can use this pillar of their ideology to frame the scheme as a guarantor of social peace. They may argue that it removes extreme immiseration and material want as one of the major drivers of conflict within and between societies. This is particularly crucial for greens in the context of competing need- and ownership-claims over scarce resources such as water, land, energy, food, and shelter. Further, as discussed in the context of (anti-)capitalism, UBI can be implemented within the existing set of political-economic institutions—in other words, it does not require forceful insurrectionary disruption to achieve far-reaching societal goals. It also does not need to actively impose interventions in business decisions or macroeconomic policies to be able to provide a social backstop against economic hardship. Finally, the antiviolent frames of green UBI advocates may also work within a particular logic of social compensation. Here, the argument would be that some structural or counter-structural violence within and between societies is unavoidable, as both climate change and the green transition will lead to significant frictions on a macroregional scale. UBI could then be conceived as a financial compensation mechanism for these struggles—a material benefit with a 'pacifist coating', if it is funded through taxes on business or industries that profit from violence and insecurity.

As its scepticism towards violent disruption suggests, green ideology shares with social democracy a tendency towards reformism. However, this does not entail opposition to far-reaching transformations. In the realm of social policy, UBI reflects this fundamental tension. On the one hand, it is a clear and transformative departure from established approaches to political economy. It reflects the ambition and radical thinking needed for a more ecologically conscious, secure, and sustainable world. In the processes necessary to achieve this goal, UBI also recognises the need to invest in every individual member of society. On the other hand, UBI remains entirely feasible within the current horizon of societal institutions and their functional logics. Rather than as a manifestation of incrementalism, the scheme may be framed as an example of 'aspirational realism' about what these institutions can and should achieve. In other words, green UBI advocates may argue that basic income would push existing institutions to the limits of their capacity and thus maximise on many social goals within the limitations of the current system. All of this could be achieved not only without changing the economic system, but also without political revolution. If implemented democratically, UBI could play a crucial part in realising a 'new bargain' between the most and least privileged members of society. Those who have benefited from unsustainable practices of the capitalist economy would concede a portion of their advantages to those who have lost out due to their excessive behaviour.

SUSTAINABILITY AND PLACE: A GREEN VIEW OF EUBI

From these arguments rooted in green ideology some clear implications follow for policy design. While we have hinted at a number of these already, the following sections break them down in further detail. As the European Greens are among the party groups that have embraced UBI most clearly in recent years (European Greens 2018, 5–6; Mehrer 2021), the EUBI based on green ideology is close to what many people will already be likely to associate with UBI intuitively. Many of the following considerations offer hints that greens face fewer historically conditioned restraints when applying their ideals to EUBI policy design than social democrats do. Again, the policy design settings we present here make no claim as such to being in line with what greens may empirically propose in the future. Instead, they represent theoretically plausible proposals in line with an ideal-typical view of green ideology.

Universality

As greens embrace federalism and are favourably disposed towards the EU in general, the green EUBI would be closely tied to the EU rather than the national level. As we outline further below, this does not necessarily imply a contradiction to green ideology's localist ideals, as the policy would not aim for extreme centralism. Rather, as far as its universality is concerned, it simply means that a green UBI in the EU context would define the 'universe' within which it operates as the entire EU *simpliciter*. However, the role of extra-state mass movements for green ideology, along with a universal understanding of how solidarity works in practice, would—perhaps counterintuitively—probably mean that the greens would not tie an EUBI existentially to EU citizenship. After all, citizenship can act as an exclusive category that prevents long-term members of society that are 'only' non-citizen residents from accessing the scheme. Consequently, the green EUBI would instead be contingent on permanent or long-term residency in the EU. Thus, migrants staying for a longer time would also receive payments after a certain point. This implies a clearly cosmopolitan view, restricted by some need for policy realism. While ideal-typical cosmopolitans might be quite willing to attempt to implement a global UBI, this would require global legislation that is currently well beyond the bounds of feasibility. Other considerations such as class issues are, by the same token, less relevant for greens, and register less strongly with them accordingly.

Individuality

Given that green ideology relies on the individual capacity to live sustainable lives while being largely detached from classical societal institutions, any genre of EUBI associated with it would be paid directly to individuals. If any alternative recipient group were to be desired, it would most likely consist in local communes, justified straightforwardly for reasons of regionalism and place-based 'ties to the land'. Similarly, greens may also consider payouts to any forms of households with shared living arrangements. In such a case, payouts may be slightly increased per capita if more individuals lived in a shared household per square metre, in order to incentivise reducing the sizes of houses and apartments. However, such approaches would clash quite strongly with some other ideals that are central to green ideology. First, green movements emphasise the need to overcome societal oppression of minority groups and to support their civil rights and liberties. If an EUBI was paid out to non-individual entities, the dependency dynamics leading to inequalities may simply be reproduced and entrenched. Second, the bottom-up, individualistic understanding of democracy favoured by green ideology would stand in tension with collective payouts—which means that, overall, individual payments would be preferred as the 'safest' option. This could then deliver on many of the potential benefits of UBI discussed above. Specifically, assuming adequacy is set at a sufficient level, individuals would be empowered to live ecologically suitable lives.

Conditionality

Green ideology is liable to adopt a relatively unambiguous stance on whether to make EUBI payouts in some way conditional. An ideal-typical green EUBI would pay out money without fear or favour to every individual, irrespective of wealth or income. This is primarily linked to the layers of universalistic ideals that underpin green ideology. Further, it avoids overcomplicating a scheme that for greens can be a powerful tool to incentivise ecological behaviour. As we will see shortly on the issue of funding, these incentives are primarily based on revenue sources. If additional incentives were implemented via payouts, this would drastically add complexity to a scheme that already has incentives built in. After all, the administrative implementation of checks on issues such as CO_2 consumption is much easier on the side of funding. Here, the consumption of goods that are marked out as particularly problematic can simply be taxed upon either production or sale. Implementing similar incentives on the side of payouts would require intrusive consumption tracking and seems neither especially feasible nor desirable, given the strong preferences for civil liberties enshrined in green ideology.

A secondary argument for payout conditionality found in green ideology concerns monetary redistribution. As greens support this goal in principle, it might be expected that a green EUBI would introduce some conditionality mechanisms similar to those discussed in the previous chapter on social democracy. However, green reservations about giving money to the already wealthy and privileged are much less pronounced than those of social democrats—and if a EUBI were to be funded through redistributive revenue sources, this issue would be largely mitigated anyway. All these arguments considered, a green EUBI is thus highly likely to just be paid out unconditionally to all members of society.

Uniformity

The dimension of uniformity is one of the key areas in which a green EUBI differs from many other proposals. After all, green ideology puts a strong emphasis on place-based individuality and localism, which implies that a uniform EUBI level across all regions is essentially off the table. Like social democrats, greens would attempt to ensure that payment levels vary between geographic areas according to their respective prevailing economic conditions. However, due to the green focus on localism, more emphasis would have to be put on achieving variance right down to the granular local level. Ideally, this would imply variance within regions, within cities, even within local boroughs or wards, if costs of living are drastically different between neighbourhoods. This is clearly an ideal-typical argument, as issues of practical feasibility may force Greens to define payout levels at a higher, city-wide or even regional geographic level. Crucially, however, national or state variance would not be a sufficient level of granularity against this background, which implies some tolerance for increased administrative complexity. The key goal here consists in allowing individuals to live ecologically and socially sustainable lives wherever they are. Furthermore, local economies should be fostered but not swamped by the injection of funds that EUBI provides. Both goals pull the green EUBI in opposite directions: if payout levels are overly uniform, this may benefit structurally weak regions at the detriment of individuals living in prosperous, high-cost areas. After all, averaging all costs of living across a larger region would lead to payouts below needs levels in high-cost areas, but above those in areas that fall below the average. This struggle is in line with the aforementioned tensions between urbanist greens and those who emphasise human connections to nature. If the latter have the upper hand, higher degrees of uniformity may be seen as an acceptable outcome, as rural communities may receive payouts higher than the value that their costs of living may otherwise justify.

Frequency

In contrast to uniformity, frequency is both less controversial and less important from the perspective of green ideology. Here, preferences for a strong state in conjunction with support for civil rights and liberties form the core argumentative basis for EUBI policy design. We suggest that, based on these principles, the ideal frequency of payment for a green EUBI would be monthly, as this would strike a balance between individual liberties on the one side and state intervention and incentivisation on the other. The state would gain some control compared to less regular payments of higher amounts. Of course, this control does not refer to direct intervention, as the operation of payouts should be a mostly hands-off process. Rather, it means that slowly feeding smaller amounts of money into the system is in and of itself a form of control. This approach prevents individuals from spending large amounts of money right away on ecologically harmful luxury goods. At the same time, monthly payouts retain many individual freedoms. Just like monthly payouts of labour income, they enable consumption smoothing over periods of several weeks. Monthly payments may also be desirable as many expenditures such as insurance payments can be timed to go out at the same degree of frequency. In addition, an incremental drip-feeding of small daily payments may steer individuals away from choosing more sustainable albeit more expensive consumption patterns. After all, the constant availability of small amounts of money may nudge some members of society towards regular micro-payments on unsustainable goods. Hence, greens must take on the task of finding the 'sweet spot' between payment intervals that are so far apart that they incentivise 'splurges' on luxury goods, and intervals that are so regular that they miss the mark of nudging individuals towards high-quality, sustainable consumption. That said, frequency is much less influenced by links to income from labour for greens than it is for social democrats. After all, labourism is hardly a prominent concept in green ideology. Thus, the need for payouts to be in-sync with established wage payment patterns would play no particular role here.

Duration

The differences between greens and social democrats in terms of the importance of labour also have implications for the duration of payouts. From the perspective of green ideology, very little speaks in favour of making UBI exclusively available to those of working age. Thus, the ideal-typical green EUBI would be paid out throughout an individual's entire life. In order to support parents in remaining independent when they are raising children, caretakers would receive payments on behalf of minors or people with special needs. All other payments would be directly made to individuals themselves throughout their entire lives. In practice, greens have opted for basic income proposals that are geared towards special subsets of the population—for instance, recent proposals for UBI just for children (Strengmann-Kuhn 2023). However, from a theoretically ideal-typical angle, it is difficult to justify such limitations. Rather, they are likely a pragmatic response to perceived, anticipated, or actual hurdles in political practice. Political actors may assume that people at more dependent stages of their lives are more 'deserving' of welfare and thus hope to achieve a UBI that adjusts to such conceptions. In turn, duration is also not the most central dimension of policy design for greens. Thus, if necessary for the formation of agenda coalitions, this is evidently an area where concessions may easily be made.

Modality

On the dimension of modality, the green EUBI has to navigate several different ideological priorities. In principle, we suggest that it would ideal-typically be paid out in monetary units, in line with the aim of green ideology to enhance individual liberties, which in a capitalist or even most non-capitalist systems still requires access to money. Such a design is easier for greens to support than for social democrats, given that greens struggle less with the relationship between income and labour. However, a green EUBI may feature a unique trait designed to maximise its principles of environmentalism and sustainability. In order to incentivise behaviour that green ideology deems 'desirable', there could be a voluntary option of receiving one's EUBI in the form of 'sustainability vouchers'. To incentivise individuals to take up this offer, the monetary equivalent value of these vouchers could be higher than the actual monetary EUBI option. In turn, the vouchers would only be applicable to specific types of consumption, such as sustainable food and transportation, or electricity and energy supplied from renewable resources. Thus, individuals choosing vouchers would give up some flexibility in spending in return for the option of being able to consume more goods that are worth supporting when seen through the lens of green ideology. This approach would solve the previously mentioned issue that payouts are difficult to use as behavioural incentives. What is key here is the voluntary nature of voucher payouts. First, a purely voucher-based system may reach the limits of what conceptually counts as a UBI. Second, since green ideology also emphasises individual liberties, an approach that *only* provides vouchers may be considered overly paternalistic.

A second twist on the modality of a green EUBI concerns its monetary form. This would, by default, be equivalent to the currency of the respective country—so, for instance, Eurozone members would pay it out in Euros. However, in principle, greens may also consider paying out UBI in local currencies that can only be spent in a certain region, or perhaps even just a single locality. In a control-oriented implementation of the scheme, local currencies could ensure that globally mobile or well-off members of society are forced to recirculate the money within the desired jurisdiction, essentially as a form of place-based 'regeneration through consumption'. If these currencies are demurrage-charged—meaning that they automatically lose value over time—the state would gain further control over the timeframes of spending. This would enable governments to prevent the accumulation of large amounts of local currencies that may lead to inflation within local economies in the long run. Ultimately, choosing such a system would make sense for certain radical interpretations of green ideology, but would contravene the goal of boosting individual liberty, while likely incurring severe resistance from other ideologies.

Adequacy

Adequacy is an important issue for a green EUBI, albeit not a fundamental one. The main reasons that would drive greens to prioritise adequacy are environmentalism and sustainability. Since green ideology is compatible with UBI primarily because the scheme can be designed to foster sustainable behaviour, payouts would need to be set at a level that enables people to consume potentially expensive goods. Consequently, a green EUBI should aim to be pitched at a relatively generous level. However, green ideology also offers a fallback scenario if such generosity cannot be achieved: incentivisation. In this second-best case, payouts would not suffice to actively enable sustainable consumption, but funding would be used to redistribute money from those with a large CO_2 footprint to those who consume less (see also funding below). In this case, even small payments would be enough to improve on the *status quo* in the view of green ideology.

Ideally, to be considered adequate, the green EUBI would at least cover 60 percent of the regional median income or 50 percent of the regional mean income, which corresponds to established definitions of being at risk of poverty. The policy would further have an additional component of interregional redistribution to enable any local community to thrive. This could be achieved by additionally linking EUBI levels in any region to an EU-wide minimum of, for instance, 20 percent of the EU-wide median income. The earlier option of receiving an EUBI in the form of sustainability vouchers would also increase the monetary equivalent a person would receive, based on particular baskets of goods designed around sustainable consumption. If, however, such adequacy levels are not feasible, greens may opt to introduce UBI as an extremely low-level payment that is fully attached to sustainable revenue sources. For instance, a CO_2 tax may be introduced, which would be regularly paid back to citizens as a flat rate. This 'climate dividend' would imply low payouts but would ensure that a CO_2 tax benefits the poor, as they consume less CO_2 than the rich.

Funding

As discussed throughout the previous sections, funding is one of the key levers that greens may use to design an EUBI according to their ideological preferences, with the main emphasis of funding schemes for a green EUBI inevitably revolving around sustainability. Ecological taxes such as a CO_2 tax, a green border tax, production-side taxes, and higher VATs on non-sustainable products could contribute to this. Such revenue sources would incentivise ecologically sound behaviour by rewarding those who do less ecological harm through net positive transfers. Moreover, pairing these revenue sources with UBI may help greens justify taxes which they would want to introduce *in any case*, but for which they would otherwise lack the requisite political support. This approach would most likely imply a specific kind of redistribution from the wealthiest members of society to the least well-off, as the latter consume less CO_2 in absolute terms. Relative to their income, ecological taxes might harm them more than the rich. However, as the EUBI would overcompensate them for these costs, they would ultimately still stand to benefit materially.

To strengthen this layer of redistribution more explicitly, a green EUBI may add another layer of taxation that does not have the same kind of ecological orientation. This could entail corporate taxes, taxes on wealth, inheritances, and high incomes, and a financial transaction tax. Although these revenue sources are not explicitly geared towards sustainability, they may ultimately have ecologically positive effects all the same. After all, they may hedge profit-maximisation and thus environmentally harmful behaviour on the production side. Any combination of these taxes could be introduced as hypothecated and exclusive EU-level resources, whereas those that remain national would partially be channelled into EU funds. Finally, to deliver on green ideology's preferences for nonviolence, a green UBI may be complementarily financed through taxes on industries entangled with—or responsible for—global incidences of violence and insecurity, such as arms manufacturers, defence and intelligence corporations, private security services, or private military contractors.

EU Policy Instruments and their Relationship to the National Welfare State

Among all the ideal-typical policy designs discussed in this book, a green EUBI is one of the most unequivocally integrationist variants. As greens support federalism and by extension almost always also the EU, their associated EUBI could be implemented directly at EU level through a regulation or an as-yet undefined new form of direct EU policy. This would lead to a 'genuine' EUBI and the introduction of proper, autonomous EU-level social policy. Furthermore, as greens are less strongly committed to national welfare states than social democrats, this EUBI could plausibly be used to replace all equivalent national monetary payments, while other support schemes would remain in place.

From a theoretical perspective, questions could be raised as to whether such strong European integration conflicts with the localism and regionalism that green ideology favours. On closer inspection, however, this is less of an issue than it might appear at first glance. First, the form of European implementation this envisions primarily conflicts with the alternative of national-level schemes. By preventing such a national outlook, an EU-level scheme may ultimately empower regions relative to the nations to which they are currently subordinated. Second, the localist ambitions of a green EUBI are realised through other channels, particularly the scheme's uniformity and its encouragement of local economies. Third, the localist alternative to an EU-level scheme—that is, a patchwork of local UBIs across Europe—would pose vast challenges of administrative feasibility. Finally, such implementations would largely circumvent the EU's institutions and procedures, which would merely raise questions about how far the scheme reflected the greens' pro-European credentials. An EU-level implementation of a scheme that responds to local necessities is thus the ideal approach for a green EUBI overall.

Technical Distribution and Introduction

Concerns regarding technical distribution follow a similar logic to the one underpinning the role of the EU. In an ideal-typical green EUBI policy, the EU would directly make payments to individual citizens. This would underline greens' support for individual liberty within a system where strong state action is allowed: on the one hand, the EU plays a crucial role by providing money; on the other, the scheme circumvents intermediaries like other governments. The EU would accordingly be required to establish its own federalised infrastructure and centrally administer the entire scheme in order to avoid national interference—and to emphasise the role of local communities as opposed to the national member states within a federal EU. In a sense, the EU would 'liberate' individuals, regions, and localities from national oversight by providing direct and emancipatory monetary means, without giving the EU active intervention capacities through punitive means-testing. In line with green ideology's preferences for reformism, and with a view to keeping track of the EUBI's potential undesired negative effects on the environment, the scheme would be introduced gradually, and would be constantly monitored by a commission for a 'just transition'. If undesired effects arise, increases in payouts would be halted and only continued once the problem in question is resolved.

In summary, the green EUBI is less concerned with the role of labour and national welfare states than the social-democratic one, but instead emphasises the importance of local communities and sustainability. It makes only a few key compromises when it comes to fostering individual independence from the markets—and thus primarily aims to incentivise behaviour through a logic of positive incentives rather than negative nudges. This stands in contrast to the social-democratic model, which incentivises wealthy individuals not to take up UBI through non-automatic payouts. The ideal-typical green EUBI mirrors some of the tensions inherent to green ideology, specifically between urbanism and individual connectedness to nature, between localism and European integration, and between sustainability and individual freedom of choice. Thus, some instantiations of the scheme are inevitable compromises, whereas others can take various routes depending on the preferred interpretation of green ideology that UBI advocates choose to draw on.

Chapter 5

Far-Left Ideologies

Far-left ideologies are a broad umbrella category for a range of political movements and ideas. We use the term 'far left' instead of, for instance, socialism, communism, or anarchism alone, or any of their many subsidiary variants, as the term has the strongest direct links to contemporary political parties in the EU while not blurring the dividing line with ideologies of the 'centre left', including green ideology, liberalism, and especially social democracy. Like social democracy, far-left ideologies have their roots in the European workers' movements of the nineteenth century, but take more radical approaches to achieving their goals. At the EU level, the ideology is primarily represented by the Party of the European Left and the associated faction of the Left in the European Parliament (GUE/NGL). The far left is often associated with a certain brand of 'soft' Euroscepticism, though the degree to which this is applicable varies considerably between parties (Williams and Ishiyama 2018).

A core value of far-left ideologies is equality (Geoghegan 2014). Rooted in historical and contemporary ideas of class struggle, the far left aims to overcome social hierarchies and strongly opposes elitism in any of its forms (March 2009, 127). In these goals, it certainly resembles social democracy, as it also emphasises liberty through emancipation and the provision of fundamental rights. Individual creativity should primarily be realised through work, as the far left struggles against the division of labour under capitalism and the alienating effects it has on individuals' relationship towards the process, outputs, and social conditions of their work (Marx 2019 [1932]). Thus, ideals of productivity and creativity are tightly interlinked, although the latter also reflects a component of intellectuality that goes beyond work conceived in a physical, often physiologically effortful sense (e.g., Marx and Engels 1978 [1845–1846], 33). All these ideas are underpinned by particular understandings of welfare, as far-left ideologies are united by their struggle against poverty and immiseration (e.g., Alexander 2015, 988). The successful outcome of this struggle, as we outline further below, is to be achieved through expropriation of private concentrations of wealth (Jud and Reiter 2023) and their redistribution into the collective ownership of society as a whole.

What sets the far left apart from its social-democratic and green counterparts is its peculiar analytical lens. Far-left ideologies often—but not always—share a common origin in Marxist social thought (Engels 2013 [1892–1893]), which gives them a particularly strong inclination towards historical and structural interpretations and explanations of the world. Industrial and latterly finance capitalism, and the exploitation of workers they bring, are the outcomes of certain identifiable developments and social causes, and exist as 'milestone' stages along a trajectory that culminates in a future proletarian workers' revolution (Boswell and Dixon 1993). The effect of this theoretical and methodological backdrop is to give the ideologies of the far left a deterministic slant, which stands in stark contrast to the more open and malleable social-democratic conception of social outcomes. It also means that the far left often adheres to expectations of rapid development that contradict the at times glacial gradualism favoured by centre-left ideologies. This especially creates a divergence in their respective ideas of social progress (Schmitt 2021). Far-left ideologies critique the past and the present, and set their store by a future-oriented idea of positive progress, whereby deep-structure historical processes based on predictable 'laws' of how society functions far outweigh the transformative power of (individual) human agency.

The worldview of the far left leads to a distinct set of premises that further set the ideology apart from the others we examine in this book. These are grounded in the principle of anticapitalism (Chiapello 2013), associated with a strict rejection of market economies as the way to operate systems of goods and resource distribution and exchange. The far left instead favours state planning as the mode of running the economy (Kaminski 1996), with the aim of replacing rather than stabilising the activities of free markets. Such an approach has implications beyond the economy as well, as it implies that the far left is committed to an idea of society built on cooperation rather than competition (Singer 1999), and is inclined to favour collectivised solutions as the way to achieve their goals (Chase-Dunn 1980, 515).

The statism promoted by the far left is of a particularly radical brand. To abolish rather than fix capitalism, workers are expected to (potentially violently) overthrow the existing system in a revolution, in order to seize control of the administrative and coercive capacities that state institutions offer (Ypi 2014). As far-left parties still face the limitations of working within the existing political system, some concrete political arguments—such as the one for a UBI we present below—may depart from this radicalism on some counts. Subsequently, the state, or the collectivity of society as a whole, takes control over the means of production (Cockshott et al. 2002) and establishes a system of economic management that ensures that every member of society benefits from its aggregate productive capital. This implies a central role of the principle of order, often manifested through (1) intervention in production by an active state with an extensive fiscal and regulatory bureaucratic function, and (2) the central, pervasive societal role of a single dominant (evidently left-wing) party.

However, the far left is not free of internal conceptual tensions. For instance, this state-oriented system could be centralised or decentralised—a perennial source of disagreement between its state socialist and cooperative anarchist variants. Both systems could also be connected in a hybrid form, based on a strongly centralised one-party government (Kalyvas 1999) that defines economic and social goals but leaves it up to regional branches to decide how to achieve these goals—which was the attempted initial model of council (or soviet) communism. There are a number of associated internal struggles relating to ideas such as vanguardism (Gray 2019), where certain sections of the working class, usually dedicated 'cadres' of the dominant party, provide theoretical and strategic leadership for the rest, acting ostensibly on their behalf in advancing revolutionary social goals. Another controversial strategy relates to entryism (Palmer 2021, 691), where far-left policies are achieved by infiltrating other political groups, generally those situated more comfortably within the centre-left ideological cluster. Ultimately, this translates to alternative approaches towards the violent overthrow of the system, as the far left may also aim to infiltrate existing institutions and transform them from within. Internal tensions also come out strongly on the question of democracy, where some far-left ideologies may still favour a proletarian workers' dictatorship as a legacy of their past exclusive, singular class identity (Draper 1987), while others—in line with the contemporary European far left, which has long since broadened its appeal beyond merely representing industrial workers' interests—take a distinctly pro-democratic, pro-system stance (Walker 1991).

The basis of a far-left understanding of sociality is collectivity in all its various forms and contexts (Freeden 1996, 426). Individual liberty (Heller and Fehér 1991, 198), which far-left ideologies typically tie closely to equality, should be enabled and achieved through the mutually supporting collective efforts of social groups, and organised via the coordination functions of central government rule, communes, or councils. However, there are again tensions within and between the far left about what specifically this interpretation of individual liberty should imply. For instance, on the issue of private property (Sayers 2011), the far left is torn between those who aim to abolish it entirely and those who only want to collectivise the most fundamental productive capital. Besides this, the far left has some very clear unifying characteristics. It supports collective movements (Millward and Takhar 2019), including but not limited to trade unions, it champions internationalism

(Imlay 2018), and it emphasises group over individual identity (Freeden 1996, 426). However, as with social democracy, issues of nationality are particularly thorny for far-left ideologies. On the one hand, nations and their institutionalisation as nation-states have historically allowed—and still to a large extent foster—the development and organisation of collective institutions at otherwise unimaginable scales. On the other hand, they regularly and sometimes viciously conflict with the far left's internationalist ambitions, which cannot plausibly be realised beyond the nation (right now) if its anti-colonialist ideals are taken seriously.

STATE PLANNING AND RADICAL REDISTRIBUTION: FAR-LEFT IDEOLOGIES AND UBI

The position of far-left parties, activists, and movements towards UBI has been somewhat ambiguous and changeable to the point of quite significant instability. Individual politicians have supported the idea of an emancipatory basic income (Blaschke, Otto, and Schepers 2010, 7–9), though at the theoretical level the far left has levelled both intellectual endorsements and critiques towards the scheme, often relying on some of the same (most commonly Marxist) underlying premises and lenses of analysis (Bregman 2016; Pitts, Lombardozzi, and Warner 2017). Yet leaving the critiques aside, there are many theoretical ways in which a UBI could be framed positively based on the assumptions of the far-left ideological family.

Equality and Liberty

One of the main pillars of far-left ideologies that any argument in favour of a UBI must address concerns labour and productivity. Supporters of the scheme may argue that in order to be sustainable and fulfilling, labour relies on a complex supporting network of resources and relationships. In the absence of such contextual conditions, the individual may lack the capacity to work on their own terms. UBI would then represent a way to ensure that every individual has minimum 'coverage' of social resources and relationships. First, it could ensure that the essential material preconditions on which all human activity relies—for instance, accommodation, nutrition, and health—can be met. Second, UBI could be framed as a minimum tangible expression of care and support between all members of society, with the aim of allowing everyone to realise their full labour capacity. Crucially, a UBI scheme could help diversify the 'relational infrastructure' on which every individual depends. What we mean by this is that any individual ultimately depends on networks and social contacts to thrive in a society. These networks are particularly important for their capacity to carry out work, as they give even highly materially deprived individuals the 'anchor' or 'springboard' they need to get access to higher-paying jobs. Traditionally, such networks were the family or the local community, which implies a fundamental dependence of the individual on what are often profoundly conservative structures. By providing a collective UBI, this material dependence could be shifted to society as a whole: everyone is materially supported by everyone else, which gives everyone more flexibility to search for jobs and decline offers of precarious employment.

Importantly, however, the labour-centric far-left case for UBI goes beyond merely such capacity to work. It also entails that the policy could allow every member of society to benefit equally from the results of their own *and everyone else's* aggregate efforts of labour. UBI could be considered a deliberate rejection of the idea that there are vast quantitative and qualitative differences between individual workers' contributions to overall production. This line of argument entails that from a macro-societal perspective, different labour inputs such as effort, dedication, and skill largely even out, especially when viewed through a lens that takes individual capacities into account. In other words: most people make broadly similar contributions to society, relative to the maximum they can physically and mentally achieve. This perspective also assumes that differences in labour output concerning the value and wealth generated have less to do with individual inputs (what we might call their 'gumption'), but are instead linked to collective interactions as well as societal attributions of value. On that basis, UBI could ensure that all workers are rewarded for the 'spillovers' of their contribution to overall societal production beyond the specific parameters of their particular employment situation. What is more, the scheme could be considered a response to shifts from labour- to capital-intensive industries. In the resulting system, labour is not the only—and perhaps not even the main—determinant of productivity. As levels of economic development and industrial specialisation cause the impact of labour on productivity to vary, it could be problematic to use it as the primary, or even sole criterion for determining the value of members to society. A universal scheme like UBI could instead be a way of distributing the social return of aggregate capital investment equally across society, freeing up people from their lives as 'wage-labourers'. Ideally, the result would be a space in which everyone can enjoy the fruits of their productivity without the constant pressure that characterises large swathes of the current political economy.

The issues of equality and liberty in far-left ideologies are further tied to questions of creativity and intellectuality (Marx and Engels 1978 [1845–1846], 33). This is closely associated with labour, as the far left sees work as more than a pure expression of economic productivity. Far-left UBI proponents may hope that the policy could enable members of society to engage in more creative work, as the time and effort they have to spend to make a living is correlatively reduced. The additional free time that could be won this way could be used by individuals to work for themselves. This work could take two basic forms. On the one hand, it could be work for marginal added income, where individuals do not reduce their working hours, but benefit from an overall increase in income, given the monetary boost provided through UBI. On the other hand, individuals could reduce their paid working hours and instead engage in tasks they consider more rewarding such as hobbies, intellectual pursuits, creative endeavours, or physical exercise—or even take part in social activities beyond labour that could strengthen their bonds with their friends, family, and communities.

What is more, far-left UBI supporters may see the policy as a way to change the very nature of work itself. Limiting the need to engage in mundane, pointless 'bullshit jobs' (Graeber 2018), the policy could incentivise and de-risk technological replacements for low-skilled and time-consuming labour. The key difference to current developments of this kind is that lower dependence on income-generating jobs may make such transitions much less harmful for workers, and could allow them to pursue more dignifying tasks that are of greater value both for society and for the workers themselves. This argument then acknowledges that a human element will always be needed in some jobs, which may benefit from greater labour supply if capacities are freed up elsewhere. Yet it is important not to mistake this perspective for the merely economistic argument found in some liberal schools of thought. Rather than creating a 'reserve army of labour' (Kaarsholm 2020) that is trapped in and dependent on exploitative work, individuals would gain the opportunity to accept and reject work as they please, thus ideally improving their working conditions and their ability to conquer as-yet underexplored niches and industries. This could be matched by the creation of a space of intellectual self-development and a societal-level shift from blue-collar to white-collar work. Through a far-left lens, however, this would not be framed in the sense of seeing blue-collar work as inherently a 'worse' form of labour. Rather, the point is to recognise the very real pressures faced by blue-collar workers, and protect them from specific detrimental harms such as exhausting physical and psychological stress. One mechanism through which such a shift could occur is training and upskilling, given that a UBI may free up time and resources for education. Whether such education is carried out purely for its own sake or to further one's career is secondary, as either step would ultimately foster valuable skills within society at large.

Two other key concepts of a far-left analysis of equality and liberty are class and emancipation (Chattopadhyay 2021, 89–109). Building on the arguments above, UBI can be framed as a way to give equal freedom to all workers, both as individuals and as members of the working class as a whole. Without context, this argument would not necessarily support the universality of a UBI scheme. After all, why would the scheme be distributed to anyone who was *not* a worker? However, a far-left argument for UBI recognises that in contemporary political economy, conditions similar to those faced by the working class—that is, waged or salaried employees—also apply to areas such as gig work, sub-contracting arrangements, and precarious self-employment. Thus, defining who counts as 'deserving'—or as a worker in a broader sense—risks leaving those who need support the most fallen by the wayside. Additionally, it would potentially undermine all-important workers' solidarity, as it segments those who are living in some kinds of dependent conditions into mutually differentiated sub-groups. A UBI could accordingly be framed as a tool of universal emancipation from market pressures, made accessible to all at the same level.

This introduces a material form of similarity and solidarity that can be reinforced in policy design (see the section on funding below). Ideally, through a UBI, the vast majority of workers could be freed from their dependence on capital, which could significantly weaken the risk of being dominated by business-owners as a class. As a result, the incentive for workers to sacrifice their own material interest to those of businesses due to a lack of better alternatives may be extensively abolished—precisely by creating a guaranteed income source to provide such a better alternative. As redistributive funding schemes could be designed so that business-owners are net contributors to a UBI constructed on far-left principles, the only issue that remains is the mere 'symbol' of gross capital flows to those who already own a significant amount. If taxes are used to offset these flows, they would be a small price to pay for major gains for the far left.

Such gains also concern the state itself, which would be elevated to the level of becoming a new basis for workers' social power. This is particularly important at the lower ends of the income distribution, as UBI could prevent (the threat of) immiseration and precarity from structurally undermining workers' negotiation power. As the scheme places a lower bound on how little workers can receive, it removes poverty as a viable weapon in the arsenal of business-owners and employers in the class struggle. UBI could further insulate workers' access to income from specific political-economic arrangements, thus ensuring that, even if workers' collective struggles temporarily fail, a basic safety net still exists 'to catch them when they fall'. This basic safety net goes beyond contemporary welfare arrangements, as it extends the privilege of passive income currently reserved to the wealthy to the working class. As an income stream for all members of society, UBI would be a way to give material substance to the principle that all humans deserve basic sustenance and support simply because they exist. Given that

UBI recipients would not have to do anything in return for such an income stream, the scheme would enshrine material wellbeing as a fundamental *de jure* and *de facto* right. Although even the wealthy would technically be eligible to receive it as well, a UBI could challenge the exclusivity of the rentier class, for instance by giving the working class a starting capital to acquire rentable assets in their own right. The associated diversification of income streams brought about by UBI could then free workers from uncertainties about potential income risks. This is particularly important when it comes to questions of investment, as workers often find themselves unable to afford to take risks, given the potentially catastrophic impacts that a loss of investment capital would have for their own and their dependents' livelihoods.

Many of the arguments we have discussed so far can be brought together under the general umbrella concern of exploitation and expropriation. At its most fundamental, far-left UBI could be framed as a simple yet effective way to alleviate the effects of exploitation on individual workers. This assumes that there is a considerable disparity between the value a worker creates and the wage that they receive in return. The difference between these two values is then appropriated by those who own the means of production, making UBI a tool of redress for structural exploitation. As a boost to workers' total income, it could help to improve the match between workers' contributions and what they receive in return—albeit under the constraint that individuals' value cannot solely be determined by their economic productivity.

As we elaborate in the section on policy design, a far-left UBI could also be set up in ways that 'expropriate the expropriators', without sacrificing its efficiencies as a universal payout. This can primarily be done by choosing revenue sources in a way that matches redistributive ideals. Thus, the scheme could bring the distribution of rewards for labour under partial societal control, making it an efficient shortcut for state redistribution—in a sense, it directly 'restores' the expropriated value that labour generates. If funded accordingly via highly redistributive taxes, business-owners might be incentivised to reduce their tax bills by increasing wages, thus reducing the amount of surplus they take. This argument operates under the assumption that higher wages give an employer a competitive advantage when trying to attract talent in the labour market, implying that business-owners would rather 'lose' money to wages than to taxes. However, UBI would not only address the process of exploitation, but also its outcomes—reducing the obvious effects of structural underpayments, such as the heightened risks of absolute poverty. The scheme thus becomes a buffer that protects workers from having to sell their property and their labour below its socially useful value. This allows them to choose whether they even want to commodify their capacity for action as wage-labour at all.

Sociality

When it comes to far-left conceptions of sociality, the differences with liberalism in particular become glaringly clear. While far-left ideologies also emphasise the value of individual identity, they imbricate it closely with group and mass identity (Freeden 1996, 426). To frame an argument for UBI—which reflects an at least partly irreducible individualism in its construction—in line with this worldview, the policy could be framed as a way of recognising a certain shared collectivism among all members of society. While the policy acknowledges individual human needs, it aims for an effective large-scale solution to the structural struggles of an entire class. A far-left UBI could thus be seen less as an individual welfare entitlement and more as a proportional share of societal-level wealth transferred from the class of capital-owners to the working class by means of a redistributive policy design.

Crucially, by distributing money to individuals directly, the scheme partly resolves the tension between individual expression and collective belonging inherent to far-left ideologies. Entitlement to UBI derives from membership of a collective, specifically a large society-level collective, but also exists with the specific purpose of emancipating individuals. In contrast to trade-union scepticism towards contemporary liberal ideas of UBI, the policy could further evolve into a common cause for activists, unions, and organisations to rally around across sectoral divides. If a UBI is promoted in this way, it could avoid the pitfalls of replacing the existing achievements of class struggle but instead act as a way to underpin and bolster this struggle with very real material power. Again, we discuss in further detail how the far left might aim to achieve this in the section on policy design. One of the key takeaways at this stage, however, is that a far-left UBI would act as a way to increase workers' solidarity with, within, and between unions while providing a clear goal for cross-sectoral industrial action. Once achieved, the scheme may significantly enhance the bargaining position of workers and by extension of unions—after all, it would give them the resources to 'hold out' for far longer, perhaps even indefinitely, in cases of protracted class disputes.

One of the major challenges of framing a far-left argument for UBI arises from the ideology's trenchant critiques of private property, especially property in capital, and particularly when this is held in excess—which might intuitively appear to be incompatible with a cash benefit scheme. However, an initial way around this is that UBI might be considered compatible with 'petty' forms of private property, since from a macro-societal perspective the levels of income necessary to help workers cover the costs of consuming goods for their own sustenance are comparatively low. Again, redistributive funding sources could be leveraged to prevent net benefits accruing to owners of 'excessive' private property. Specifically, far-left ideologies challenge the idea that revenue from the sale of products should exclusively remain the private property of those who own the means of production that went into creating these products. Instead, as argued above, the workers who 'activate' these means of production through their labour should also have a stake in the ownership of products, and consequently also in the revenue that results from their sale. If instituted properly, a UBI funded by taxes on such sales could redistribute revenue to workers and elevate the societal significance of human need over arbitrarily prevailing social rules that define what distribution of exclusive property claims is 'deserved'.

Building on this, far-left actors could frame UBI as a way to break with the idea that capital and the means of production themselves can be privately owned *at all*. Such resources could be considered public rather than private—which is, after all, one of the most commonly shared aspirations of the ideologies that comprise the 'far left' grouping. However, unlike the implementations of communism familiar from the USSR, China, or their various geopolitical and geoeconomic satellites, a far-left UBI could make such resources *de facto* public by taxing and redistributing them, instead of nationalising them entirely. The idea that underpins such an approach is that production presupposes in one form or another interaction between groups of individuals—including the division of labour, resource supply chains, regulatory frameworks, the accumulation of collective knowledge, and credit systems. Further, production always has some form of collective externalities beyond the specific purposes that any given product is intended for. Hence, far-left UBI proponents could easily argue that production is never a purely private matter anyway—in which case, a redistributive UBI would be one powerful way for society to then raise an ownership claim over capital and the means of production. A far-left argument for using the associated resources for a cash benefit instead of in-kind services and goods is that basic monetary payments are ultimately the most efficient way to respond collectively to the otherwise individualised needs of workers in society's many diverse contexts.

A peculiarly complex issue for far-left ideologies' conception of sociality concerns nationality and internationalism. More so than in other areas, cosmopolitan and communitarian ideas of welfare clash fiercely in this domain. A far-left UBI would be treated both as a resource and a relationship that is integral to rooting a distinct national identity, realised in a system of social rights. Like other identitarian concepts such as language, territory, and history, a far-left UBI could underscore that far left sociality is connected to a specific place. The policy could act as a form of currency to smooth interactions between the inhabitants of a common area. Building on this, the inclusivity of such a scheme heavily depends on preferences for or against cosmopolitanism. An inclusive UBI would emphasise that within *de facto* existing nations, interdependent communities have formed that share modes of production and its associated forms of class structures, exploitation, labour, and property—framed more as a given fact than a normative goal. In response to this, UBI allows the inhabitants of a nation to be fundamentally equal at a minimum level of income in the same way that their common language, territory, and shared history lay the groundwork for basic equality in other realms of sociality. This view constitutes an inclusive take on UBI, as it does not actively utilise the nation as a vehicle of exclusion, but rather uses UBI as a vehicle to include everyone who happens to reside in a nation under a basic sense of commonality. Such an approach is more open to cosmopolitan ideas but feels the need to respond to existing forms of 'othering' by at least undermining their consequences for those who move into a territory and may otherwise be disadvantaged.

Against this view stands an exclusive view of UBI that lends itself to communitarian ideas of sociality. It uses UBI to demonstrate societal differentiation, and in particular the advancement of one's own society beyond the economic mode of other countries that do not have a similar scheme. Crucially, however, cosmopolitan UBI supporters on the far left can extend the scheme to apply to a larger unit such as the EU by recoursing to ideas of internationalism. They may argue that key dynamics of political economy and of class struggle—especially today—span beyond national borders and thus constitute a shared reality and belonging in the socioeconomic realm. A supranational UBI could then introduce a 'pro-worker' policy that accommodates this common realm, recognising that the 'functional geography' of capitalist exploitation is hardly limited to the contingent inheritance of national borders. What is far more important for the far left than national identity is that a UBI would respond to place-based and sectoral differences in the prevailing political economy of different countries, regions, cities, and so on. Workers' remuneration may not map neatly onto existing administrative subdivisions, which means that a far-left UBI would in principle be open to finer-grained variation of payout levels (see policy design).

Anti-Capitalism

Weaving together several of the implicit threads so far, one common intuitive characteristic associated with the far left is the idea of anticapitalism (Chiapello 2013). One of its key elements concerns the link between the economy and other sectors of society. A far-left UBI would not just be geared towards reallocating wealth between classes, but also towards pursuing equalising and liberating effects in areas such as the governmental system, legal frameworks, moral norms, or caregiving structures. Simply put, the assumption here is that intervening in the economy can benefit workers in noneconomic terms as well. Specifically, introducing a far-left UBI could respond to labour-eroding developments such as automation and AI. As these developments may free elites from their dependence on workers, they may ultimately also result in further imbalances in, for instance, political power: if capital owners do not need workers anymore, workers lose access to even the fairly limited capital flows they can currently control. As a result, they struggle to survive and lose the resources they need to organise in interest groups or compete for political office.

This logic can be scaled to other realms and societal resources as well. In one sense, this is based simply on the sheer fungibility of UBI: money transferred can be used to acquire any other resources needed to participate fully in a social community. What is more, political, legal, and cultural resources that are equally and freely accessible 'on paper' may in practice still require a baseline outlay of money. This can simply be rooted in opportunity costs: if every available hour of the day must be used for paid or unpaid work to sustain a living, little further room is available for political participation. A UBI alongside interventions like living wages, working time reductions, and wage and wealth caps could level the playing field. The basic logic underpinning this argument is that economic power translates into the ability to secure and deploy administrative and repressive power, influence over regulation and the legal sector, as well as ideation and communication, for instance through media outlets. To counter this, a far-left UBI would not only need to provide basic resources to everyone, but crucially also need to redistribute these resources from the wealthy to the less well-off. Arguably, it could do so more efficiently than targeted benefits, as fewer people would (by definition) fall through the cracks. After all, the actual process of redistribution would be achieved on the side of tax revenue rather than on the side of payouts in the fiscal transfer equation.

Another prominent element of far-left anticapitalism is a generally shared preference for state planning (Ellman 2014). In this respect, a UBI could be framed as an acknowledgment of the fact that markets only imperfectly respond to human needs, which was an implicit factor in the earlier discussion about the insufficient compensation that waged employment offers for the value created by labour. In a purely market-based labour remuneration system, workers are left to engage in individual pay negotiations within their workplace, modified into slightly larger-scale negotiations insofar as they are unionised and benefit from collective bargaining. However, the far left may argue that this does not sufficiently and systematically address the needs of the working class. After all, trade unions are still splintered up by sector. This is the result of a fundamental dilemma, as 'one big union' that speaks for all workers could not properly differentiate between sectoral needs, but sectoral unions weaken the power of the working class as a whole. Hence, the far left may advocate for UBI as an additional state-led initiative to close the gaps within this system that cannot be addressed by more targeted schemes.

In a less problem-driven approach, the far left could also aim to use UBI to remedy the shortcomings of previous iterations of state planning. The economic failures of state socialist and soviet communist governments during the Cold War, in particular, have eroded trust in the idea that the state should be entrusted with highly planned economic governance. Far-left actors may hope that a UBI can showcase that modern states have gained—or more accurately, *never actually lost*—the capacity to implement effective large-scale measures that remedy economic hardship beyond the 'band-aid' approach of means-tested welfare schemes. To achieve this goal, a far-left UBI would need to effectively react to changing economic realities and to variation across regions. The policy would then take the form of a 'low-stakes' exercise of state capacity, given that it would not need to intervene directly in labour markets and business operations. What is more, the scheme is in principle compatible with a wide range of economic models. The only economic modes that can theoretically be ruled out for the implementation of a UBI are a purely *laissez-faire* free-market economy—which would reject any state intervention—and purely centrally planned economies which would not see the need for UBI, as more direct tools of intervention are available.

The final element of an anti-capitalist far-left argument for UBI consists in the pervasive ideological embrace of cooperation and collectivism over competition. Here, the starting premise is that the policy could be a way of weakening the pressure to compete on the labour market, as workers do not have to secure jobs simply to cover their costs of living. Workers could receive the option to 'opt in' or 'opt out' of competition and reflect on whether the 'marginal utility' they receive from competing is worth the stress and struggles associated with it. What follows from this is that UBI may take away one of the major threats to worker solidarity, namely employers imposing personal loss on workers as a result of withheld wages during industrial action. The impact of losing out on benefits by going on strike would be much lower if a sufficient basic income was secured for everyone. UBI could thus be framed as a material underpinning of more durable workers' movements. This, in turn, could force employers to offer better-remunerated work, as well as in-work opportunities for workers, which together could further decrease class differences. However, for the far left, a UBI would primarily be an intermediary stage that opens the door for further socialisation policies. Far-left supporters of UBI may hope that the scheme gives the working class the material strength—as well as strategic confidence—to campaign for a more expansive societal-level model for workers' support, resting on more granular supplements to workers' income within business operations. If UBI is a social dividend, so the logic goes, then this can be replicated at the level of individual firms too. Beyond regular salaries, bonuses could be expanded from merely the management levels (disproportionately of 'white-collar' tertiary, quaternary, or quinary industries) to all employees across all sectors. Accompanied by enhanced democratic control of workers over companies, this may contribute to achieving, or at least *pro forma* replicating, increased societal ownership of the means of production without the 'sledgehammer' approach of outright nationalisation.

Statism

The last pillar of a far-left argument for UBI is statism. The role of the state in far-left ideologies can best be described as instrumental: it is not an inherent end of far-left principles or strategy in itself, but rather serves the purpose of achieving other, more fundamental goals. Part of the reason for this ambivalence is the residual suspicion—again a legacy of Marxism—that state structures as they exist in capitalist society can never fully escape their intended function as instruments that allow the ruling class to wield power over workers (Hay 1999, 154). This ambivalence towards, and at times even rejection of, state power stands in tension with other far-left approaches such as state planning. A UBI could be framed as a tool to resolve this issue. It may allow the far left to make the best of the existing state institutions, putting them to use in order to achieve equality and emancipation, albeit without creating an oppressive apparatus ready to be taken over by a (new or already-established) ruling class. The guiding assumption here is that the state currently holds a large degree of untapped potential to be more assertive against—rather than on behalf of—private enterprises. Implicit in this claim is that the existing portfolio of social policy measures is insufficient. However, crucially, it also means that the principle of state action is already legitimised, turning the focus away from *removing* it and instead towards *subverting* its existing tendencies. In other words, the biggest hurdle—namely achieving legitimacy for state intervention at all—has already been overcome. UBI would then simply be a particular expression of a larger aim to put all members of society in touch with structures of collective self-management.

Through a UBI, individuals could meaningfully feel the material benefits of being subjected to a state administration. This means that both UBI and the state are instrumental in their own interrelated way: UBI helps to cement support for state action, while the state can be used to implement UBI as a tool to realise broader left-wing goals. The increased legitimacy of the state is particularly important for the far left to achieve deeper reforms such as a reorientation away from market capitalism. UBI is one possible method of achieving this, which could also be accompanied by an expansion of administrative bodies tasked with social policy matters, as well as the establishment of permanent bodies of workers' representation in state institutions. Given the far left's relaxed sympathy for a judicious dose of social disruption, very much unlike social democracy, liberalism, or Christian democracy, there are no reasons to treat any of the existing state institutions as sacrosanct here. UBI could thus be used as a tool to materially support the working class in their efforts to restructure the state in line with their interests. The assumption here is that UBI enhances the wealth and collective power of the working class, which can then be pooled to strengthen and create new institutions that act in workers' interest. Specifically, workers may combine their enhanced bargaining power and presence in state bodies to extract concessions on workers' co-determination within sectoral regulations or at a more granular level within the management structures of businesses themselves. Alternatively, they could aim to abolish some of the functions of the state as it currently exists and replace them with workers' assemblies. Any embrace of such arguments by far-left actors clearly depends on the radicalism involved, and the particular 'shade' of far-left ideology they happen to represent.

The same question of the degree of radicalism of far-left arguments also plays into their relationship to democracy. UBI can be designed as a policy that interprets democracy in a majoritarian sense. It provides every member of society with equal resources, rather than favouring, for instance, minorities or vulnerable groups. This can become part of a far-left argument for UBI if those who choose to deploy it assume that workers and employees in a broad sense—as opposed to more restricted readings such as the industrial working class—constitute the largest group in a given society. Under this assumption, empowering this largest group with resources that are taken from the wealthy minority could give the far left structural electoral advantages in the long run. Such advantages are primarily a concern for party politics, but could also be framed as a tangible benefit for workers themselves. Through the materialist lens of far-left ideologies, the biggest value of democracy for workers is not their mere procedural inclusion but rather the resulting influence over policies that could benefit their interests. UBI could, as argued earlier, be framed as a way to act on these interests. Importantly, a far-left UBI would need to be protected from reactionary turns in democratic politics: comparing the far-left UBI to the Christian-democratic one, for example, shows clearly how fundamentally different goals could be marketed under the same label. Thus, the far left would likely aim to institutionalise their vision of a UBI within the societal framework much more firmly than some other ideologies.

Fears of the working class being split up into multiple ideological fractions could drive exactly such an impetus. As social policy questions can quickly cause tensions between groups of workers, divided by sectors, markers of identity, and other social characteristics, the far left would not only aim to 'protect' UBI against retrenchment by constitutionalising it, but also use it as a tool to unite all workers under one universal umbrella. Once implemented, the far left may further hope that UBI could democratise spheres of society beyond only the political domain. Here, the far left exhibits some similarities to social democracy, although driven by different underpinnings. While social democracy cherishes the value of democracy as such, the far left may see democratic empowerment in the economic sphere as a tool of class struggle, and therefore one of the key purposes of a far-left UBI. The goal here would be to rebalance the relationship between capital and labour within production processes. The state would provide workers with the means to push through democratic involvement in business decisions, thus ultimately weakening capital-owners. It is worth noting that UBI under this logic is more of a short-term substitute than a long-term solution. Instead, the institutionalisation of workers' involvement within businesses would take priority to ultimately achieve a more comprehensive democratic transformation of contemporary political economy.

Far-left proponents of UBI can further tap into the preferences for centralism (von Beyme 2014) held by many of their associated ideologies to frame the policy as the universal provision of equality from a single vantage point. In another case of a 'maximinimal' approach, the far left could aim to maximise the level of minimum equality that a central administration can feasibly provide for as many people as possible. While in theory more radical approaches would be conceivable, a far-left UBI would express the point that any state must take seriously the realities of national and international political economy. The working class may have cross-spatial reach, but it is also often fragmented and limited by boundaries. The resulting tensions and frictions imply that even a central administration would struggle to settle on policies that appease all workers. UBI could be a simple first step to put in place a baseline in this regard. However, for the far left, these tensions and frictions also speak in favour of implementing a UBI centrally, as the state could be considered to 'stand above' sectoral divides. Still, because of sectoral and place-based differences in the structure of the economy in any given society, a far-left model of UBI could not simply be applied in one blanket form. On that basis, far-left centralism cannot be allowed to undermine the earlier requirement of ensuring that UBI is calibrated to the requirements of each context.

This could represent the biggest test of the central state's capacity to deliver UBI, as it requires permanent state institutions to have already developed extensive bureaucratic 'depth'. Local administrations must gather data as granularly and as close as possible to where workers live to ensure that the central government can design payout levels appropriately. Central provision thus depends on decentralised information—although how precisely this decentralisation should be structured is not necessarily clear. For instance, it could follow existing geospatial boundaries, or impose new ones that track more closely the sectoral divides within the working class. What is more, any attempt to decentralise information-gathering and adjust UBI to local needs has to reconcile its conceptual tension with the far left's commitment to centralism and universality. It is not hard to see this becoming the source of internal struggles between far-left UBI proponents. One way out of this dilemma could, again, be a 'maximinimalist' approach where UBI is first introduced over the largest territorial area possible, and then tweaked sectorally and in a place-based way over time. In a different way to social-democratic gradualism, this stepwise approach would aim to start with payouts at a high level straight away but recognise that a measure of 'trial and error' is unavoidable in centralised policy planning. Rolling out the scheme at high levels, both in terms of the number of recipients and immediate payout levels, explicitly rejects any approach that prefers to implement UBI for carefully selected subgroups of the population first. After all, such an approach would create artificial divides between in- and out-groups within society. Far-left ideologies reject this both on intrinsic principle, and with a view to avoiding any undermining of collective class solidarity. This thinking is generally at the heart of why far-left ideologies might embrace UBI in the first place.

The final element of a far-left argument for UBI concerns the idea of revolution (Ypi 2014). Here, the far left's framing for an argument in support of UBI strays quite some way away from other ideologies, particularly from social and Christian democracy. A far-left UBI would be framed as a way of institutionalising a radical overhaul in societal attitudes towards what 'human worth' means. UBI offers a way to connect the idea that work is—and of right ought to be—more than just wage-labour with the reality that workers ultimately need money to survive. Its core purpose is, after all, to decouple monetary means at least partially from work, thus allowing the latter to be understood in a more holistic way. Such a fundamental change to the logics of the labour market could give workers the latitude to produce for someone *other* than their employer—not least for *themselves*—and to conceptualise their human activity as more than this labour as well. They could dedicate greater time and effort than before to carrying out socially beneficial tasks. Such change could be justified by recognising that human beings have both an instrumental and an intrinsic value. Instrumentally, they 'do good' for society beyond what they can produce for mere market exchange. Intrinsically, they are multifaceted beings who have a value *as such* and thus need to be empowered to realise their interests. A far-left UBI, so this argument goes, could be used as a starting point for a wholesale transformation of state institutions, with the aim of embedding these values in the fundamental structures that govern society.

This transformation should also extend to the underlying political economy under which society operates. A UBI could build out some of the existing functions of the state and act as an entry-point for more far-reaching transformations of capitalism. It would normalise the idea that all workers' interests must be taken into account *equally* when defining the appropriate transfers that redistribute wealth and income among society's members. Seen through a far-left lens, these transfers would be considered less interpersonal and more classist and structural—proportional transfers from each member of the class of wealthy asset-owners, business-owners, and beneficiaries of economic rents, and proportional transfers to each member of the salariat, gig workers, subcontractors, or the self- or wage-employed. UBI could be framed as a key tool in the vanguardist arsenal to shift the state's class character away from structurally reinforcing the domination of the owner class. Instead, it should institutionalise at least a 'class compromise', if not an outright reversal to working-class political control. Again, these aims can be realised only if the policy is designed in a very particular way, as elaborated further below. Beyond these policy design choices, however, a far-left UBI relies on a number of other policies to accompany it. It can achieve its comprehensive goals only if it is one pillar of a bigger revolution. In the far-left worldview, UBI is not considered a silver bullet that can, and will, reconcile all tensions in society. More than that, the far-left argument for UBI explicitly warns that the scheme must not be considered the endpoint of progressive change. At its most parsimonious, it can be seen as a radical expansion of social benefits that need to be accompanied by radical advancements across all areas of the welfare state—and beyond. This could, for instance, include universal basic services, but *in extremis* also a revolutionary overthrow of capitalism as such. Whether in such a scenario a UBI would be maintained in the long run depends on the alternative system that is put in place, and thus remains open for debate.

TOWARDS EMANCIPATION: A FAR-LEFT VIEW OF EUBI

Building on these arguments, a far-left EUBI would entail the most dramatic social changes of all the policy designs we discuss in this book. While some of the following considerations run counter to what communitarian far-left actors may demand, they are firmly rooted in our discussion of far-left theoretical principles. As we have subsumed various neighbouring ideologies under the 'far left' label here, many alternative ideal-typical EUBI designs could be specified if a more granular approach was chosen.

Universality

Universality is the first area in which far-left preferences can potentially clash, mainly down to differences between far-left interpretations of communitarian and cosmopolitan approaches. A communitarian far-left EUBI would have an exclusionary core built into its formulation, in the sense that it would be developed and implemented primarily by the EU's member states. Its European dimension would derive from parallel attempts to create an EU-wide policy learning and cooperation framework between workers across the bloc, but the scheme would ultimately be a *national* one, reserved for citizens of the various *national* communities. In contrast to this, a cosmopolitan far-left UBI would build especially on the constituent ideologies' goals of eradicating hierarchy and exploitation, and elevate the international dimension of politics and the economy. Thus, everyone who finds themselves in Europe for anything more durable and substantial than touristic purposes would receive an EUBI under this ideal-typical scenario. This would include short-term migrant workers, with the explicit aim of protecting them—as among the most vulnerable members of the EU polity—from exploitation, discrimination, and social dumping. Taking all the previous arguments into account, we consider this cosmopolitan version to fit better with the core principles of far-left ideologies overall. One crucial argument for it is the fear of undermining collective solidarity if the working class is split up by arbitrary divisions. While such an argument would theoretically lead to a global UBI, a European version can currently better respond to far-left requirements concerning centralised state planning—given that an extensive roster of European institutions and well-established policy capacity already exists at the supranational level.

Individuality

Another point of tension within a far-left model of EUBI concerns the individuality of monetary awards. On the one hand, these ideologies are virtually synonymous with an embrace of collectivism, and in particular emphasise the need for workers to organise within society through councils, unions, and other collective bodies. On the other hand, one of the signal drives that binds together the members of the far left is a shared striving for individual (worker) as well as collective (class) emancipation. Both principles pull EUBI policy design in opposite directions, as one hints that the preferred system would see payouts to groups, while the other could justify fully individualised payments. This tension could be resolved by transferring money directly to individuals, but by collectivising the revenue sources that stand behind these payments (see the section on funding below) and by organising funding so that workers are the main beneficiaries of the scheme. As a result, a far-left EUBI scheme would enhance collective group solidarity while at the same time ensuring that individual workers are still adequately protected and valued. As is the case with an EUBI designed in line with green principles, caretakers of children, the aged, or the disabled could again receive the money on behalf of those 'in their charge'.

Conditionality

Irrespective of the arguments that can be leveraged in favour of a far-left EUBI, one of the most difficult hurdles it must overcome is the scepticism that any such scheme would face due to the simple fact that it is giving money to the privileged as well as disprivileged members of society. As we alluded to earlier, the best way of resolving this issue is by adjusting the revenue sources on which the scheme relies (see further below). However, in addition to this, a far-left EUBI could very easily introduce a number of additional procedural mechanisms to discourage the wealthiest members of society from claiming the money to which they would be entitled. As with the social-democratic ideal-type for EUBI, these would entail tapering off automatic payments as individuals' income and wealth increase. To remain classifiable as a UBI, this would again have to be accompanied with a formal right for even the wealthy to claim UBI all the same—although the far left would likely embrace stronger mechanisms to discourage this. These could include high bureaucratic hurdles, as well as creating a repository of publicly available information about who actively claimed UBI—perhaps restricted to those above a certain wealth and income threshold, or who fall within the upper deciles of the society's wealth and income distribution. The latter would be a form of political-economic 'public shaming': the 'negative' equivalent of the social-democratic donation mechanism where those who voluntarily abdicate their UBI are publicly praised.

Uniformity

As we have seen above, far-left ideologies are generally receptive to arguments that speak against fostering high degrees of uniformity among the members of society. As with the ideal-types we have previously described, the far-left EUBI would thus correspond to regional or sectoral needs. There is a wide array of options available here to specify this requirement more precisely. One level of variation could quite simply be the local level, defined at the granularity of local boroughs or even wards, which would aim to do justice to everyone's exact needs and social situations, set against the average prevailing conditions within their immediate contexts. This would require immense resources but by the same token could be seen as a powerful demonstration of state capacity. UBI levels may also vary between sectors, based on each one's particular income levels and employment practices, though this runs the risk of further dividing the working class. In yet another scenario, UBI levels may be defined at the national rather than the local level, in line with some far-left tendencies towards embracing a national form of collective solidarity ahead of any others. This aligns with the inclination among several of the same far-left strands towards state planning, which would mean that the EUBI would be linked not only to national income levels, but also to a variety of other factors such as intended or expected levels of regional growth, productivity, and other forms of socioeconomic development. These would need to be assessed on a regular basis, most likely by a dedicated committee of experts and workers' representatives, in order to ensure that the central state's 'picture' of the degree and nature of interregional variation remains as accurate and up-to-date as possible. How precisely this would be translated into granular variation within the EUBI levels distributed among the workers resident in different regions is simply not clear from a theoretical perspective, especially given the diversity of far-left ideologies involved.

Frequency and Duration

In the light of the far-left tendencies towards state planning, as well as the relative enthusiasm of some of its constituent ideologies for an extensive bureaucracy, this model of EUBI would be paid out more frequently than many of the others, in order to avoid large capital accumulation at any given time, and to retain control over society's overarching capital flows. An appropriate payout frequency to match this ambition could be a weekly one, to ensure that the most vulnerable members of society are never 'too far away' from their next opportunity to have a sizeable share of their everyday costs taken care of. This would give the state a strong degree of involvement and would also make public intervention more prominent in the everyday lives of EUBI recipients. This may, in the long run, normalise a more active role for the state, and may also increase public trust in the state's capacity to address socioeconomic issues. To retain the EUBI's emancipatory potential—that is, to safeguard all members of society from hierarchy and exploitation in all their forms at every age and stage of their lives and working trajectories—it would be paid out throughout the entire lifespan of every individual.

Modality

Regarding the modality of payments, different intra-ideological principles come into conflict for the far left. State planning preferences point towards vouchers—which, after all, would allow the state to exercise a high degree of central control over consumption behaviour. However, the goal of individual liberation and emancipation points more firmly towards cash payments, as these provide EUBI recipients with a degree of fungible choice that avoids the top-down restrictions that voucher schemes implicitly impose. Importantly, for many far-left movements, state planning is geared more towards the systemic structures of the economy and not so much towards individual behaviour. A far-left EUBI would therefore be paid out in monetary form, maximising workers' emancipation in parallel to other structural transformations of prevailing political economy, and giving workers greater flexibility to act as ready allies for the state in the task of eroding capitalism 'from within'. Accepting the fact that capitalism is and for the foreseeable future will likely be the prevailing economic system, and that under capitalism, those who have greater command over money and other currencies of wealth have greater power, the far left would aim to give workers as much access to monetary means as they possibly can. Less fungible forms of payout would then fail to empower workers relative to employers to quite the same extent, as access to money is required to credibly decrease dependence on work for income in a 'one-to-one' ratio. Crucially, this does not mean that a far-left EUBI would sacrifice its member ideologies' extensive preference for state planning, as centralised high-frequency payouts and redistributive funding would provide ample reason to maintain a strong role for the central government.

Adequacy

While many other areas of policy design are subject of intra-ideological conflicts within the far left, adequacy acts as an important—and highly welcome—point of agreement. The main point here is that any form of far-left EUBI would be far more than simply a tool for poverty relief. It would also serve to collectivise capital gains and fully emancipate individuals from the depredations of market forces. Thus, EUBI levels would under no scenario be lower than the at-risk-of-poverty threshold in the given European region (see the Introduction), but would in fact also ideally be supplemented through the proceeds from increased capital gains. The aim would be to maximise the minimum monetary entitlement that everyone enjoys through centralised state action. The exact EUBI levels would again have to be determined by a committee of experts and workers' representatives, whose decision would in this case be bound by specific minimum standards, such as the at-risk-of-poverty rate and pre-agreed goals and targets for society-wide redistribution and individual emancipation. Among all the ideal-typical policy designs we discuss in this book, it can safely be assumed that the far-left EUBI would aspire to reach the highest possible payout levels.

Funding

As we have alluded to at various points throughout this chapter, funding is one of the key levers that the far left can use to make a UBI a redistributive tool that not only supports but also forms part of the overarching class struggle between capital and labour. An ideal-typical and fairly radical funding approach would consist of two pillars, socialisation and taxation. Based on the well-established far-left principles of anti-capitalism and redistribution, some productive capital and banks would be placed into collective societal ownership—most likely, although not strictly inevitably, through direct nationalisation. A predetermined proportion of the revenues associated with these new public assets would be hypothecated and channelled into the EUBI, to provide a stable source of 'core funding' for all future EUBI payments. Depending on quite how radical the far left is prepared to be, this approach could also be varied to embrace different extents of socialisation. For instance, a less radical version of this EUBI would not seize all the means of production—that is, it might leave certain industries or sectors 'untouched' and still open to market forces—but instead shift focus more towards the second pillar of taxation. This pillar would consist primarily of high taxes on wealth, land value, corporate profits, inheritance, automation, and luxury goods. Taxes on extremely high incomes—or on particular sources of income such as passive rents or dividends—could also factor into the overall revenue, but policy design would need to ensure that the vast majority of workers would remain unaffected. By taxing these factors, the far-left EUBI would become a prodigious redistribution apparatus that constantly cycles funds—especially excess revenue from productive capital—back to the working class. Due to the centralised nature of the scheme (see the section on EU policy instruments below), some of these resources would be generated by EU-level taxes. However, the socialised productive capital would initially remain national, as long as no far-reaching political integration of the EU has yet taken place.

EU Policy Instruments

In principle, there is much to speak in favour of implementing a far-left EUBI centrally at the EU level. Cosmopolitan conceptions of human rights and internationalism, coupled with clear preferences for centralised state action, could make an EUBI a tempting option to deliver on the idea of a 'social Europe', and construct a scheme of genuinely EU-level social policy. Within the current framework, the closest legislative instrument that matches such an ambition would be a Regulation. However, the kind of implementation that far-left approaches to EUBI have in mind would require a significant Treaty change—especially as the far left would aim to institutionally entrench the

EUBI as resolutely as possible, for instance by constitutionalising it. If Treaty change is on the table anyway, enshrining the scheme in the Treaties would be one effective way of achieving this. Perhaps more importantly, introducing an EUBI would come with a specific additional precondition for the far left: radically strengthening the power of workers within the EU's administrative apparatus. Otherwise, there would be a risk that the EU would be skewed towards business interests—including using an EUBI to undermine workers' rights, for instance via welfare retrenchment (see next section). One step to bringing about a transformation of the EU in line with far-left preferences may be a more fundamental democratisation of the EU, amid a long-overdue overhaul of its institutions in general, in order to give the majority of wage-earners stronger representation, and a stronger voice relative to other EU-level interest groups. This may, just for purposes of illustration, imply introducing formal veto powers for trade unions and workers' bodies within the European Economic and Social Committee—which would also need to exercise a significant role in the design and implementation of any EUBI scheme. What is important here is that the far-left EUBI does not fit simply or comfortably into the policy framework of the EU as it now stands. Thus, introducing it would also mean a dual disruption of the current system: first, its introduction would require fundamental institutional reform; and second, the scheme itself would redefine what European social policy can be.

Relationship to National Welfare States

If EU reforms that strengthen workers' powers at a European scale were to be achieved, the far-left EUBI could be implemented without the risk of welfare retrenchment. By implication, the scheme would be a kind of 'bolt-on' complement to existing national welfare states, and would only be allowed to replace those policies that are (1) intended for poverty relief, (2) purely monetary, and (3) set at a value no higher than the value of an EUBI. The limitation to poverty relief (e.g., social assistance) is needed to ensure that the EUBI has an additional emancipatory effect beyond poverty prevention. If other emancipatory monetary policies (e.g., unemployment benefits above the poverty threshold) were to be replaced, this effect would be weakened or even cancelled out as a result. However, any replacements for welfare policy would undermine the net benefit that workers and the most disadvantaged members of society would get from an EUBI. Hence, the ideal-typical scenario for the far left would be to avoid any form of welfare retrenchment and design an EUBI as a purely additive scheme.

Technical Distribution and Introduction

Assuming the level and forms of political integration and transformation outlined above actually take place, the EU under a far-left EUBI would make payments directly to individual citizens and residents. A dedicated federalised infrastructure to do this would be created, and the EU would centrally administer the entire scheme. Considering the revolutionary leanings of several segments of the far left, any such EUBI would be introduced swiftly—the sooner, higher, and more granularly, the better. To avoid any delays during the time that the centralised system is being set up, national infrastructures would temporarily be coopted for implementation over the course of a transitional period. Payments would start immediately at the at-risk-of-poverty threshold, and be subsequently adjusted in accordance with the expert committee's recommendations as quickly as possible. If necessary, any initial funding shortfall in implementing this scheme at the desired level would be addressed by taking up public debt, shared collectively at the EU level.

All things considered, the far-left model of an EUBI would be strongly redistributive and would largely be able to achieve its most fundamental impact by making radical choices on the funding side of the overall EUBI 'equation'. If in doubt, the goal to achieve individual emancipation from the hierarchies and exploitation that characterises life in capitalist society would trump the desire to use central state planning to achieve the far left's societal aims—although a certain measure of state planning remains key to making an effective far-left EUBI a reality.

Chapter 6

Liberalism

One of the oldest ideologies we discuss in this book, liberalism as a tradition of social thinking coalesced out of several disparate strands of radical, republican-democratic, and anti-mercantilist thought prominent during the seventeenth and eighteenth centuries (Dahrendorf 1991). Its long history produced some of the most diverse political positions concerning social protection, making liberalism a particularly interesting and at times highly rewarding lens through which to analyse UBI. Liberals remain a dominant force in Europe to this day, and have long been the third-largest political group in many European national legislatures as well as the European Parliament, typically behind Christian democrats/conservatives and social democrats (e.g., European Parliament 2019). At the EU level, they are mostly organised under the Alliance of Liberals and Democrats for Europe Party, which together with the European Democratic Party form the Renew Europe group.

As the name suggests, one of the key pillars of liberalism concerns individual liberty (Ryan 2017, 365)—a principle that comprises a set of specific freedoms, including freedom of thought, speech (Meyer 2020, 8), action (Dewey 1935, 225), assembly (Inazu 2012), and trade (Wissenburg 2006, 20). Implicit in this list is a tension between several different interpretations of liberalism that is particularly prevalent within the contemporary EU: Is liberalism primarily meant in political-economic or sociocultural terms, which is often reduced to a binary between liberalism 'of the right' and liberalism 'of the left'? In its most radical forms, the more economic strand of liberalism, for instance, heavily emphasises the role of free commerce in free markets (Friedman 1987), while the more cultural understanding of liberalism focuses on issues such as expression and individual identity (Kymlicka 1989).

In short, there is not just one 'liberalism', but rather many 'liberalisms', and tensions between these different liberalisms cut across the principles that underpin the overarching ideological family label. Generally, liberalism in all its forms builds on strong rights. These could entail the right to property (Gaus 1994) and land, which would emphasise economic freedoms, while the liberal ideal of autonomy and consent also implies that society should provide its members the right to freedom of contract (Flanigan 2017). However, liberals may also champion individual rights to privacy (Warren and Brandeis 1890), electoral enfranchisement (Kahan 2003), welfare (Lombardi, Miyagishima, and Veneziani 2016), and healthcare (Cappelen and Norheim 2005). Depending on how these rights are to be fulfilled, they can stand in conflict with economic freedoms. More fundamentally, however, liberals are united by the idea of providing individuals with civic and human rights (Mahoney 2008), the latter of which are considered universal beyond national borders.

The tensions between political-economic and sociocultural ideas inherent to liberalism are resolved under the principle of equality. Here, the ideology favours equality of opportunities (Miller 2013, 93–114) and basic resources over the equality of outcomes that is more prominent within the social thinking of social democracy or the far left. This can, in principle, also entail fiscal redistribution and support for public services, as liberal ideas of justice presuppose that every individual has some basic opportunities for self-fulfilment (Christman 1991).

Another pillar of liberal society is the idea of tolerance (Kautz 1993). Liberalism emphasises the need to accept individuals for who they are, culminating in pluralist societies that mediate between particularistic interests. These societies should be democratically organised, specifically through representative parliamentarianism (Selinger 2019) and must be built on a strong constitution that underpins the rule of law (Tucker 1994). Liberalism accordingly rejects absolutism and instead strives for the creation of societies in which individuals deliberate and engage with one another to solve both individual and collective problems (Charney 2014). In cases where these disputes become unresolvable merely through debate, there is a clearly defined scope for a judiciary to step in to adjudicate between their relative merits.

Liberalism presupposes a very specific way of social thinking. It paints humans as fundamentally reasoning, rational beings who maximise their utility—with a political anthropology that remains variously consistent with the ideal of *homo oeconomicus* widely posited by neoclassical accounts of economic liberalism in particular (Read 2022, 311–22). This implies an understanding of individuality rooted first and foremost in self-interest and particularistic thinking. However, liberal philosophy also emphasises human emotionality alongside critical thinking and reason (Hobhouse 1911; Paine 1877 [1794]). As humans are seen as capable of abstraction and reasonability, education and enlightenment (as one of the products of education) is a central element of liberal thought (Schmidt 1999). Such a rationalist view does not, however, imply that liberalism ignores the effervescence of human creativity.

On the contrary, the ideology embraces it, placing particular emphasis on its value for invention and scientific progress (Avnon and de-Shalit 1999, 3).

Importantly, liberalism does not deny the social components of human nature. It emphasises organicism (Cabrera 2023, 8), the view that individuals as members of a society form part (quasi 'organs') of a larger organic collective (quasi 'organism'). However, this idea of a collective stands in opposition to (e.g.) far-left understandings of the same concept, as liberalism remains ultimately centred around the discrete individual. Conflicts between individuals exist but should be resolved in a way that allows for sufficient harmony to sustain the fabric of society on which all individuals depend to some degree. Many of the rights that individuals enjoy in society are given to them by virtue of being human (McManus 2020), which gives liberalism strong universalist and internationalist tendencies (MacMillan 2007) and connects it to ideas of cosmopolitanism (Langlois 2007).

Despite its extensive emphasis on the reasoning, creative, discrete individual, liberalism also features a well-developed understanding of social order. For individuals to be able to pursue their goals, the state must provide a basic modicum of security and stability through some limited intervention and activism. By establishing reliable institutions, the state plans for the future to ensure that individual freedoms do not end up *de facto* or *de jure* inhibiting themselves. This can imply a certain area of unresolved tension within liberalism between support for leaving free markets to their own devices and instead embracing state intervention precisely to prevent this—and there are disagreements between different strands of liberalism as to how far exactly state intervention should go (Bellamy 1993, 29). Historically, liberalism also further exerted its order through state action in the context of colonialism and imperialism (Williams 2018), as the universalist ideas to which liberalism aspires spilled over relatively easily into narratives of 'freeing' other peoples from moral or intellectual 'infancy' or (perceived) oppressive rule—especially if paired with specific ideas of a 'general interest' and a 'common good'.

Finally, in terms of human progress, liberalism shares with social democracy its conceptualisation of social developments as inherently open-ended, rather than as deterministically driven towards a fixed end-point. This is rooted in the idea of free will and choice that underpins liberal assumptions about individual behaviour—and social behaviour as an aggregate of this (Pabst 2013, 219–20). Liberalism then balances ideas of evolutionary struggle (Freeden 1976), in which every individual fights for themselves, with a broader humanitarianism (Reid-Henry 2013), which entails a certain degree of protection from oppression. Ultimately, liberals hope that charting an unerring course towards individual freedom will be the best way to let humanity flourish and improve itself over time.

UNCONDITIONAL FREEDOM BEYOND THE STATE: LIBERALISM AND UBI

Regarding UBI, liberalism occupies a remarkably specific niche. On the one hand, UBI is often considered quintessentially a liberal idea in light of its intense focus on individual independence. On the other hand, it is quite rare to find liberal activists or politicians openly promoting a UBI—especially in the European context, although a few exceptions exist on the international stage (Yang 2018; Luterman 2019). To put this another way, theory and practice diverge unusually strongly when it comes to liberal support for UBI.

In UBI debates, liberal viewpoints have found fairly strong representation since the idea first emerged. For liberals who are in favour of social protection in principle, UBI can appear as more-or-less a natural fit when taking into account the principles that underpin liberal ideology in general. Among those principles, we specifically focus on the following ones here: liberty and rights, autonomy, justice and equality, democracy, and individuality and sociality.

Liberty and Rights

Perhaps the most intuitive, instinctively characteristic feature of liberal ideology revolves around the high premium it places on individual liberty and rights. This is typically associated with freedom of action and its derivatives, with the ideal goal that individuals have the capacity to exercise their will and agency in society. This ability, however, depends on the availability of at least a basic range of resources (White 1997; Fitzpatrick 2010). Accordingly, liberal supporters of a UBI can frame the policy as a tool to ensure that these basic resources are provided in the highly universalisable form of income and wealth. A UBI thus 'buys' individuals access to freedom of action, so that they can make their own agency socially impactful. As liberal societies are organised around systems of trade and exchange—whether purely marketised or subjected to some state interventions—marketisation without any kind of resource 'floor' may place hurdles in the way of those who lack basic monetary means. This issue extends far beyond the question of mere consumption choices: liberal supporters of UBI may frame the policy as a vital guarantee of freedom of assembly and movement that gives the members of society the means they need to participate fully within it.

In this regard, the ability to move is particularly important for liberals, as they conceive it as a key feature of society *as such*. If individuals receive the ability to reach and achieve their goals 'in social space', they can interact with each other more seamlessly and take collective action (Bauböck 2009). As a result, society becomes more than an abstract concept or the mere aggregation of its individual members: achieving physical proximity and relational connection with others becomes a way to foster societal meaning through individual action. However, the movement necessary for this ideal is often (very literally) effortful and costly. As individuals often do not *ex ante* have the means to realise true freedom of movement, they have to rely on some external support—which, in turn, could be provided by a UBI (Allegri and Foschi 2020). Similarly, liberals may frame UBI as a guarantee for freedom of thought and speech. First and foremost, it would enable members of society to 'vote with their pocketbooks'. Expenditure choices are already a vital and ubiquitous measure of public opinion in free-market societies, as they have become a way of expressing views on societal issues beyond mere questions of taste. However, for these mechanisms to function seamlessly, a minimum of available capital for all is required to make 'marketised voting' compatible with ideals of individual freedom of action (Smith 2021). After all, poverty and a lack of income can be seen as a form of exclusion and denial of voice in a liberal society. A liberal UBI may then be a crucial way to ensure that all members of society can—and will—be 'economically heard'.

This logic of participation also extends to the political realm itself, in that UBI may be framed from a liberal perspective as a tool to give genuine force to the ideal of electoral enfranchisement. This means that the policy represents a form of both economic *and* political empowerment, which is increasingly important for being a member of a community with a meaningful say in what shape this community takes. As a regularly replenished resource that members of society can wield to intervene within the political and economic domain, UBI would act as a backstop for individual powerlessness, rather than imposing a maximum ceiling on influence. This would allow liberals to combine ideals of participation with a continued freedom to acquire and accumulate wealth—on the grounds that arbitrary domination via political oppression or economic exploitation are quite simply less of a concern, given that individuals cannot fall below a certain threshold. This legally acknowledges and reinforces the protection of individual agency from those who have accrued more political and economic power. Not unlike the equal value of political votes, a liberal UBI might thus be framed as a way to hedge 'multiple-tier' social identities. In turn, politically empowered individuals would gain control over the specific design of UBI through democratic processes (see the section on democracy below), and in something of an ironic twist would also invert historical requirements for minimum level of property-ownership in order for citizens to be permitted any political involvement. Universal political rights give every individual a stake in defining universal social rights: rather than having to own a minimum of wealth to be politically enfranchised, it is political enfranchisement that comes with receiving a minimum of wealth.

Beyond individual action, property and land in particular carry strong ideological associations with liberalism. While liberals emphasise the links between individual action and wealth, they implicitly favour systems that allow individuals to become economically active in the first place. UBI could thus be framed as a way to guarantee access to some minimum level of ownership, and a way to ensure that all members of society have consistent and reliable means to acquire possessions. It thus acts as a form of 'entry-level' capital endowment that allows everyone to 'enter' the property system. The scheme further stabilises individuals' ability to continue to operate within this system, no matter what economic choices they make. In a nutshell, it dissociates the right to mere survival from the striving for nonessential property. In and of itself, UBI can also be seen as a claim to property *itself*, both individually and as a share of the collective. It represents a defined entitlement, in the form of a financial asset that is allocated in perpetuity to all individuals in a society. It is thus effectively a fractional stake in the wealth of the nation as a whole, which every member of society is responsible for 'stewarding' through their economic choices. Finally, with respect to land ownership specifically, UBI might be seen as a way of making land more attainable in societies in which nearly all areas are already associated with some preexisting ownership claims. As land is often inherited, it is detached from the ideal-typical liberal processes in which ownership is the result of (conscious, reasoned, deliberate) individual action. Depending on how a UBI is funded, it may make funds available for individual market actors to establish their own claims on land possession.

In its ideological roots, however, liberalism is not solely focused on marketisation. Liberal arguments can also be made for quite extensive welfare policy frameworks (Lombardi, Miyagishima, and Veneziani 2016; Cappelen and Norheim 2005), which, in turn, accordingly play into framings of UBI as well. Unlike socialists or other members of the far left, liberals are less inclined to focus on the large-scale aggregate of social problems and the systemic pressures associated with them. Instead, they emphasise what they consider to be the 'microfoundations' of social precarity, that is, individual circumstances and actions. To address these, liberals might opt to propose a UBI that provides an individual-level minimum below which nobody can fall, precisely in order to enable individuals to 'pull themselves up by the bootstraps'. A key argument here is that the best way to address individual problems is highly dependent on situation and context. Thus, according to liberal ideology, it requires considerable input from individuals themselves. This would imply that true welfare cannot be fully achieved if it relies on a monolithic structure that caters centrally to the diversified needs and preferences of individual recipients. UBI, so the liberal argument goes, could act as a bridging device that allows state welfare institutions to provide a simple universal solution to a wide range of particular problems. Additionally, the policy would sharpen the principle of positive rights in a way that specifies what individuals need as members of society—and by extension, who they are. Liberals would aim to achieve this goal by rebalancing welfare provision away from presumed need in favour of freedom of choice. In this effort, UBI may create flexible, fungible resources that can cover for gaps in existing systems of social provision, which may lead areas like healthcare, housing, transport, childcare, and unemployment support to become more individualised and less paternalistic.

Finally, at the heart of individual liberties lie civic and human rights (Mahoney 2008), which may lead liberals to frame UBI as an automatic and guaranteed positive material provision of citizenship. While means-tested or otherwise targeted welfare entitlements act as a 'special right' reserved to a certain group, designed to help that group overcome a particular disprivilege, they leave unoccupied space for truly society-wide 'in-cash' guarantees. A liberal UBI could step in here as a form of material 'equivalence' and inclusion, which gives all members of society a crucial point of mutual noncompetitive relatability. It would add a humanitarian dimension to the range of rights individuals enjoy as members of a society. Instrumentally, this right would entail the means to help individuals participate in social practices; intrinsically, it would recognise their basic needs and deservingness *as* fragile human beings. A liberal UBI would thus be something more than just a charitable act by the state. Instead, it would provide legal acknowledgment and grounding for the fact that human life consists in more than mere survival. By extension, internationalist liberals could further emphasise UBI as a way to integrate the strenuous requirements of human rights commitments into domestic rights frameworks. This is particularly relevant in contexts where state capacity itself might fail to take over all elements of the public goods and service infrastructure required to provide more targeted interventions. Societies could thus use UBI to signal global 'advancedness' and comparative advantages on the world stage. In the context of an increasingly global competition over talent, such signalling may establish a nation as a global norm-leader and attract highly qualified inward migration and investment.

Autonomy

A second pillar of liberal ideology consists in autonomy, a principle that has now been most prominently embraced by contemporary libertarians as the self-declared successors of the 'classical' liberal tradition (Zutlevics 2001). One of its key features concerns privacy, and liberal UBI advocates may hope to use the scheme to achieve a more privacy-respecting system of social security, compared to the potentially intrusive and stigmatising receipt of in-kind benefits. While the latter may label individual members of society as 'deficient' in specific socially valorised respects, UBI has inherent potential to respect individual personhood and dignity by emphasising anonymity. Not only are payments generalised, but they actively avoid intruding into individuals' consumption patterns and general behaviour. Under a liberal approach, individuals' decisions on how to spend their UBI would be left entirely to their own considerations.

Liberals might place further value on the idea of a UBI for enabling purchases of possessions that are primarily destined for the personal use of each individual. Ownership of these possessions is *prima facie* uncontested, and sole rather than joint. This sets the scheme apart from support measures that grant temporary access to (semi-)public goods—again, catering to the privacy preferences of liberal ideology. In extreme cases, a UBI designed based on liberal ideas can even become an option for individuals to *shield* themselves from the public if they wish to do so. This is true in both a social and a physical sense. Socially, a liberal UBI would allow people to cut back their dependencies on others down to the bare minimum. Physically, it would enable individuals to buy the materials and the time they need to erect boundaries around themselves and whatever else they happen to own. Although this is often (and very readily) criticised through the lens of other ideologies, liberals might place considerable value on this opportunity as a deeper recognition of the fact that individual sources of fulfilment can lie both within *and outside* collective engagement. Even if such behaviour was collectively undesirable, liberal ideology would maintain that the ultimate decision of whether to engage in isolation should resolutely be up to the individual and their personal choice.

Liberal autonomy, however, is not just a matter of privacy. It also extends to the realm of contract and consent (Flanigan 2017), including the concept of a 'social contract' (Froese 2001). In a similar way to greens, liberals might frame UBI as an integral part of such a social contract that defines the benefits that accrue to all members of society. Liberal ideology emphasises that these benefits are paid in return for individuals' legally established contributions, including but not limited to conforming to norms, obeying laws, exercising 'good citizenship' in support of other people, participating in consumption and market exchange, and upholding social institutions. In a sense, UBI adds a rewarding rather than a punitive layer to social conformity, given that an ideal liberal society might prefer to leave such conformity up to individuals' own preferences and voluntary determination.

Leaning on more familiarly social-democratic terminology, liberals might also see UBI as an expression of social solidarity among all members of society, irrespective of the other bases of difference between them. Liberals might support UBI as a *desideratum* that stabilises the social contract by making members of society *want* to consent to the social arrangements that they happen to be surrounded by. In absolute terms, the tangible material benefit that flows automatically from membership in society may contribute to this quite significantly. Relative to what is available in other societies, UBI could easily look like a uniquely advantageous social offer that makes individuals favour choosing membership of one national community over another. The scheme would essentially be a way of 'enhancing' membership in society—a way to make citizenship in *this particular* society a 'marketable' and 'profitable' proposition. In turn, UBI could make individuals' consent to membership in society more substantially meaningful, as it carves out for them a certain level of autonomous, 'system-independent' empowerment. Against this backdrop, individuals technically do not have to go along with many social practices as they lose their fears of abandonment and retribution. Thus, UBI would increase the significance of the repeated choice an individual makes to participate in society moment by moment, day after day, given that this behaviour would be less forced and likely a more authentic expression of their 'ideal' choice.

Although this is often overlooked in contemporary political discourse, liberal ideology also relies on the principle of moderation in order to stabilise individual autonomy (Carrese 2016). The argument here rests on four considerations. First, autonomy is not fundamentally feasible without finding a way to preserve for individuals an unassailable core of self-direction and non-interference. However, second, such autonomy is also stunted and unequally distributed in society if it is defined as relying *purely* on the capacities and resources over which individuals have direct personal control. After all, these resources are often partly lacking, if not wholly absent, which implies that precisely the free-market economies that liberals are inclined to favour may be *particularly* prone to ultimately hampering rather than fostering autonomy. Third, autonomy is not possible without acknowledging the inevitability and generative potential of at least a baseline of *interpersonal* (inter)dependence. Fourth, and somewhat cutting across this argument, autonomy is realised only passively and incompletely if it is defined as (co-) dependency on others' agency, rather than as maintaining 'independent' distance to at least some degree. These arguments appear at first glance to be partially (or even completely) contradictory, and thus to pose conceptual problems for the ideal of autonomy in interdependent societies. Hence, liberals may want to use a scheme like a UBI as a theoretically and pragmatically appealing 'middle way' for personhood that can navigate between pure atomism and pure collectivism. Even if 'pure' autonomy is impossible, a liberal UBI may be a successful attempt to edge in its general direction.

In another sense, UBI could be framed as a middle way between two competing understandings of autonomy. On the one hand, some liberals might favour the argument that autonomy is fostered by the existing structure of society, including and especially by its welfarist institutions. Only through collective support, so this argument runs, can one truly be independent. On the other hand, autonomy could instead be presented as the full or as-full-as-possible removal of any extant social institutions, thus boosting choice within contexts that resemble or replicate a market framework, and affording individuals the opportunity to dedicate their personal space and effort to participating in other social activities. In this approach, while the familiar regulatory structures defining business ownership might disappear, entrepreneurship tendencies *as such* would be left untouched. In between these two options, a liberal UBI might aim to maximise independence from welfare institutions while maintaining the empowerment brought about by collectively financed support schemes. This could be framed by liberals as the polar opposite of collective codetermination in a post-monetary system of centrally planned resource allocation. However, the specific autonomy brought about by a liberal UBI would also have clear limits. The scheme would be geared towards being strictly 'basic' to provide moderate boosts to individuals' economic capacities. This should be enough to satisfy the needs of survival and low-level flourishing, but not enough to facilitate a life of luxury—which would instead be reserved for the gains made through market activity. The result would not be a post-work society where everyone is independent from employment. Rather, it would rebalance wealth flows to slightly adjust their currently extensive contingency on labour activities, which still leaves space for work to supplement individual income.

If any form of autonomy was to be achieved in a liberal society, this would need to satisfy ideals of tolerance and plurality. While the second of these would be an inevitable *result* of the considerations outlined here, the first would be its necessary *precondition*. Liberal UBI advocates might frame the scheme as, in a sense, an institutionalised acknowledgment that there is not just one way for individuals to meet their social needs—or, indeed, even only one 'right' category or definition of social needs *at all*. Other measures of social difference (cultural, religious, etc.) are a fact of life that political economy *simpliciter* is poorly equipped to cater to. All the same, they strongly shape how individual members of society conceive of and pursue their own welfare. Thus, a liberal UBI could aim to deliver 'difference-neutral' support as a way of enabling without at the same time also delimiting individual capacity for action. This would relieve the state of the dubious responsibility of having to enter the complex terrain of deciding which social practices to support financially, and to what extent.

Moreover, liberals might regard UBI as a way to recognise that tolerance is not just something that can be done passively—but rather, as something that requires active support in order to create potential for real diversity. Certainly, giving individual members of society (negative) rights that protect them from discrimination and create a 'safe space' where they can pursue their social activities is one of liberalism's cardinal, essential goals. However, this by itself does not equate to a guarantee that marginalised individuals in particular can actually follow up on their rights, since after all this often depends on material capacities which would have to be provided via a UBI or something like it. Liberals might frame UBI as a way to ensure that society can enjoy its own plurality without succumbing to fragmentation. The universality of a UBI provides all the individuals that receive it with capacity and opportunity, without raising any correlative expectations towards anything like homogeneity in how these individuals go on to exercise this capacity. If one applies a view of society as a mass aggregate of many interlinked but mutually demarcated private spaces, there is a risk that individuals find themselves in a binary choice between conformity or secession—either following the rules of the collective, or having to break with it completely. Liberals might hope that UBI adds a more fluid range of options to this view. Individuals in disagreement with collective rules, or so the idea at least goes, would not have to withdraw from society by refusing to participate in societal processes or, *in extremis*, leaving the community entirely. Rather, they could enjoy a space where they can pursue their own conception of an independent 'good life' while maintaining communal ties where they prefer.

The final ingredient in liberal ideas of autonomy concerns individual creativity and invention (Avnon and de-Shalit 1999, 3). This is in some ways close to some of the essential considerations found in green ideology, and assumes that humans are, at their core, imaginative and above all generative beings. What sets this creative potential apart in liberal ideology is its stronger emphasis on 'creation' in an entrepreneurial sense. Accordingly, one way to see a liberal UBI would be as a universal 'start-up fund' that leaves individuals space to do whatever they see fit with their income while enabling, in principle, their specific ability to engage in productive, exchange- and profit-oriented free enterprise. As a flexible, fungible asset, the scheme would act as a 'blank cheque' investment in millions of individual aspirations. Such nonjudgmental 'seed funding' provided by an 'angel investor' state may foster inventiveness and the development of new products, while leaving the need for 'proofs of concept' up to the impersonal fluctuations of market forces rather than the willed, wilful, and above all biased selections by gatekeeping investors who first must be won over. The best ideas, so the hope, would survive while the risk everyone who contributes to this progress takes on is collectively buffered.

This could lead to what liberals consider 'true creativity'. Rather than adhering to socially imposed parameters of what constitutes creative labour, individuals could pursue their own aims through UBI. After all, it removes the conditionality that premises the receipt of money on individuals steering their creativity in the direction demanded by their employment conditions. Occupational responsibilities, professional routines, employment schedules, senior management expectations, or corporate strategic imperatives may lose their perceived inevitability, their 'bite'. In other words, individuals would receive a material reward for giving their originality and self-direction free rein. As a consequence, liberals may hope to liberate creativity from productivity without eradicating the latter entirely in a market-based economy. Individuals could dial back the proportion of their time they spend on narrowly framed labour for income. This could free them up to engage in purposeful action in both non-economic social domains and economic pursuits—*and* also in seemingly purposeless action, such as recreational activities, that does not instrumentally serve any specific ends whatsoever.

Justice and Equality

Though autonomy is certainly one of liberalism's central principles, the ideology is far from blind to issues of equality and justice. A key pillar of liberal ideas of justice concerns the opportunities that individuals have available to them. Ideally, every individual should be given the opportunity to advance in life (Christman 1991). However, this raises a dilemma for liberalism, as free-market societies can easily lead to self- or externally imposed disconnections with large parts of society and its activities. Hence, individuals may miss out on what are demonstrably vital and enriching parts of the human experience. Similarly, materially speaking, some goods may be *technically* available, but not actually meaningfully accessible to lower-income individuals in particular. This is not as such a problem for liberalism in principle, as stratified access to goods is simply a plausible and acceptable result of market competition. However, if the lack of accessibility extends to essentials, this can rapidly become an issue for the long-term viability of this social state. Implicit in this argument is a 'two-tier' opportunity structure that conceptually separates luxury and essential opportunities, where the latter may be opened up for universal pursuit through a UBI scheme.

Further, a UBI may be a way to redress the sheer extremity of the divide between the 'cans' and 'cannots' that is inherent to a hierarchy between different goods and opportunities. It may partly equalise the provision of opportunities across members of society in a way that does not eradicate but instead fosters individual agency. This argument is underpinned by the assumption that the opportunity that matters the most is situated at the lowest level of the available range of incomes. According to this logic, the most basic of goods necessary for survival makes the biggest difference for whether or not individuals can pursue and realise their agency. Thus, the difference in opportunities between those who cannot access the bare necessities at all and those who can just about access enough to barely satisfy what they need is considered far more substantial than the quantitative value might suggest. By contrast, the difference in opportunities between those who can access everything and those who can access only their bare necessities is considered far smaller, no matter the quantitative difference.

Following this logic, full equalisation of society becomes unnecessary as long as a healthy degree of *sufficiency* has been attained. Liberal UBI advocates can frame the policy as the way to guarantee this goal. It institutionalises individual opportunity, with its fungibility reflecting the societal desire to foster potential without imposing limitations. The crucial difference between those who have nothing and those who have only a little—or even those who have seemingly unlimited wealth—is, according to the liberal view, not just the literal amount of money they happen to possess. Rather, it is the more intangible independence from having to make forced choices concerning how to exercise their agency that is at issue here. Thus, the most effective way of relieving the 'cannots' in society from this dependency is quite simply to give them money that they can turn into opportunity however they please.

To a minimum degree, such ideas of equality and justice also have implications for resource and fiscal redistribution that rapidly get lost in the way that liberalism is represented in everyday politics. A commitment to liberal ideology entails a fairly pronounced assumption that the most effective way of redressing social injustice is *not* to intervene in the structural frameworks of society. After all, such an approach would be both circuitously indirect and could cause a 'chain reaction' of unforeseen consequences. Rather, liberalism aims to meet the more parsimonious aim of giving everyone access to basic resources, for which UBI could be one of several possible tools (Birnbaum 2010b). This would simply rectify some basic material outcomes of otherwise free societal processes. Ideally, this could be achieved with a funding structure that leaves the gains from individual effort more-or-less untouched, leaving the redistribution of resources limited instead to wealth that is *less* attributable to individual agency. In this regard, one of the most appealing aspects of UBI for liberals is its relative restraint when it comes to levelling new expectations towards state capacity. UBI can tap into already advanced tax-and-spend systems and replace other costly schemes, thus potentially slimming down states' financial administration. Despite being a relatively large-scale intervention, the scheme fits rather neatly and efficiently within liberalism's principles of justice.

In addition, UBI might help address liberals' scepticism towards certain forms of public services. The basic argument here is that such services are often not enough to let the worst-off in society fully participate in social activities. Many of these services are instrumental to achieving a certain task—for instance, public transport as a necessary prerequisite to exercising freedom of movement—or act as safety nets—as is the case with health and social care provision. This facilitates participation and lowers the risks of social activity for large parts of the population, but does not put the majority of 'ordinary' social engagements within the reach of those who are struggling to get by. UBI would be a clean, clear social intervention that would enable individuals regardless of their financial situation to make the most of the benefits that public services provide. Liberals may hope to achieve this outcome as a way of individualising a social justice system that otherwise builds on 'subgrouping', whereby only certain eligible groups can benefit from many support schemes. UBI extends and expands an otherwise granular system that recognises societal diversity to some degree, but may miss many of its key facets. In principle, socially minded liberals who favour public services can combine them with UBI to offer a hybrid of equality and equity, in recognition of the fact that it is impossible to fully plan for all the circumstances that can affect individuals. In this respect, a framework of social justice provision that includes a UBI could offer a broader portfolio of measures that respond to population-level similarities of circumstances while also allowing room for individual-level variation.

Democracy

Like many of the other ideologies discussed in this book, liberalism places great emphasis on the importance of democracy. However, some of liberalism's other ideals, especially those geared more towards the economic domain, may occasionally cause tensions to emerge with its democratic political goals. This is particularly pressing for liberalism, given its firm commitment to representative democracy and parliamentarianism (Selinger 2019). Liberal UBI advocates might frame the policy as an example of how democratic political institutions can produce interventions that successfully counteract the outcomes of other social domains without having to sacrifice liberal values overall. The fragmenting effects of high concentrations of economic power may even drive more market-oriented liberals to worry about their potential risks for democracy. Parliaments that pass a UBI could then be presented as 'protectors of the people', which ensure that liberal social orders work for, not against, the public interest. This, in turn, may help liberals lower revolutionary pressures—which may *prima facie* be oriented against market capitalism, but would almost inevitably spill over against parliamentary democracy as well.

In the same way, UBI could be considered a way for political representatives to signal that they are meeting their delegative responsibility of acting in the interest of voters as individuals instead of faceless masses. After all, the policy may satisfy the basic material needs of all members of society in a continuous and guaranteed way, rather than just as a 'one-off' solution. Accordingly, democratic institutions would also gain a tool to help them adjust to changes in their society's political-economic conditions over time. This is particularly relevant in situations where the costs required to cover basic needs rise rapidly, and society increasingly makes support for democracy conditional on its capacity to help individuals make ends meet. More generally, UBI may become a simple and effective way for liberal politicians to satisfy their duty of trusteeship towards society as a whole. This could boost the legitimacy and authority of political leaders and institutions by showing that they can produce tangible 'society-level' improvements that reach every individual. Ideally, this could limit political apathy and disengagement with elections among populations disenchanted by long periods of political-economic neglect. UBI is somewhat unique for liberals in this case, as it allows them to demonstrate this kind of state capacity without relying on extreme interventionism. Moreover, it strikes a blow against a plebiscitary logic that insists that all 'society-wide' decisions must be left to the exclusive legitimating device of a referendum. Under the current means-tested welfare policies, such referenda are likely to lead to society-wide sectarian divides over who is (and is not) considered 'deserving' of receiving welfarist support.

Another major part of liberalism's ideal of democracy consists in its commitment to constitutionalism (Hardin 1999). Under this principle, one of the main arguments for UBI is its nature as a 'positive right'. Taken to its extremes, the policy's 'bare bones' could be written into the constitutional arrangements of society and thereby placed 'beyond the reach' of everyday politics. Liberals may well choose to take such a step, on the grounds that they could see the policy as a vital unifying and anti-sectarian tool to bridge social divides. UBI is in principle simple and general enough to be included in a 'basic law' of a community, as opposed to the more carefully circumscribed, subgroup-oriented measures that would be far harder to 'constitutionalise' in an appropriately generalised way. By making the protection of material necessities part of the rule of law, a liberal UBI could give the worst-off members of society a 'last resort' if the risks they take in a market-based society end up harming them.

Moreover, the scheme would protect property rights, as individuals would not immediately have to sell off their possessions as soon as they hit hard times. A constitutionalised UBI would be one aspect of welfare policy that is placed at a greater remove from the reach of austerity and retrenchment. This could future-proof societies against the ever-changing headwinds in the policy climate that are inherent to democratic institutions. A UBI as a constitutional right could also be one way to make individuals and their basic material agency eligible for judicial protection. What separates this from many of the other established approaches in this regard is that this protection would be direct and delivered on behalf of individuals themselves. Alternative approaches such as the constitutionalisation of collective bargaining and interest group rights would be farther removed from liberalism, as they imply only indirect protection rights for individuals *as individuals*. Furthermore, a constitutional right to a basic fiscal transfer could also strengthen access to legal recourse against fraud, theft, and exploitation, which may be a better way of protecting the social identities of the most vulnerable in the 'grey zones' of the bureaucratic system.

In more recent years, deliberative democracy has become increasingly fashionable in the EU, as evidenced by the Conference on the Future of Europe. Deliberation is also a vital element of liberalism (Charney 2014), including a basis for its arguments in favour of a UBI. The hope in this regard is that the policy would democratically destigmatise individuals by removing many of the exclusionary aspects of welfare policy. This is fundamentally linked to democratic deliberation, as partisan and factional discussions can quickly become hostile to the most vulnerable, particularly when they are clearly demarcated as subgroups of society. The most precarious members of society may thus become voiceless in the very debates that decide whether they are deemed 'worthy' of social solidarity. Hence, they cannot properly defend their right to basic resources, which renders them vulnerable to becoming subjects of political 'horse-trading', for instance in coalition-forming negotiations. To enable proper deliberation without such toxic exclusion of those most dependent on the societal change that democratic institutions seek to develop, UBI could be a powerful liberal tool to foster a deeper engagement with the causes of interpersonal inequalities.

Providing all individuals with regular cash flow, 'no questions asked', creates a 'floor' of day-to-day expenditure that the state has to finance in a sustainable way. From a liberal perspective, it is clear that this expenditure cannot simply be funded through creating debt. The search for revenue sources thus forces politicians to make tough decisions about what is 'just' and what is not, which may ultimately preserve the economic health of society by preventing the emergence of extremes of wealth and income. While usually more typically associated with green ideology, debates on acceptable maxima and minima of wealth and income can also be linked to liberal thought, particularly when it comes to maintaining the functionality of markets. Essentially, the 'antitrust' aim of monopoly prevention would be scaled down to the level of individuals. What is more, liberals may consider UBI a way of raising the level of the political debate by encouraging a depolarising shift to technocratic determination of payout levels and implementation. Two mechanisms are at play here: on the one hand, sources of division in the realm of social policy may be removed; on the other hand, UBI is a policy that affects all members of society, meaning everyone has a stake in being involved in the debate. Liberal UBI advocates might hope that this could lead to a highly involved but ultimately more consensualist discourse—although there is no guarantee as such that the heightened political interest might not lead to the exact opposite as well, sowing divisions between 'pro-' and 'anti-UBI' factions.

Individuality and Sociality

Arguably one of the most prominent pillars of liberalism in contemporary debates concerns individuality—which always stands in a specific relation to sociality. Both principles are underpinned by issues of self-interest and particularity. If we follow the arguments above, liberalism aims to strike a balance between (1) enabling individual market gains and (2) protecting minimum standards for individual agency. In the context of this tension, UBI can be considered a policy that respects both minimum needs and the ability to individually move beyond them. Liberals could frame the scheme as an acknowledgment of the idea that members of society have interests that pertain to them as discrete individuals, irrespective of the social relationships they enjoy. On one side of the liberal coin, the needs that UBI addresses are those that satisfy the most basic individual self-interests, including survival and activity. However, on the other side, the policy can also capture other self-interests that cannot be predicted or presupposed, for instance those that arise once individuals have successfully 'played the market' in their own favour. Society may simply not conceive of some interests as valid or relevant, even though they are a crucial part of some individuals' agency. UBI essentially guarantees that social policy carves out a niche for individual self-interest beyond what society may collectively want to provide through targeted services. Thus, it lets social policy reflect an equilibrium of interdependence, where individuals navigate between strict atomism and full self-dissolution in collectivity.

This harks back to the arguments concerning autonomy, in the sense that it conceptualises individuals as self-contained but also mutually networked nodes within society. As a consequence, individual agency requires protection from the potentially harmful agency of others, while simultaneously relying on support from a community made up of these same others. This tension is inherent in liberal conceptions of society. However, the ultimate choice of where to draw the boundaries concerning mutual dependence must fall to individuals themselves. This choice, as the liberal argument for UBI has it, could be supported through the provision of a basic income. Within the context of social interaction, UBI could also be framed as risk insurance against unforeseeable developments in the material and relational foundations of societal order. If individuals engage in social interaction and choose to increase their mutual dependencies, social crises can be detrimental to the equilibrium stability of this 'social system'. One response to such crises that liberals often reject is a one-off expansion of state capacity to address the competing needs of individual members of society in a regulatory way. UBI could be a hands-off, permanent buffer against such potentially arbitrary needs for intervention. This would enable welfare policy to flexibly react to changes in social contexts 'by default'. After all, UBI would allow individuals to reallocate self-oriented expenditure to adjust to changes that may affect them in unique ways, which cannot properly be addressed through centralised decision-making. In other words, the state hands large parts of concrete decision-making over to the people, while at the same time empowering them to get through crises more-or-less 'under their own steam'.

Crucially, an inherent counterpart to self-interest in the liberal worldview consists in organicism (Cabrera 2023, 8), the conceptualisation of society as an organic whole. To achieve organicism while maintaining individualism, liberals may use UBI as a tool to foster social harmony in the presence of individual independence. The policy could underpin a societal settlement in which the mere necessities of life are taken into account, and where societal institutions are attentive to individual needs and interests. UBI could thus embed 'social caring' into the basic structure of a community, such that becoming and remaining a member of society is an act of recognising the worth of all other members. This could emphasise the crucial importance of every single individual for society to function as a whole, enshrined in a legal-normative settlement of universal justice. Dynamics of rejection, disrespect, and dehumanisation that underpin interpersonal and intergroup conflicts may be hedged if everyone is provided with a monetary minimum. Hence, the liberal UBI would be a means of allowing society to make the most of its disparate individual agencies and the opportunities that arise from them.

As liberals see society both as the sum of its parts and as a collectively networked entity, they may use UBI to ensure that no individual's agency becomes overly self-destructive or jeopardises the overall network at the expense of others. This is not to be confused by the collectivism inherent to, for instance, communist ideology. Rather it refers to the idea that individual freedom must not restrict the freedom of others (e.g., Rawls 1971). In a nutshell, UBI could be seen as a way for society to distribute its aggregate wealth among its constituent parts in the most efficient and least disruptive way required to sustain itself. This is, however, not a meagre exercise of societal self-preservation, but rather a more ambitious expression of society's common good. Liberal supporters of a UBI might argue that societal wealth cannot be attributed solely to the agency of any single individual, but that it is the legacy of many iterations of 'joint and several' activity by its many members. Thus, UBI would encapsulate individual claims to a common wealth in which all members of society have a stake: to preserve these individual claims, this common wealth must also be preserved. This, in turn, requires the preservation of all of society's various nodes. Hence, beyond being a claim, UBI could also be framed as a way to stabilise the very wealth that underpins said claim. One way to communicate this is as a prophylactic investment in the general health of the societal body. This investment accrues initially to individuals but is then circulated among them through expenditure choices, thus fostering previously unaffordable forms of social activity and ultimately fiscally rejuvenating the network as a whole.

Liberal society is, however, not necessarily limited to the nation-state. Liberalism is also closely associated with a commitment to internationalism (MacMillan 2007), which has implications for the way that liberals may frame UBI as well. This is particularly relevant for a European version of the scheme. Liberals may hope that UBI could strengthen cross-border social solidarity among individuals who are members of a supranational community that decides to implement the scheme. This may thicken an international identity among them as humans *as such*, supporting ideas of human rights to a dignified life. By virtue of being universal, UBI would be an inherently inclusive entitlement that accrues to all members of a community. Thus, if a national community joins into a supranational one that provides the scheme, individuals would immediately benefit from it, allowing them to relate more tangibly to liberalism's internationalist ideals. This could, in turn, also strengthen international institutions both in terms of the portfolio of policy competences they take on, and in the public support they enjoy. Institutions like the EU may find themselves suddenly able to pursue the maximisation of minimum standards in a wholly new domain of social policy.

From a liberal perspective, supranational action towards mitigating place-based differences is highly desirable, as such differences are essentially arbitrary from the perspective of the individuals who happen to live in one place rather than another. UBI may be a useful tool for liberals in this regard, as it can semi-independently sit alongside existing rights to which individuals are entitled under national frameworks. Thus, the policy is a low-stakes form of internationalisation that strengthens individual rights without explicitly taking away anything from national communities. Social justice would become less place-dependent, reducing the impact of the 'postcode lottery' of birth. In a way, UBI would thus continue the virtues that underpin cross-border schemes such as foreign aid and investment in state- and capacity-building, and additionally turn them 'inwards' to benefit the domestic population as well. It would further increase the material attractiveness of the society that implements it to individuals who happen to fall outside of it. Hence, implementing UBI *ab initio* over as large a geographical area as possible increases the share of the world population whose basic needs are met 'at the stroke of a pen'. Within this area, pressure on internal migration would fall as individual needs could be met even in less prosperous regions.

Societal Stabilisation

Beyond these elements of liberalism, there are a few further arguments for UBI that its liberal proponents might field when it comes to the stability of society. The first group of these arguments concerns the potential tensions between markets and state intervention. To strike a balance between the two, a liberal UBI could be framed as a form of public-private partnership that centres the individual and aims to maximise their agency without channelling public funds through government contracts with private providers. As the money flows right into the pockets of individuals, UBI would show that structural intervention is possible while keeping the role for government and business intermediaries minimal. The result could be a *de facto* cooperation between state and markets that does not stifle the diversity of market actors but rather creates extensive leeway for individuals to become such actors themselves.

This state-led guarantee for individual market access could ensure that no member of society is so radically disprivileged that they are fully 'priced out' of basic consumption. In turn, the liberal model of a UBI relies on the continued existence of market consumption to provide choices of sufficient quantity and quality for individuals to realise their agency. To put this somewhat bluntly: without markets, a liberal UBI would be essentially pointless; without the state, it could not exist. However, beyond its introduction and maintenance, a UBI would require comparatively little ongoing state intervention. It strikes a careful balance between 'activist' and 'nightwatchman' roles for the state that acts more as a 'corrective at the margins' to avoid catastrophic individual and social outcomes. This could be achieved without onerous public policy measures as UBI would require administrative effort only at the point of being introduced, while merely relying on occasional 'maintenance' thereafter. This argument lends itself to structuring the implementation of a UBI via a sovereign wealth fund that has the capacity to generate 'passive national income' and thereby reduce the need for active management over time.

In a similar vein, liberalism carries a highly specific concern for security and stability, on the grounds that these are vital for ensuring that individual autonomy is meaningfully realised. Liberal UBI supporters may regard the policy as a useful way of recognising that material resources are the fundamental, irreducible basis of social security. First, guaranteed access to fungible assets is the most versatile way for individuals to be able to respond appropriately to any challenges or threats they may confront at a personal level. Second, social insurance systems ultimately rely on the transfer of material wealth in order to assure their members that they will be protected in times of need. UBI would hence be an effective way to make security personally felt by all individual members of a society.

What is more, it could be a way to avoid social unrest as it staves off extremes of inequality and places a lower bound on social deprivation and insecurity. Though liberals do not subscribe to goals of absolute equality in outcomes, they nonetheless include all citizens under the same notion of equal citizenship and humanity. Thus, if some individuals starve while others have all of their needs met, this may lead to radical dissatisfaction and distrust concerning the unifying capacities that citizenship has to offer. UBI could at least reduce the risk of society losing its legitimacy in this way, and lower the perceived need for violent social change and associated institutional overthrow. Yet UBI may be beneficial from a liberal perspective on less violent questions of policy stability as well. As its expenditure requirements are relatively predictable once implemented, UBI could become a mainstay of public policy that lends itself effectively to long-term planning—especially if sustainable funding structures are chosen to support its implementation from the outset.

This, in turn, links to principles of planning and institutionalism. Here, liberal ideology takes a minimalist approach without, however, going so far as to reject the state *as such*. While liberalism far more than other progressive ideologies certainly takes the view that state action should be limited, it is still committed to the view that the development of societal institutions is key for making individual interactions more meaningful. UBI can thus be seen as a form of 'state planning' that avoids the slide into authoritarianism. The state does not assume commanding authority over its citizens, but rather boosts individual autonomy—and a liberal UBI would aim to prove the point that there are areas where simple interventions can be both large-scale ('universal') and fairly light-touch ('basic'). This acknowledges that state planning does not need to be prescriptive, but can leave extensive space for and even encourage open-ended individual agency. A liberal UBI would then be one of the most parsimonious ways in which a state can fulfil its essential *raison d'être*. It would recognise that for society to be a political community in any meaningful sense, it requires political institutions that engage in administrative management of some kind. If the goal of a community then consists in fostering social justice under the limitations that liberalism imposes, UBI in fact represents a very minimalist and *laissez-faire* variant to institutionalising administrative management. This implies that the policy represents a gentle form of planning that does not require expansions of state capacity—or for that matter of political activity in any form—to the detriment of individual agency. As UBI may be feasible within the existing parameters of institutional expectations and does not require a vast apparatus of information-gathering, it would avoid paternalistic invasions of individual lives—and could function without creating any new costly and time-consuming burdens for state bureaucracy.

THE MEANS OF VOLUNTARY ACTION: A LIBERAL VIEW OF EUBI

The EUBI that follows from these arguments can be characterised as falling overall into a relatively minimalistic form, which stands in particularly stark contrast to its far-left counterpart. These differences apply in many regards and lead to some fundamental opposition, especially regarding how such an EUBI should be funded. The liberal EUBI also differs from approaches by social democrats, greens, and the far left in its fundamental goals, as it aims to liberate the individual from state scrutiny rather than from the markets.

Universality

In theory, liberal ideology aligns well with the basic idea of UBI, as it also embraces universalism quite explicitly. Since liberals also support economic ideas of free markets and growth, universalism in the case of an EUBI implies that all EU citizens along with all economically active non-citizens would receive payments. Those who have been economically active in the EU for a specific period of time in the past would be eligible as well—though the exact length of this period would have to be defined through democratic processes without leading to far-reaching discriminatory structures. Ultimately, whichever eligibility criterion is chosen, along with the scheme itself, would be constitutionalised in line with the arguments discussed above.

A possible alternative liberal view concerning universality could be that the scheme should transcend the borders of the EU entirely. In its most radical form, liberalism is perhaps the ideology most likely to put forward a global UBI, with the aim of giving concrete meaning to universal human rights. One might counter that within the definition of a European UBI, this approach would not really be applicable. All the same, an EUBI that spans the entire continent rather than only the specific territory of the EU may be more desirable from the liberal perspective. Yet the main reason this approach can be ruled out even for an ideal-typical liberal EUBI consists in legislative capacity. In practice, the EU already has a well-established legislative capacity that would be easier to amend than it would be to introduce an entirely new policymaking space across the continent—notwithstanding the existence of institutions such as the Council of Europe or the European Political Community (both in their own way profoundly liberal projects). While the arguments we enumerate here primarily follow theoretical considerations, this pragmatic view is difficult to discard. After all, trying to impose a policy on sovereign communities without democratic legitimacy fundamentally contradicts liberal ideas. Thus, even from a theoretical standpoint, a UBI within the boundaries of the EU ultimately comes out as the preferred solution.

Individuality

As one of liberalism's central concepts, individuality is among the most important dimensions of liberal UBI design. Due to the strong focus on individual freedom and autonomy, a liberal EUBI would be paid directly to every individual member of society. It would be paid only to caretakers if those they take care of are fundamentally unable to make informed (that is, reasoned) financial decisions on their own—or if they explicitly request financial 'stewardship'. Such cases should be extremely rare. For young children, caretakers would receive partial payments with the rest being paid into a sovereign wealth fund. The older these young people become, the more money they would receive themselves, delivered in accordance with something akin to a 'tapering off' system. Once young people are officially considered of full age, they would receive the money paid into the sovereign wealth fund in their names as a basic starting capital. Accumulated interest would be retained in the fund to contribute to long-term funding without accumulating public debt. Alternatively, a simplified liberal EUBI might be paid out to every individual directly without any restrictions whatsoever. However, this would disregard the complexity of liberal ideology, particularly when it comes to (1) its conception of society and interdependence, and (2) its requirements for long-term stability concerning funding.

Conditionality and Uniformity

When it comes to conditionality, liberal ideology suggests a relatively clear picture for the procedures around an EUBI. Due to the fairly intense liberal opposition to bureaucracy and state paternalism along with preferences for individual autonomy, it is to be expected that no criteria would be applied concerning eligibility for receipt. This means every individual would receive their payments directly in line with the minimal limitations defined under universality and individuality *regardless* of any other social attributes they might have. This would not only include individuals who deviate slightly from socially desired consumption patterns, but also, for instance, criminals and others who dramatically flout societal norms. However, this does not mean everyone would receive the same amount of money. Concerning uniformity, a liberal EUBI would vary depending on sub-national economic conditions (see section on adequacy), which would be defined based on dedicated EU-wide research without political interference. Such conditions would deliberately be crowded out of the democratic process to avoid politicisation and division, in the by now well-established tradition of fostering technocratic impartiality and a healthy separation of institutional powers. Furthermore, these criteria would be kept as simple and objectively measurable as possible in order to limit arbitrary intervention and keep the administrative burden low.

Frequency

The frequency of payouts in an ideal-typical liberal EUBI is one of the key elements that set it apart both from more left-leaning designs and several of the common proposals in contemporary basic income debates. Just as liberal ideology aims for individual autonomy while rejecting paternalism, liberals also trust individuals to distribute consumption based on their own considered individual judgment. It can be fairly supposed that payment frequencies of a liberal EUBI would therefore be less regular than would be the case with other ideologies—which may further contribute to the liberal goal of reducing bureaucracy wherever possible. Besides the basic starting capital (see section on individuality), a liberal EUBI could, for instance, be paid out yearly to give individuals more flexibility regarding choices for large one-off spending decisions. However, a counter-argument against this approach concerns the idea of shielding society and its individual 'nodes' from destructive crises, on the grounds that individuals who have already spent their income once a crisis hits would be overly vulnerable. However, liberalism is likely ultimately to 'stick to its guns', and entrust individuals with the ultimate decision of whether to take such risks or not. What is more, a key liberal argument for a UBI is that state-guided social policies cannot account for individual-level crises and their own specific requirements. Large one-off payments may thus be necessary in the eyes of liberals simply to cater to entirely legitimate individual needs, which would make a yearly payout cycle the most appropriate delivery schedule for a liberal EUBI.

Duration and Modality

Based solely on the primary ideals of liberal ideology, there is no particular reason to radically limit duration and modality in a UBI policy design. Not only would stark limitations contradict liberalism's individualistic core, but they would also cause the scheme to miss out on many of its potential benefits. This concerns economic activity in particular, as liberals hope to empower and encourage individual entrepreneurship as well as economically beneficial action in general by providing universal 'seed funding' and basic risk insurance. Thus, to include the elderly and the young in individually autonomous economic activities, the ideal-typical liberal EUBI would be paid over the course of an entire lifetime, factoring in the specific arrangements for young children outlined above (see section on individuality). This also responds to preferences for fully flexible and individually determined retirement ages and other work decisions. In order to maximise individual autonomy and to minimise paternalism, the liberal EUBI would further be paid out in monetary form, corresponding to the respective official currency of the EU member state in which EUBI recipients happen to live. For instance, for the Eurozone, this would imply payouts in euros; for member states that have opted out of the Eurozone, payouts would be in their national currency (at the 'spot' exchange rate). Following modern liberal preferences for financial investment, the EU could offer an optional yearly opt-in system that would invest an individual's EUBI in a sovereign wealth fund, thus temporarily replacing cash benefits with shares in products on the financial markets.

Adequacy

The liberal EUBI would ideally aim to enhance individual independence and prevent individual poverty. However, preferences for free markets along with the widespread liberal support for fiscal austerity measures would suggest arrangements that link the total value or generosity of the system to the available funds (see section on funding). Thus, liberal EUBI levels would fluctuate in line with economic developments across the EU as a whole. Lower limits would be introduced only if various other social policies were to be abolished in order to still live up to ideas of humanitarianism. Rather, the liberal EUBI would be strictly capped at lower levels than the other EUBIs we discuss in this book. For instance, it may not exceed 40 percent of the respective sub-national median income to limit distortions to the markets, keep taxation low, and to remain in line with ideas of 'survival of the fittest' in both labour and welfare and social policy competition. If revenue sources earmarked for UBI exceed costs at this limit occasionally, they would be paid into the sovereign wealth fund to bolster the overall 'health' of the scheme. If such excesses became the norm, taxes would be lowered. The exact subnational EUBI levels would be linked to a simple set of criteria, based on data compiled by EU-wide teams of researchers. These criteria could entail median and mean incomes, but also inflation rates, purchasing power parities, and other indicators of economic development. Crucially, these criteria must be relatively easily measurable and should translate into EUBI levels based on a standardised formula to avoid any additional bureaucracy and paternalism.

Funding

In line with preferences for free markets, the ideal-typical liberal EUBI would avoid high taxes on capital gains, income, and wealth. Some taxation in these areas could be possible in principle if liberals decide that overly extreme forms of wealth generation from passive income such as capital gains are not in-sync with ideas of individual effort, performance, or creativity. However, such approaches would be strictly limited, with the tax base shifted instead onto more self-evidently 'unearned' sources of income such as inheritances, depending on the interpretation of liberal values. Again, some may consider inheritances not to be in line with the ideal of individual action determining wealth. However, the main parts of funding should be based on revenues from public investment and on flat taxes, including VAT. A sovereign wealth fund could be set up at the EU level to be able to move larger sums more swiftly. Additional national sovereign wealth funds could add a layer of risk reduction, while all taxes would remain national due to the coordinative nature of the scheme (see section on EU policy instruments). Abolishing other welfare state offerings and public expenditure—that is, using the simplifying effect of the EUBI to 'clean house' at the national welfare level—should free up resources for the EUBI. Overall, a liberal EUBI would be the version of the policy that aims most aggressively at 'streamlining' state action, although the most socially oriented liberals may draw the line at such 'downsizing' of the public finances when it comes to the most essential public services.

EU Policy Instruments and Relationship to National Welfare States

While supportive of globalisation and internationalism, the liberal EUBI would also aim to avoid interfering too much with national sovereignty regarding social and fiscal issues. This is the case as democratic legitimacy is central to liberalism and supranational institutions may be considered still somewhat lacking in this regard—at least so long as their 'democratic deficit' remains unaddressed. The liberal EUBI would thus be based on Recommendations and coordination. More concrete decisions on matters like funding would be left to EU member states. Although only voluntarily, it can be supposed that national welfare states would be replaced in large parts. This should reduce bureaucracy and free up funding while also reducing paternalism and enhancing individual independence from the state. Some public services would be replaced with private, free-market offerings which citizens could individually purchase—for example, using their EUBI—although again, social liberals may voice reservations in this regard. Needs- and means-tested social transfers would largely be replaced by the EUBI, and the entire process would reduce the overall size of the public sector, implying not only one-to-one replacements, but also intentional net welfare state retrenchment.

Technical Distribution and Introduction

As the liberal EUBI would be based on Recommendations and coordination, national infrastructure would be used for distribution. The EU would assist member states only on demand by taking over tasks that national administrations lack the capacity to fulfil. The scheme would be introduced gradually to avoid economic shocks and disruptions to the markets, and this slow introduction would further be monitored by a board of independent researchers with a special focus on economic impact.

All in all, the ideal-typical liberal EUBI stands in stark contrast to its counterparts from several of the other progressive ideologies. It would replace welfare states, reduce the role of the state overall, emphasise voluntary action, and leave as many decisions to the individual as possible.

Chapter 7

Christian Democracy

Christian democracy has long enjoyed a strong basis in European nations. Particularly dominant in countries like Austria, the Benelux, and Germany, this ideology enjoys close historical links to Christian churches and faith communities, and is typically associated with conservative values (Kalyvas and van Kersbergen 2010). However, as we argued in chapter 2, Christian democracy features some key elements that can also be considered (at least residually) progressive, especially if contrasted with the various classical accounts of conservatism (Schmidt 2016, 411). In the EU, Christian democracy is represented by the European People's Party, which for a long time has been the largest political group in the European Parliament. However, many of its member parties do not identify as traditionally Christian-democratic anymore, as the ideology has increasingly been electorally outperformed by conservative and liberal parties in many of its heartland states (Gottfried 2007).

To start by addressing an obvious rejoinder to the idea of categorising Christian democracy as a broadly progressive ideology, there were and are some significant reactionary facets to it (Pombeni 2013, 312). These are largely related to its commitment to a specific understanding of centrism (Gottfried 2007). Christian democracy tends to frame itself as almost 'neutral' between left- and right-wing politics, emphasising the importance of moderation and anti-extremism. Often, this implies a deliberate equivalence between the far left and the far right in Christian-democratic rhetoric (CDU 2020). However, as discussed throughout the previous chapters, these principles are also (partly) shared by social democrats, liberals, and greens.

Another conservative element of Christian democracy concerns its interpretation of order, where the ideology emphasises values of stability and protection of the *status quo* (van Kersbergen 1994, 44–45). In its more religious interpretations, this harks back to ideals of a divine order of the world (Almond 1948, 751) and the sanctity of naturalism. Similarly, Christian democrats' emphasis on tradition implies that they value familial units as essential social institutions and, to a certain degree, respect familial accumulation of (basic) wealth (Clemens 2013, 193). Thus, the Christian-democratic 'utopia' is quite different from the ideas inherent to other ideologies. Instead of an unknown, novel future, it refers to nostalgia and romanticism towards a shared 'heritage' (Wolkenstein 2023, 637), thus rejecting political experiments that depart too drastically from these ideological legacies (e.g., Carrel 2017).

So what, if anything, could be considered 'progressive' about Christian democracy? The answer to this question is rooted in its stance towards capitalism. While the ideology defends private property (Invernizzi Accetti 2019, 140–42; Pombeni 2013, 319–20), it also rejects excess based on Christian values (Invernizzi Accetti 2019, 142–43), and further promotes trade unions and social dialogue in a social market economy (Gabor 2012, 319). These ideals are much less prominent than in social democracy, for instance, but they are present nonetheless. Christian democracy may not be radically anti-capitalist and may fundamentally adhere to ideas of economism (Oudenampsen 2022), but this approach is distinctly different from market radicalism, as it is open to a (somewhat) strong welfare state (Schmidt 2016, 411). The well-established hostility of Christian democracy towards communism (Greenberg 2015, 327–28) is closely linked to its support for (parliamentary) democracy and cross-party collaboration (Hanley 1994, 190)—again, principles that are found in other progressive ideologies as well.

What sets Christian democracy apart from these other progressive ideologies is its strong emphasis on subsidiarity (Wolkenstein 2023, 643, 648). Territorially, this can imply that political matters should be decided at the level that is closest to being affected by them, or which is responsible for their implementation. At a more interpersonal level, it can further entail that the state should only be active when societal actors cannot sufficiently take over a task on their own behalf. This defines Christian-democratic statism and sets it apart from liberals to the political-economic right and social democrats to the political-economic left. On the one hand, subsidiarity can have a conservative side when it goes against (e.g.) European policy integration or social provisions. On the other hand, it can also legitimise social actors from civil society against the overweening power of market institutions, and empower local communities to be more independent from national oversight.

The progressive facets of Christian democracy are not limited to the role of the state and social partners. Christian democrats also hold quasi-progressive views of sociality, albeit from a different perspective than the other ideologies we discuss in this book. Christian social values form the basis for a view of society where humans form an organic whole, tied together in smaller groups and at larger scales by notions of (often religious, or at least more broadly cultural) community (Kalyvas and van Kersbergen 2010, 196). In this community, individuals are enabled to act on their human will (Kraynak 2004, 93–94) and willfulness, albeit within carefully defined parameters, exercising rights that are conceived as fundamentally natural or potentially 'god-given' (Fanning 2021, 81, 184). Adhering to some facets of biological essentialism (Ostrowski 2022a), Christian democracy then promotes the idea that certain traits are inherent to human nature (Invernizzi Accetti 2019, 53 ff.).

Despite Christian democracy's general support for the *status quo*, the ideology promotes specific types of change. This change, however, is by design anti-revolutionary, and instead follows the idea of natural and gradual growth (Galetti et al. 2011, 9), allowing members of a community to reap opportunities that present themselves while preserving a certain degree of consistency.

SOCIAL ORDER THROUGH SOCIAL WELFARE: CHRISTIAN DEMOCRACY AND UBI

It is fair to say that Christian democracy is hardly the first ideology that comes to mind when we consider the forefront of UBI movements in contemporary policy debates. However, based on its ideological values, it could easily attach itself to the debate in a way that is both intellectually profitable and stands to develop the debate in a series of intriguing new directions. If Christian-democratic parties chose to prioritise UBI, they could frame the policy in a way that would align with most, if not all, of their ideals.

Order

In line with Christian democracy's careful balancing act between conservative values and progressive concepts, the ideology can draw on rather unique arguments to justify UBI. One of the key pillars of such justifications revolves around the idea of order. Here, UBI could be framed as a guarantor of stability. This is a largely standard response in the Christian-democratic lexicon: whenever Christian democrats develop concerns over deep tensions within current society that they consider vital to address immediately, welfarist policies typically present themselves as a ready solution.

A UBI in particular could address a few specific Christian-democratic concerns. First, it could be seen as a more-or-less stable equilibrium that guarantees minimum protection and thus social stability for society as a whole without necessarily radically redistributing resources. The latter may perhaps be the option favoured by other ideologies such as the far left, but would run counter to Christian-democratic ideas of the stability of society as a whole, as it would necessarily imply considerable disruption to existing social relations. In other words, UBI could prevent those who 'lose out' in socioeconomic struggles from resorting to vengeful violence aimed at (re)acquiring larger parts of society's wealth.

In addition, Christian democrats may hope that UBI can achieve social stabilisation not only at the societal, but also at the individual level. While one-off endowments may fundamentally disrupt the financial basis of people's lives—'disrupt' here understood in a clearly positive sense—UBI would not be a one-shot 'fork in the road' moment that fully reshapes people's life trajectories. The basic nature of UBI could instead support everyone to satisfy their fundamental needs without incurring a reasonable likelihood of suddenly being stripped of their support. This, again, would imply stability both in long-term policy design and in the predictability of its likely outcomes. Finally, UBI as a policy has the potential of remaining 'as it is' somewhat indefinitely, with payment levels remaining relatively stable in real or nominal terms. Unlike several of the other ideologies we discuss, Christian democrats may latch onto this as a way to raise policy focus on the long-term affordability of the scheme.

Another important element of order concerns the *status quo*. Here, a Christian-democratic argument for UBI would see the scheme primarily as a present-focused policy, aiming to fix some of the failings of the current societal settlement. This would concern first and foremost the reduction of severe poverty, including homelessness, food and fuel poverty, and the dangers resulting from extreme climatic temperatures. In all of these cases, the policy would respond to an immediate problem, namely the lack of monetary means at an individual level. A Christian-democratic UBI would aim to remedy this and thus enable individuals to live their lives in greater prospective dignity: individuals may both perceive their own lives as more dignified, and also be seen and treated with greater dignity by their respective communities. The policy would shift upwards the lower bound of wealth and income without necessarily forcing an upper bound. Accordingly, a Christian-democratic UBI would aim to 'optimise' a balance between maintaining the *status quo* of political economy while improving social welfare in clear and tangible ways. This tallies with a measure of respect for the principles of the existing policy framework, which aims to identify the 'worst off' and support them through targeted schemes.

A Christian-democratic UBI would not entirely challenge this system, but rather introduce an additional, universal layer to close any of its remaining gaps. The scheme would thus assume that any member of society is liable to financial constraints, and would therefore offer a safety net for the whole population. On that basis, the scheme would not necessarily impose any expectations on society or its members to change in order to be deemed deserving of support. A degree of variation can be introduced here depending on the importance that is placed on 'moral' behaviour. Christian democrats could frame UBI as primarily a tool to prevent decline without the baggage of a 'directional expectation' of fundamental change. While the stability that

UBI provides may be seen as a precondition for any future progress, the compatibility of the policy with a wide variety of future developments means that societal choices remain at the core of deciding whether and how the *status quo* should change.

Sociality and Individuality

The second pillar of a Christian-democratic argument for UBI concerns sociality and individuality. Here, in a way that exhibits certain parallels to green ideology, Christian democrats may conceptualise society through the lens of organicism and natural essentialism. This means that members of society are viewed as analogous to different parts of a 'collective body' that fulfil different functions and must each be protected at a baseline survival level in order to safeguard the 'health' of the whole. On that basis, a Christian-democratic UBI could ensure that society can 'keep going' without going beyond coverage of the bare necessities. As money raised for the scheme could directly go to recipients, the losses along the way would be fairly minimal.

The Christian-democratic interpretation of the necessary minimum would likely be parsimonious, aiming above all to maintain people's physiological and environmental wellbeing. Membership of society would imply an expectation that these needs are met, while anything above and beyond them constitutes optional 'add-ons' that individuals can pursue 'under their own steam'. Underpinning any argument for UBI is then the assumption that these basic needs can be fully met through money and the goods and services it can buy. Finally, as alluded to above, a Christian-democratic UBI could be framed as key to ensuring a harmonious coexistence between members of society. More conditional schemes may run the risk of causing frictions by introducing asymmetric resource availability. Thus, a Christian-democratic UBI would, in a figurative sense, ensure a constant flow of resources that circulates to every part of the 'societal body', preventing stagnation and guaranteeing a well-functioning society 'in good order'. More pragmatically put, UBI would be a way of making capital available to everyone in society, in order to stabilise the functioning of markets through consumption.

Perhaps more obviously linked to Christian-democratic sociality is the role of the religious community. As Christian democrats often operate in extensively multicultural or secularised societies, where appeals to Christian religious doctrine and institutions *as such* do not command automatic legitimacy, they could frame UBI as an expression of the inherent dignity of individual beings in a context that removes religious authority from political influence. The scheme could be conceived as a reflection of the human capacity to make reasoned and moral choices—after all, it leaves spending decisions up to the recipient. This is underpinned by a set of beliefs in humankind's ability to improve on the failings of earthly existence by aiming for a more elevated state of being, which are replicated to varying degrees and in different conceptual language in multiple faith systems beyond Christianity. Building on this relative 'consensus position', UBI itself could be framed as an expression of a reasoned morality, as a humanitarian intervention within one's own society. The mutual recognition of humaneness and the idea that members of society are inherently alike in their fundamental humanity could then be 'implemented' through a social policy that works within the realities of a secular system.

In a more religiously connotated context, a Christian-democratic UBI could be framed as the secular and bodily equivalent of a divine intercession to alleviate human suffering, and as a precondition for humans to turn to higher sensibilities. Religiously defined expectations towards moral and reasoned choices would become significantly more meaningful if these choices are carried out without the pressure and limitation of physical necessities: once people have an actual choice without severe constraints, their actions become much more 'accessible' for moral judgement. In a more positive framing, moral actions may become more attainable when individuals are able to lead lives without constant struggles for survival. Conversely, if the Christian-democratic argument for UBI is intended to centre a certain type of 'desirable' moral behaviour, the policy could be designed to incentivise such behaviour. In this vein, UBI could be seen as the basis of a strong community of charity and shared values. Like any welfare policy, it expresses the acceptance of material sacrifice by the wealthy for the good of those in need. Christian democrats could argue that all members of society have a powerful human capacity that deserves to be realised as far as possible. Though religious organisations already try to achieve this in a grassroots, 'bottom-up' way, they remain largely fragmented. In order to deliver on the 'salvific task' of full-scale poverty alleviation, Christian democrats may turn to UBI as a consensual tool that can reach beyond the boundaries that divide the various confessions present in their society.

Inherent to many of these arguments is a specific conception of the human will. The basic proposition here is that humans are free to exercise their individual will as a vital element of human uniqueness. Humans, so the argument goes, are able to formulate aims for their conscious action that (partly) depend on reasoning and individual circumstances. However, the latter can impose an important limitation on the worst-off, least advantaged members of society that prevents them from enacting what makes them human. Christian democrats may see in UBI a way to give everyone the capacity to make meaningful choices by counterbalancing the costs that otherwise lead to *de facto* forced actions. The scheme could thus make it possible for members of society to assert themselves, their preferences, and their interests.

At the same time, UBI could also be a tool against unrestrained wilfulness, by individuals on their own account or towards others around them. In particular, it would give everyone a 'power base' from which to resist overreach by more privileged members of society, who use their comparatively greater wealth to impose forced choices on the less privileged. While the scheme enables a basic expression of individual will, it thus also limits exorbitant enactments of desires by the rich and powerful. In a more general sense, then, the basic level of UBI encourages people to think responsibly about how to allocate their finite resources—in which ways, and to what ends. Finally, UBI itself is also an expression of a 'social will', as it is a decision by and on behalf of society as a whole to provide a baseline level of support to everyone. The scheme then extends to all the welfarist principle that material well-being is one of society's core interests. The 'universal will' takes precedence over the 'targeted will', thus reinterpreting welfarism as an essential characteristic rather than a special feature of society.

The final element of Christian-democratic sociality and individuality pertains to rights such as the individual claim on one's surroundings (Invernizzi Accetti 2019, 140–42). UBI could be framed as a recognition of this claim that is assured and safeguarded by the structure of society. On the one hand, the scheme is a claim against other individuals, more specifically the 'best off' based on moral ideas of the evil of poverty and the undesirability of inequality, which mirror critiques of extreme wealth as a source of social tensions. On the other hand, UBI represents a claim on society as a whole. Since negative rights such as those designed to grant protection from interference do not suffice to guarantee a viable life, actual protection also requires the positive right to a minimum of resources.

More generally, the rights-based Christian-democratic case for UBI builds on the idea that membership of society should be fundamentally equal for all. This runs into tensions between civic equalities such as political, legal, and moral rights as well as obligations, and economic inequalities resulting from free will. Thus, UBI may be framed as a right in order to reconcile this tension and subordinate the economy to politics, law, and morality. Citizenship would receive a clear economic component without fundamentally interfering in some of the most important social domains: UBI neither 'crowds out' other rights and duties of citizenship, nor does it render capital accumulation and enterprise growth impossible. This, in turn, leads to the last important argument concerning rights, which holds that freedom cannot only be guaranteed by formal rights, but also requires practical underpinnings. A legal right to act in a certain way may fall short if the material *de facto* ability to act on this right is not also given at the same time. UBI could thus be seen as an economic enforcement mechanism for political and legal status—a low-intervention policing effort to ensure that social rights are actually met.

(Anti-)Capitalism

As mentioned at the start of this chapter, Christian democracy has a complex relationship with (anti-)capitalism. One of its cardinal features is its resolute support for private property, with the caveat that it reserves considerable moral criticism for any tendencies to excess (Invernizzi Accetti 2019, 140–43; Pombeni 2013, 319–20). UBI could thus be framed as a way to give all members of society something they own individually. However, it would also be a recognition that market capitalism provides only the opportunity for—but not a guarantee of—private ownership. As capitalism alone does not give everyone a 'life-start endowment' to enter the market, UBI could 'derisk' this system. Since it is awarded through regular payments, there is no pressure on anyone to manage the funds they are provided with all at once, and their basic security is smoothed over time. This stabilises private property over individuals' lifecycles and the variable contextual conditions they face. In a way, UBI can be conceived as an open-ended annuity whose total value is linked to society's overall wealth. This annuity is paid out in the most liquid form possible, maximising freedom of choice and expressing society's faith in individual responsibility. Recipients are then empowered to meaningfully participate in market exchanges without sacrificing their personhood through degrading labour.

What is more, Christian democrats could see UBI as a way of bridging the public and private spheres. As a societal-level investment in individuals, it highlights a key implicit assumption that underpins contemporary political economy, namely that the system of private property ultimately rests on a public consensus. In order for everyone to buy into this consensus, UBI would provide all individuals with a stake in its continuous operation. As a result, all members of society can access at least *some* property to ensure a shared base-level of personhood in a marketised system. This logic effectively converts collectively generated wealth into private, individually awarded and received benefits. Implicitly, it acknowledges that value-creation is not solely the result of individual effort but requires a set of complex interactions as well as a universal consensus on the attribution of value to particular products. UBI then essentially 'rewards' individuals for willingly accepting and perpetuating this consensus.

While embracing free markets, Christian democrats also tend to support trade unionism in principle and in practice (Gabor 2012, 319). In line with this, they can build an argument for UBI premised on the idea of solidarity between all forms of labour. The scheme could reflect a shared aim across industrial sectors that consists in weakening the ability of capital owners to enforce precarious working conditions. By giving workers an employment-independent source of material power, UBI may allow workers to reject an inhumane 'race to the bottom' of employment. The policy may remedy the difficulties associated with organising collective solidarity across major differences in employment structure, for instance pertaining to sectors or contract types.

Through a Christian-democratic lens, UBI may further be seen as a pillar of a more collaborative, corporatist approach to resolving capital-labour tensions with support and mediation by the state. The scheme could give unions the scope to focus on more ambitious goals than securing basic labour conditions, such as pushing for enhanced labour representation including codetermination as equals on boards, or semi-permanent state-mediated industrial dispute resolution mechanisms. From the perspective of workers, UBI may also broaden what trade unions offer them as collective and social groups. The policy could allow them to turn into cooperative structures rather than narrowly organised vehicles of class struggle, including strengthening unions' roles as forums for exchanging best practices across sectors. This could strengthen and build on the already well-established union provision of work-oriented legal and financial advice, as members' contributions become less essential for strikes. Similarly, portfolios regarding education and skills provision, cultural activities, and optional insurance schemes could be enhanced in similar ways. And even in a more basic sense, when it comes to membership, UBI may give workers more leeway for joining unions and paying their fees.

Christian democracy's complex stance on capitalism culminates in the idea of the social market economy (Fanning 2021, 183–202), which in many respects resembles the equivalent concept embraced by social democracy. In the vein of the fundamental 'compromise position' that lies at the heart of this political-economic system, UBI can be seen as a classical mechanism to balance the activities of the state and the market. It strengthens the ability of state policymaking to affect market outcomes, while providing a means of stabilising markets themselves. Up to now, welfare policy is often designed as a parallel sector of the economy that does not raise the same expectations of private consumption on the recipients of public goods and services. To a large degree, social policy also represents a series of 'fixes' and 'adjustments' that *ex post* recompense those who 'lose out' for particularly harsh market outcomes. By contrast, UBI could be framed as an *ex ante* strategy that reshapes the assumptions and premises under which market competition operates. It strengthens the 'starting position' of market participants through a relatively simple and low-level intervention. In this respect, the scheme suits the basic outline of a social market economy rather well and remains compatible with a wide range of further political-economic approaches, including both protectionist state interventionism and free-market *laissez-faire* policies.

In this way, a Christian-democratic UBI could underpin fair competition by ensuring that nobody is structurally disadvantaged to the most extreme degrees imaginable. Those who benefit the most from market interactions could never gain complete dominance over any single member in society, as UBI would effectively preserve the ability for everyone to compete at least to some basic degree. What is more, the destructive power of 'loss' due to market risks would be reduced, giving everyone regular access to new attempts at risk-taking. In a framing that echoes one of the main opportunities of UBI for economic liberalism, the scheme could also be seen as a way of providing regular 'seed funding' for entrepreneurship, boosting the range and number of private enterprises. Finally, UBI sits within a portfolio of provisions to ensure that market capitalism is steered in a social direction. The policy itself cannot be the sole guarantor of prosperity, as it only acts as a societal limit 'at the margins' for what outcomes markets can produce. This means that its impact hinges on being paired with additional regulations and targeted investments to ensure that the most basic needs for survival are covered without UBI as well. Only then can a UBI be reasonably expected to be used for long-term planning and entrepreneurial goals.

Statism

With regards to statism, Christian democracy's core commitments centre strongly on the principle of subsidiarity (Wolkenstein 2023, 643, 648). In an ideal political system where the responsibility for many issues is devolved to the lowest possible unit, UBI could extend the current logic of 'block grants'—lump-sum budget allocations transferred from central government to place-based local authorities—to an even lower level. Rather than regularly paying money to communities at the subnational scale, the individuals themselves would become the direct recipients of support. The Christian-democratic approach to arguing for UBI would accordingly rest on the assumption that financial decisions are best taken at the individual level. Matters would be less clear when it comes to the question of how to deal with UBI in the specific context of the nuclear family, on which Christian democracy—uniquely among the ideologies discussed here—places a high degree of emphasis. Here, a number of options are available: the scheme can be split up into separate transfers to individual family members or grouped together into a single larger figure distributed to each family unit (see policy design).

In another link to subsidiarity, Christian democrats could use UBI to adapt to a modernised understanding of welfare provision beyond confessional actors. In several West European welfare systems, Christian-democratic subsidiarity has been realised by tasking confessional welfare associations with the provision of social services. However, confessional divides are becoming increasingly diffuse, and the growth of societal pluralism implies that individuals now exercise far more choice than they used to previously, especially when it comes to the social groupings and ties they participate in. Thus, an individualised approach to welfare could be a way to 'update' subsidiarity in light of these background developments, while playing to the specific strengths of centralised state coordination. Depending on policy design, bureaucratic hurdles could be minimised without imposing overly demanding expectations on the state to guide UBI recipients in how the money is to be used. In such a system, there is no reason to lose place-based context as an important justification for subsidiarity, since UBI payout levels could very easily be varied across territories in response to local socioeconomic conditions—reflecting differences in wages, income levels, and purchasing power. The main question for policy design that follows from this is how granular such adjustments should be. Concerning the specific context of a European UBI, the appropriate level of provision would also need to take some application of subsidiarity principles firmly into account (see policy design).

Within the pillar of statism, democratic rule is another key and eponymous element of Christian democracy. On that basis, the ideology could frame UBI as a way to shore up the democratic manifestation of a particular political theology and values derived from Christian doctrine. Specifically, values such as charity and welfarism, mercy, neighbourly and fraternal love, and forgiveness for mistakes can practically and metaphorically be read into the aims and operations of a UBI. Similarly, the mutuality of 'second chances' may be represented by the scheme just as well as the awareness of imperfections before divinity, expressed through a tolerance for pluralism of values. Arguments concerning poverty and prosperity that have their roots in a number of the more radical strands of Christian social thought, such as liberation theology, also lend themselves effectively to the idea of UBI, as outlined earlier in relation to the provision of minimum socioeconomic protections. All these concepts then connect to democratic ideas, as UBI could be conceived as one way of giving the state a 'moral character' entrenched in democratic institutions. By designing policies that are given the stamp of democratic approval in a way that ensures that they also represent religious values, especially those with cross-faith resonances, Christian democrats could weave their ideas into the institutions of increasingly non-Christocentric societies.

Beyond such potentially strategically loaded approaches, UBI could be framed as an example for a responsive representative model of democracy that provides institutional answers to widely felt popular needs. It may present a way of conveying to the public that democratic governance is *for* the people and has the interests of society and its aggregated members at its core. The legitimacy of the scheme would not necessarily need to come from an election victory that is won based on party manifestos that promise UBI. Instead of this more procedural criterion, Christian democrats may derive their legitimacy from the more substantive consideration that UBI benefits society, rather than from it being approved by a majority. This would make the policy an explicit mechanism to offer opposition to plebiscitary and populist tendencies that place welfare for the most vulnerable members of society at the mercy of the majority, which is one of the major foundations of welfare chauvinism.

Building on this logic, UBI could be instantiated as part of a democratic societal framework *beyond* majoritarian changes: in a similar way to the liberal UBI, some Christian democrats may be tempted to institutionalise the scheme within the existing charter of social rights or the founding documents of a community. Writing fiscal policies into constitutions is not new to Christian democrats—as evidenced, for instance, by the 'debt brake' that forms part of the German Basic Law (Milbradt 2016)—but is not without its risks. Thus, a Christian-democratic UBI may be developed through the alternative route of quasi-corporatist bargaining between and within stakeholder groups, for instance between government departments, political parties, or national and regional governments.

Collaboration between actors is more generally a part of Christian-democratic approaches to statism, especially where political parties are concerned (Hanley 1994, 190). As we discuss in the later chapter on agenda coalitions, UBI may be seen as a measure that brings together the central ideas of various ideologies in such a way that it could act as an abstract conceptual and concretely instantiated consensus point. Such a consensus could include elements of rights, citizenship, justice, democracy, and an alignment with the natural world. The reason UBI in particular could be especially interesting for Christian democrats who emphasise consensus in this way is the fact that it balances several important and otherwise contentious goals implicated in the key divides between the ideological left and right, progressives and conservatives, radicals and reactionaries, as well as in a thematic sense between individuality and sociality, state- and market-centrism, as well as liberty and equality. In short, the scheme may be seen as an attempt to resolve some long-standing ideological disputes through at least a baseline agreement.

What is more, UBI could be seen as a powerful tool for coalition-building not only between political parties, but across a wider range of social movements, including trade unions, pressure groups, and civil society organisations. The ostensible simplicity of the scheme along with its fungibility makes it compatible with different sectional interests, especially given that material empowerment lies at the root of many struggles over status and recognition. The common hope for a range of groups with very different social interests and preferences would be that UBI could act as an instrumental mechanism to achieve other goals such as enhanced education, cultural activities, or the flourishing of diverse identities. Hence, the scheme could become an accessible entry-point for developing shared manifestos to put organised pressure on a state to acquiesce.

If Christian democrats were to pursue such coalitions, they could frame UBI as 'non-ideological' in that it places equal value on all the potential states of society that can result from individual and collective action. Depending on how exactly it is designed, the scheme does not explicitly and actively favour any one specific outcome in the progress of humankind. As a blanket universal measure, it is not set up *ex ante* to reward certain kinds of behaviour. Rather, it expresses a fundamental *a priori* social attribution of value to all members of society, regardless of what their values might be. This, of course, does not rule out further ideological disputes over other forms of public spending. However, these could be seen as second-order concerns once a baseline of material sufficiency is achieved through UBI.

Tradition

As discussed above, Christian democracy operates at the fringes of what could be considered 'progressive'. One of its more conservative-leaning elements concerns the importance of tradition (van Kersbergen 1994, 33). Although we focus on progressive arguments in this analysis, we cannot ignore this pillar of Christian democracy, given its importance for the ideology. The result is a set of arguments that are quite different from what the other ideologies we discuss centre in their social reasoning and rhetoric.

The first element of a Christian-democratic framing of UBI rooted in tradition connects to cumulation. In essence, this refers to the phenomenon that developments over time accumulate smoothly (van Kersbergen 1994, 33) due to a choice or event that occurred in the past. Against this backdrop, UBI could be presented as a logical continuation of past interventions in welfare policy. It would not only use existing welfare infrastructure to roll out a more comprehensive system of payments, but it also entails a set of more ambitious claims towards which the entire history of social policy has been geared. First, it addresses the idea of steadily emancipating people from low-wage labour, thus continuing the history of unemployment and in-work benefits, minimum wages, and working time reductions. Second, UBI builds on the ideational history of first entitling some and subsequently all members of society to state-funded financial support as a right, either in cash through direct payments such as tax credits, or in kind by providing services. UBI could also continue 'newer' developments like the tendency to unify benefits into single payments, as represented, for instance, by the Universal Credit system in the United Kingdom.

In all of this, UBI does not need to be intended or designed to replace the whole established welfare system. Rather, it could non-destructively add to it or replace only some selected schemes that would become redundant once a UBI is introduced. Many other policy areas build on separate justifications beyond merely ensuring that there is a social 'floor'. For instance, public transport not only provides mobility and thus opportunities to every member of society, but also fosters environmental sustainability. Such additional goals remain valid even in the presence of a complementary cash benefit. While UBI could be framed as a device to limit bureaucracy, it does not need to stand in conflict with established and tried-and-tested schemes. Instead, UBI could add a new tradition to Christian democracy's canon of political heirlooms. After all, Christian democracy aims to preserve what it deems good but is not averse to policy innovation as long as it is done with a view towards the long term. This implies that a Christian-democratic UBI would need to be feasible and equipped with a clear outline for its future development. In that case, UBI would be a reform that can beget future reforms without itself at any stage being too disruptive to what society can absorb.

Another key element of tradition relates to the tension between familiarity and flexibility. A Christian-democratic UBI would need to respond to this, for instance by being delivered in the same way as established benefits payments. What is more, the scheme would need to conform to the assumptions that already exist around financing and distribution in order to accustom both public administrators and taxpayers to it. The somewhat unique advantage of UBI for Christian democrats is that it can meet its expectations around familiarity while remaining flexible enough to live up to the ideology's economistic expectations. Varying payout levels in real and nominal terms in response to government finances, population demographics, inflation, bureaucratic capacities, and other contextual factors could be done relatively easily and to significant effect, given that the scheme is unconditional and hence does not need to take into account complex considerations of eligibility.

On the side of recipients, familiarity is also something of a given with many if not all possible UBI schemes. After all, a UBI merely provides them with the additional financial capacities to do more of what they prefer. In this sense, UBI is what its recipients make of it: it is simply a capital injection that is perfectly fungible within the market frameworks that are already in place, and with which we are all familiar as members of society (even if we only enjoy very differential access to them). UBI seamlessly blends into preexisting financial means and leaves decisions about whether to stick to familiar consumption patterns or to try out something new entirely up to the individual.

Another important idea for Christian democrats linked to tradition is consistency. As a regular payment equally delivered to all members of society,

UBI is an intuitively good fit with this aspect of the Christian-democratic worldview. The scheme's cost is easily calculated if policymakers can agree on a fixed level for payouts, and can thus be easily forecast for future budgets based on predicted population growth and planned payout adjustments. This consistency also introduces reliability into the lives of UBI recipients, who can count on a predictable income stream at a known level, similar to employment income—albeit with a rather lower risk of being laid off.

To ensure this consistency, Christian democrats may aim for UBI levels that are enough to enable individuals to take meaningful long-term decisions without being so high that they incentivise reckless behaviour. Accordingly, the scheme can also help smooth individual recipients' consumption patterns. Importantly, unlike unconditional one-off payments, UBI is not an emergency measure or short-term spending spree but rather a structural solution to deprivation. Its universality could further help reduce political clientelism by obviating the opportunity for governments to pay income supplements selectively to their own electoral or sociodemographic constituencies. The lack of arbitrary restrictions allows UBI to be distributed to individuals irrespective of their ideas and values while being removed from the vagaries of electoral fiscal cycles.

Of all the ideologies discussed in this book, Christian democracy is perhaps most insistent on promoting centrism (Gottfried 2007) and anti-extremism. For framing an argument in favour of UBI, this means an emphasis on balance. As alluded to earlier, UBI could be presented as a careful balance between the demands that the political left and right raise against contemporary political economy—taking into account both sides' arguments and proposing a consensual compromise. It is orthodox in the sense that it rests on the same premises and assumptions as the prevailing approaches to political economy, but it also errs towards the slightly provocative side of conventionalism, on the grounds that it promises change without revolution. Further, the scheme can be designed in a 'pro-establishment' way that aims to reframe but nonetheless reaffirm existing structures and systematic logics such as the relationship between state, market, rights, and property.

Another element of balance that Christian-democratic UBI proponents could embrace treads a fine line between more 'classic' and disruptive elements of social policy. The scheme could provide an alternative to mainstream political economy that is nonetheless well-known in current welfare and social policy discussions, and firmly focused on the present. As already mentioned above, the potential ideological 'neutrality' associated with UBI—which we partially draw into question in this book—could persuade Christian democrats to see it as a 'sensible' and 'reasonable' policy. It is possible to identify many similar balance-related framings, emphasising the ways in which UBI offers a principled but not dogmatic proposal, a measured policy that avoids both sudden shocks to and the ossification of the existing system.

Such arguments run somewhat parallel to social democracy's incrementalistic approach to policymaking and suggest that a Christian-democratic UBI would purposefully be designed to oppose the extreme left and its idea of a far-reaching socialisation of production. Instead, Christian democrats would aim to widen access to private property and capital while maintaining the existing system of money for exchange. Thus, Christian democrats may hope that a UBI would highlight the role of the individual as the key unit in any new approach to political economy, as opposed to alternative ideas that emphasise collective units such as economic classes, sectors, or decentralised worker-owned and cooperative enterprises. If more radically disruptive reforms are on the table, UBI could be framed as a tangible and feasible policy within the current system that protects citizens without the risks and violence of a revolution. A Christian-democratic UBI could effectively acknowledge the structural flaws of capitalism but demonstrate that they can be remedied via an equally structural approach that falls short of wholesale system overthrow. Christian-democratic UBI supporters may thus try to split off moderate forms of left ideology, especially social democrats and greens, from their more radical peers.

This resistance to radicalism is, however, hardly limited to the left. Christian democrats would also face incentives to design a UBI that can oppose the policy aims and expectations of the extreme right. In its rejection of unrestrained *laissez-faire*, a permanent guarantee of access to basic means clearly opposes the anti-inclusive tendencies of ideologies such as fascism or libertarianism. Christian-democratic UBI proponents effectively promote the need for a universal criterion of value for all individuals that is broader than the mere capacity to be productive. By adjusting or building out existing welfare systems rather than fully abolishing them, UBI could, again, allow Christian democrats to split off moderate forms of right-wing ideology from extremists as well. In this respect, its similarities to a liberal UBI become particularly important.

The final element we subsume under Christian democracy's tradition-oriented tendencies concerns its appeal to moderation. In line with this idea, Christian democrats may choose to emphasise the basicness that lies at the definitional core of UBI. While they may hope that the policy addresses some structural flaws of contemporary political economy, they could see UBI as a 'medium-intensity' intervention: the state reallocates resources, but not beyond basic needs and without centrally deciding on more specific measures. Furthermore, the concept of constructing a cash flow that covers social minima could be considered less invasive and thus more moderate than salary caps or the full equalisation of material resources. Hence, UBI could be one example of 'sufficientarian' and 'satisficing' policymaking.

In another sense, Christian democrats may see UBI as a way of reinvigorating past ideas of welfare. This argument would frame UBI as a 'road not taken', on the grounds that previous welfare debates have favoured selective and insurance-based policies explicitly aimed at specific target groups. Rather than being revolutionary, UBI could thus be framed as a moderate response to the shortcomings of past decisions that only became clear once a certain amount of time had subsequently elapsed. The more progressive-leaning UBI advocates are able to frame the policy as a recollection or redeployment of historical ideas of charity, philanthropy, social security, or welfare, the more they may be able to convince more reactionary forces within Christian democracy of the idea as well.

This could lead to a carefully delimited decontestation of the next stages of societal progress. As even reactionary forces have a hard time offering total blanket opposition to any and all forms of social progress, they can instead seek to 'work with' the idea of change in the hope of guiding it in a direction they find more palatable than what would happen if they simply 'boycotted' any engagement in the debate. Although this leads us firmly away from the territory of progressivism, it is strategically important to consider for progressive Christian democrats who are facing existential ideological struggles within their own parties. They may be able to frame UBI as a moderate 'necessary concession' in order to prevent more radical 'turns to the right', perhaps conceived as a way to hamper the momentum of left-wing projects.

Utopia

In contrast to ideas of tradition, Christian democracy also promotes its own visions of utopia. These are—perhaps counterintuitively for left-wing actors—closely linked to nostalgia for a shared 'heritage' (Wolkenstein 2023, 637). The basic idea here is that nostalgic and perhaps glorified recollections of the past can inform a desirable future, whereby UBI in particular can be framed as an expression of the old principle of *noblesse oblige*. As a redistributive policy, it relies on an assumption that those who are better off in current societal arrangements have a duty of care towards those who are struggling. This responsibility is also mirrored on the side of the state. By laying claim to govern a society, a state assumes a role of stewardship towards all of its members. In this context, UBI can be seen as one way of realising this universal and nostalgic duty of care that aligns with the realities of modern neoliberal capitalism.

Christian democrats could further frame UBI as an attempt to dial back the dehumanisation of post-industrial capitalism. As contemporary political economy relies on forms of partial employment and underemployment that put workers into precarious conditions and hamper their ability to accumulate capital, this undermines Christian democrats' ideas of the 'good entrepreneur' and the worker who starts their own small enterprise. UBI could essentially become a wage supplement that gives workers the power of autonomous choice needed to realise the utopian promises of a market-based society. The scheme also implies an attempt to hark back to a time before the emergence of a dehumanising bureaucratic state that uses means-tested welfare schemes to group individuals into categories of desirability. In this vein, Christian democrats may think of UBI as a way to emphasise that humans are not an undifferentiated mass that collectively uses one-size-fits-all public services, but rather an agglomeration of individuals, each of whom can exercise decisive command over their own personal uniqueness. In short, the appeal of UBI here is that it is abstract enough to work for modern policymaking, but also embraces the concrete diversity that people exhibit in society today.

Close to nostalgic visions of the past is the idea of romanticism. This element is illustrated well by juxtaposing UBI as an aspirational and empathetic policy to otherwise highly realism-driven approaches to welfare. A romanticised Christian-democratic argument for UBI would critique the idea that humans cannot be trusted with a payment that has no strings of conditionality attached. The same line of argument may also see the instrumentalisation of people and nature in pursuit of profit and productivity as unsustainably destructive. Instead, social policy could be framed as having an intrinsic value of responding directly to the suffering of those living in immiseration—and of those fearing such a condition.

This romanticism, however, does not mean that Christian democrats lose sight of the elements of moderation and modesty discussed earlier. Rather, they may see UBI as a way of steering idealism about welfare policy towards the points of acknowledging that specific concessions need to be made to ensure feasibility and sustainability. After all, UBI would only provide a basic floor. Even a strenuous commitment to equality, so the argument goes, cannot change the fact that state approaches to material (re)distribution need to work within often exogenous logistical and financial constraints. Through a UBI, Christian democrats may aim to 'discharge' their welfare responsibilities in a way that requires little maintenance and thus leaves administrative resources available for other schemes. One result of the policy would then be a transformation of an entrepreneurial state into a philanthropic state. This state plays a vital role for investment, albeit not only in areas such as industrial policy, but also in the sense of social investment that directly supports people themselves. UBI could effectively represent 'human capital with a human face', in the sense that it supports individuals in their self-development, while valuing them as members of society beyond their productive contributions.

Although utopian visions of a better society are an important part of Christian democracy, they are not generally accompanied by support for major experiments at a state-wide scale. On the contrary, Christian democrats would, ideologically speaking, rather operate on the safe side wherever possible. For advocates of UBI, this means that the policy could be framed as simple to grasp and sleek in design. No vast expansion of administrative organisation is required, costs are quantifiable and simple to anticipate, and a prodigious array of experimental evidence in favour of the policy has already been gathered. A Christian-democratic UBI also does not require a fundamentally new legitimation process, as it is designed to merely patch deficiencies in the existing system. Accordingly, the scheme should minimise the risk of dramatically overturning the current finely poised societal balance and pushing vast swathes of its members into social or ideological *anomie*.

Another important element for Christian democrats to consider is how to design UBI in a way that minimises unforeseen externalities. When it comes to framing an argument for the scheme, Christian democrats could rely heavily on the existing empirical research on it, making it less of a 'natural experiment' and more of an implementation of gathered knowledge. While this argument is primarily a step in the direction of 'de-risking' UBI, the scheme itself can also become a buffer that Christian democrats can deploy against experimentalism. As discussed earlier, it can be seen as an alternative to more radical proposals for shifts away from the current societal settlement. Thus, UBI becomes a pressure valve for legitimate desires for change that prevents them from spiralling into speculative adventurism in the realm of policymaking. In short, if society is to change, Christian democrats would set out to gain as much control over the endpoint of this change as they conceivably can.

Social Change and Progress

Despite everything discussed so far concerning the Christian-democratic hesitancy towards social change, there are some distinct elements of progress built into the ideology. These largely rest on the concept of natural growth—that is, the idea that change occurs naturally but should not be forced by radical disruption (Galetti et al. 2011, 9). UBI could be framed as a reflection of this idea applied to society, recognising that societal complexity is growing constantly, and thus requires changes in the ambitions and functions of the state and social policy. Following this argument, it is no longer possible to achieve human prosperity through broad-brush policies without taking into account the particular needs of individuals. One single state system cannot address every sliver of human life if it does not focus on providing individuals with the means necessary for their own pursuit of happiness. By implication, the scope to achieve improvements through state action still exists, but it requires an individualistic approach.

As Christian democrats aim for manageable and moderate approaches in more-or-less all areas of social policy, they could aim for a UBI that rests quite heavily on individual action and less on state control than, for instance, a green UBI. Such an approach could be linked to the idea of natural growth, in that it could be framed as the logical continuation of the historical emergence of the welfare state. Responding to societal change, UBI would expand on this development and extend access to it to a growing number of societal groups, just as many prior welfare reforms did in their turn up to now. UBI could then be seen as the logical conclusion of a long-term tendency. Nevertheless, the policy would be a constrained intervention all the same. It provides a basic level under which no member of society can fall, and thus creates the conditions for further growth without unnecessarily predefining its direction. We alluded to this idea before, as it runs through various elements of Christian-democratic ideology. Through this lens, a Christian-democratic UBI would not only be the continuation of welfarism in general, but of a specific concept that we also discussed above: the social market economy. UBI does not intervene in other social domains such as religion, culture, or education directly and thus permits a moderate interpretation of *laissez-faire* policies. However, it still gives everyone the security needed to pursue their own goals in these domains as they see fit.

The preference for natural growth inherent to Christian democracy goes hand-in-hand with pronounced anti-revolutionary tendencies (Galetti et al. 2011, 9). Here, UBI could be framed as a reform of the welfare system that can only function within the basic logic of the social market economy—since in a system that operates without money and markets, a UBI would be essentially pointless. Additionally, the scheme simply reduces the drop-offs between those who are eligible for welfare and those who are not. Thus, while limiting the pressure on income through work overall, it reduces the degree to which the welfare system disincentivises taking up work at a low level of pay. After all, the material reward from work is higher if welfare payments are not entirely lost with increasing income.

This means that Christian-democratic UBI proponents may hope to combine preferences for productivity with a policy that effectively incentivises anti-revolutionary tendencies. After all, if the market economy fails, so does UBI. This gives recipients a stake in systemic stability. Accordingly, the scheme would be designed to actively prevent a complete overhaul of society. Instead, it would provide a clear solution to the problems of those who otherwise fall by the wayside and thus strengthen human dignity by deeming all—not just select groups—'deserving'. Ideas of common humanity and shared membership of a social community are thus merged with the condition that systemic disruption must be avoided. Accordingly, a Christian-democratic UBI would be designed to alleviate pressure for change, thereby undercutting revolutionary tendencies. Lying between surface-level tweaks of existing policy instruments and deep structural overhauls of the state as such, the policy could be the furthest that Christian democrats may be willing to go in terms of fostering or entertaining paradigm shifts (Hall 1993) in social policy.

STABILISING THE NATION: A CHRISTIAN-DEMOCRATIC VIEW OF EUBI

The Christian-democratic EUBI falls in between some of the policy designs discussed in the previous chapters. In line with the Christian-democratic aversion to revolutionary changes, this EUBI would be among the less disruptive models for how to instantiate the policy. In some regards, the arguments presented here imply some potentially contradictory tendencies. As with any of the other policy designs discussed in this book, the following remarks should thus not be interpreted as an attempt to find a single definitive concept for a Christian-democratic EUBI—not least because, up to this point, Christian-democratic parties have tended to resist rather than spearhead the case for implementation in UBI debates. By implication, an EUBI has hardly been high on the agenda for these parties at all. Especially in comparison with green parties, a Christian-democratic EUBI may thus seem like a primarily theoretical exercise. However, given the arguments outlined above, changes in political discourse—especially those associated with a radicalisation of electorates on political-economic questions—could change this quite rapidly.

Universality

For Christian democrats, universality is defined by high ideals of human nature which, in principle, span across the entire globe. However, the ideology's notions of belonging and community inhibit an overly cosmopolitan approach here. In an effort to avoid disruptive change while embracing subsidiarity, a key concern for Christian democrats, the defining criterion for access to an EUBI would thus need to be national citizenship. This implies that all citizens of an EU member state would get access to the UBI provided by that same state—subject to a specific role for the EU (elaborated further below). However, legal constraints would lead to a hierarchy emerging between migrants. Due to European non-discrimination rules, citizens from other EU states would also have to receive access. Member states could then decide whether or not to grant access to third country nationals as well. While on paper, Christian ideals of welfarism and humanitarianism would speak for an open approach, Christian-democratic parties have in practice shown a tendency towards welfare chauvinism (e.g., Zeit Online 2013). On that basis, even while they would not be necessary from an ideal-typical perspective, exclusions of third-country nationals from a Christian-democratic UBI are ultimately highly likely.

Individuality

In the previous sections, we elaborated on a theoretical area of tension between individual receipt and the significance of the nuclear family for Christian democracy. As in the cases of the other ideal-types, there are good arguments that lie in favour of the Christian-democratic EUBI being paid to individuals directly. This would limit state interference in the questions of where societal change should be steered towards, and could enable a greater fit of the policy to an individualised world. However, due to the importance of the family and of societal institutions as well as subsidiarity between non-state caretakers and the state, a tweak could be built into UBI to make it align better with Christian-democratic ideals. Specifically, caretakers could receive their EUBI much more easily for those they take care of than in the case of, for instance, the liberal EUBI. This means they would receive the full EUBI for their children at least until these children are of full age and—in line with subsidiarity—until other nationally determined criteria of individual independence are fulfilled. Such criteria could, for instance, include higher ages, finishing school, or moving out of the parents' household. Importantly, a more family-centric understanding of Christian democracy could lead to payments being delivered centrally to households and then distributed within each household as its members please—although this would come quite extensively at the cost of individual independence.

Conditionality

When it comes to conditionality, a few potential specificities of UBI may come to light through a Christian-democratic lens. With an eye on Christian values and morality, it is tempting to propose a scheme that makes receipt conditional on specific forms of behaviour that fall in line with these ideas. However, not only would this be difficult to achieve within the conceptual confines of UBI, but it would also run counter to many of the arguments for a UBI outlined above, especially concerning the non-involvement of the state in the directionality of societal change. In order to embrace individualism to the fullest extent possible, it is likely that an ideal-typical Christian-democratic EUBI would therefore choose to apply no further conditionality criteria.

Uniformity

Concerning uniformity, the principle of subsidiarity is key. It causes potential inconsistencies within this ideal-type, as the EU would have to leave it up to member states to decide whether, and how, to apply subnational variation. Thus, all the other elements discussed under this ideal-type may diverge, as not every member state will necessarily prefer the Christian-democratic proposals, either in their 'pure' form or in some hybrid combination. Ironically, a Christian-democratic approach to implementing an EUBI could thus consist in setting up a plethora of national UBI schemes that run fully against Christian-democratic ideology. Assuming, however, that the national implementation of an EUBI also adheres to Christian-democratic ideas to some extent, its uniformity would leave room for variation. First, the EUBI would be adjusted to national economic indicators, meaning that every member state would have its own specific payout level. Second, further voluntary subnational adjustments would be put in place to also implement marginal ideas of subnational and local subsidiarity within each member state.

Frequency

The frequency of UBI payouts for UBI would likely be in line with the widespread interpretations of UBI and, for instance, be highly compatible with social-democratic proposals in particular. As Christian democrats consider individuals able to make willful decisions but also embrace moderation, the Christian-democratic EUBI would shy away from extremely short or extremely long timespans between payouts. This is also in line with the interpretation of state 'stewardship' that protects citizens from the temptation of excess. Conserving established income and expenditure patterns, the EUBI would be paid out in line with the nationally most common timing of receiving income from work—for example, at the end of every month. This would further avoid the introduction of an EUBI causing any disruption of economic cycles, and build on path dependencies which often rest on long-standing social institutions. What is more, the introduction of more regular payouts could, in principle, be regarded as an unnecessary regularity of state intervention. Although automated payouts should theoretically not increase the administrative burdens on the public sector if carried out more frequently, the symbolic implication that an approach that overly relies on 'drip-feeding' could have runs against the role of the state inherent to the social market economy.

Duration

The duration of payments is one area in which Christian democrats can adjust policy settings away from the 'default' idea of UBI to get closer to their ideological goals. In order to achieve social stability for the individual and for society as a whole, the Christian-democratic EUBI would technically be available throughout an individual's entire life. Concerns such as those that preoccupy labour-centric social democrats are less of an issue here, and the main reason for Christian democrats to even consider limiting payout duration would be more strongly focused on ideas of frugality, probity, and prudence. Especially in the earlier stages of the scheme's development, arguments could be made along the lines that, in order to afford UBI, it should be limited to certain phases of life. Ultimately, based on theoretical argument alone, such considerations should not affect policy design. However, the considerations around subsidiarity and the traditional structures of family and society mean that caretakers would receive the EUBI for some parts of an individual's life (see section on individuality).

Modality

Modality then becomes a relatively straightforward prospect, especially compared to green ideology and social democracy. As Christian democrats embrace the social market economy with tendencies towards an interpretation in favour of free markets, they would pay the EUBI out in monetary form. In line with the arguments presented above, Christian democrats' complex relationship with capitalism primarily aims to fix the inherent imperfections of a market-based system, thus stabilising this system against revolutionary overthrow. Monetary payouts would push recipients to 'buy into' this system. On the one hand, they would stabilise the markets through consumption stimuli and by preventing the worst effects of poverty. On the other hand, they would transform any anti-market movement into a movement against the very basic income that keeps many citizens afloat.

Adequacy

One factor that complicates the issue of a UBI for Christian democrats consists in the potential for any such scheme to crowd the traditional providers of welfare out of the social policy system. In its monetary form, the Christian-democratic EUBI would face a tension between aiming for poverty relief based on religious considerations, and trying not to interfere too much with the role that churches play for social security in conservative welfare states in particular (see also Esping-Andersen 1990). In order to live up to poverty relief while staying firmly in the moderate range of the ideological spectrum and embracing the social market economy, the Christian-democratic EUBI would be lower than some other EUBIs. To retain subsidiarity, this could, for instance, mean an upper limit of 50 percent of the national median income, a lower limit of 20 percent of the national median income, and room for national decision-making regarding where precisely within that 'corridor' the payments should fall. Such decisions could, for instance, take into account existing other welfare programmes as well as entrenched preferences for fiscal austerity. Importantly, without complementary welfare systems such as social services and targeted benefits, UBI levels would need to be increased to have their desired effect of improving the position of the 'worst off' in society. After all, Christian democrats also aim to enable entrepreneurship and moral behaviour, which in both cases necessarily goes beyond mere survival. Against the background of the Christian-democratic preferences for path-dependencies and against systemic disruption, the ideal scenario for this EUBI would be to build on and complement existing schemes. However, there are some caveats to this, as we discuss under the section on the relationship to the national welfare state.

Funding

In order to avoid disrupting societal hierarchies for the sake of stability and anti-experimentalism, the Christian-democratic EUBI would avoid touching accumulated wealth as much as is feasible while still giving the scheme sufficient funding to be viable in the long term. The emphasis for funding the scheme would lie on taxing income and consumption, the latter for instance through a VAT as well as dedicated 'sin taxes' on consumption that is considered 'undesirable', such as gambling. In this way, Christian democrats can incentivise 'moral' behaviour 'through the back door' without having to steer societal change through payouts. This logic is similar to the analogous approaches of other ideological ideal-types, underlining the crucial role of payouts for (E)UBI design. In order to sharpen the scheme's embrace of moderation, luxury goods could also be taxed along with specific financial transactions, such as on trading in financial instruments underpinned by derivative rather than inherent value. Due to fiscal austerity and the wish not to disturb the balance of the social market economy, more funding would come from rolling back existing welfare schemes. At this point, a complex area of internal tension arises. Christian democracy aims to build on rather than abolish existing welfare schemes in principle—here again the role of tradition is of central importance. However, the ideology also suggests restraint when it comes to public involvement and expenditure, which would imply severe resource limitations for the policy. Nonetheless, at the same time a basic minimum should be secured for all members of society through EUBI payout levels. Thus, Christian democrats have to optimise these factors to reach a satisfying balance. Even in a purely theoretical, ideal-typical scenario, a Christian-democratic EUBI would thus have to negotiate a principled compromise, leading to some increases in taxes, to some welfare retrenchment, and to some limitations to the scheme's generosity. All the taxes listed here would be organised at the national level, in line with the general thrust of the Christian-democratic EUBI.

EU Policy Instruments

As suggested already, the involvement of the EU itself in a Christian-democratic EUBI would be fairly minimal. Based on the principle of subsidiarity, the scheme would be 'enforced' via a Recommendation. This implies that while the EU does play a role, it is largely relegated to a passive or reactive 'monitory' role of watching from the sidelines. It can provide encouragement and assisting frameworks of coordination. However, a more binding policy—especially a Regulation—is out of the question, as it would fundamentally violate the idea of an EU built on subsidiarity. Ambitious Christian democrats may still argue for a Directive, which would have to be implemented by member states through their respective processes of national legislation. However, this would already constitute the farthest-reaching intervention of the EU in social policy to date. Accordingly, a Recommendation is both theoretically and practically the most fitting approach here. Residual tendencies of centrism within the ideology could, meanwhile, imply a combination of a minimum threshold Directive with a Recommendation for optional top-ups. Still, if in doubt, a simple Recommendation seems the more plausible solution.

Relationship to National Welfare States

As suggested under the section on funding, existing national welfare schemes could partially fall victim to Christian-democratic frugalism, even though the preservation of traditional institutions runs counter to some important pillars of the ideology. To free up funding for the EUBI, some retrenchment could be expected. Such replacements would, however, primarily concern schemes like social assistance—that is, any (unconditional) cash benefits paid by the state in order to provide poverty relief. This could be seen as a moderate compromise to reconcile the internal tensions of the ideology, as it would not undermine any public good that pursues goals which a UBI itself cannot credibly live up to. Rather, Christian democrats may frame the replacement of monetary schemes as their natural progression into a more comprehensive, joined-up social welfare system. Crucially, Christian democrats would avoid replacing any welfare schemes provided by churches, communities, families, or other traditional societal institutions. In other words, the Christian-democratic EUBI would primarily aim to remove welfare schemes that are not in line with the conservative image of the 'proper' welfare state, wherever it is deemed necessary to fund the new policy.

Technical Distribution and Introduction

As the Christian-democratic EUBI would work through Recommendations and coordination, it would be implemented by member states using their own infrastructure. In line with preferences for anti-experimentalism and moderation as well as to avoid disturbing the economy and breaking with national traditions, the Christian-democratic EUBI would further be introduced gradually and extremely slowly under constant supervision by national committees checking primarily for economic, but also for social and cultural effects of the scheme. If undesired and unexpected externalities were to occur, the rollout of the EUBI would be temporarily halted until the relevant issues were fully resolved. By the same token, at any point at which the costs of the scheme exceed the available designated revenue sources, its introduction would again be temporarily halted until revenue catches up to avoid incurring a new source of public debt.

In short, the Christian-democratic EUBI focuses strongly on national action and subsidiarity. It would strengthen conservative welfare schemes but remain progressive in its ideals of individual social stability. Of all the schemes presented in this analysis, it would be the least disruptive to the existing frameworks and operations of European political economy.

Chapter 8

Agenda Coalitions for a European Basic Income

The policy designs for an EUBI we have presented over the course of the previous chapters are designed to align closely with the respective theoretical principles of each political ideology. By implication, this means that some of them differ in several fundamental ways. In this chapter, we turn to the question of what happens if these separate visions of an EUBI are forced to confront one another in processes of coalition-building—specifically, of forming an 'agenda coalition' with the intention of implementing a UBI across the whole EU. Despite their fundamentally unique characteristics and (in some cases) significant differences, we argue that the five progressive models for an EUBI are far from irreconcilable, and that many of their flagship elements also show signs of significant overlap. To get a better grasp of such overlaps and differences, the table overleaf concisely summarises (in simplified form) the key elements of each ideology's ideal-typical EUBI at a glance (see table 8.1).

Many of the considerations presented above may invite a measure of controversy among proponents and opponents of the general idea of UBI alike. While some elements of the different ideal-types stretch the boundaries of what one might consider a UBI in its 'classic' form, all schemes contain strong elements of 'universality', 'basicness', and 'income'. Considering the essential purpose and advantages of constructing ideal-types as an analytical lens, these approaches should also not be regarded to be the *only*, the *definitive* viable options within each ideological framework. On the contrary, one of the most forceful aspects of this list is quite simply that it demonstrates how diverse EUBI policy designs can be, underlining the point that the number of concrete policy designs for the general idea of an EUBI is potentially limitless.

The same goes for the 'European' part of an EUBI. Some of the ideal-types we have presented are 'less European' than others, as they leave voluntary

Table 8.1. Ideal-typical EUBI policy designs

	Far Left	*Social Democratic*	*Green*	*Liberal*	*Christian Democratic*
Universality	All EU denizens	All EU citizens, children first	All long-term EU denizens	All EU citizens and economically active denizens	All EU citizens derived from national citizenship
Individuality	Directly to individuals	Directly to individuals, shares for unions	Directly to individuals	Directly to individuals	Directly to individuals with tendencies towards caretakers
Conditionality	No automatic payouts to the rich, bureaucratic hurdles	No automatic payouts to the rich, 'donation' databases	—	—	—
Uniformity	Varies with national conditions and development goals	Varies with national conditions	Varies with regional conditions	Varies with subnational economic conditions	Varies with national economic conditions
Frequency	Weekly	In line with established wage payouts	Monthly	Yearly	In line with established wage payouts
Duration	Lifelong	Lifelong, but modality varies	Lifelong	Lifelong	Lifelong with tendencies towards caretakers
Modality	Monetary	Monetary for the young and elderly, vouchers during working-age	Monetary with optional vouchers of higher monetary value	Monetary with optional shares of sovereign wealth fund	Monetary

	Far Left	*Social Democratic*	*Green*	*Liberal*	*Christian Democratic*
Adequacy	At least at-risk-of-poverty level, topped-off through capital gains	At-risk-of-poverty level	At least at-risk-of-poverty level, including EU-wide minimum	Varies with economic performance capped at 40% of subnational median income	Between 20% and 50% of national median income
Funding	Collectivised capital and banks, redistributive taxes	Redistributive taxation on non-EUBI income and wealth	Primarily ecological and redistributive taxes	Revenues from public investment, flat taxes, savings from welfare state retrenchment	Nondisruptive taxes, savings from welfare state retrenchment
Instruments	New centralised EU policy	Directive	Regulation	Recommendation	Recommendation
Welfare State	Remains intact	Remains intact	Remains intact	Retrenchment	Retrenchment, except conservative elements
Distribution	Directly by EU	Through national infrastructure	Directly by EU	Through national infrastructure	Through national infrastructure
Introduction	Right away at high levels	Slowly and gradually	Gradually	Slowly and gradually	Slowly and gradually

implementation up to individual EU member states. This runs the risk of creating a nationalised patchwork, which may provoke all the concerns about welfare magnetism allegations that we discussed earlier in the book. This issue could be resolved by forcing all policy designs into the requirement of being implemented at the EU level. However, this would obscure precisely those ideological differentiations that our ideal-type approach was supposed to highlight. Given that these proposals are ideal-typical, which is to say purely hypothetical scenarios, they also assume that proposals relying on EU Recommendations would be implemented nationally in accordance with the respective theoretical policy preferences at play. Thus, the same logic that justifies assuming an ideal-typical EUBI being implemented at the EU level also justifies assuming that Recommendations would lead to national implementations in line with the policy design characteristics we have outlined.

In practice, concrete EUBI designs might—and most probably would—look fundamentally quite different, in that they might constitute mixed types or perhaps even take entirely different approaches to development and implementation. Such differences could be rooted in many factors that do not necessarily have to stem from the same motivations. For instance, intra-party variations in EUBI preferences could require policy designs to undergo significant adjustments already before a party even enters electoral competition. External political pressure from opposing parties could further limit the (perceived) political options available to a party and incentivise them to push for a proposal that is not perfectly in line with intra-party preferences. The same could also result from the perceived need to respond to public demands, while power resources and institutional limitations could present hurdles that would prevent a party from either achieving its goals or from even considering them worth proposing. What is more, even if we take as read that our theoretical arguments offer a complete overview of what each ideology promotes, theory does not always match political practice on all counts. Political parties are diverse, malleable organisations that do not neatly map onto the (already somewhat porous) boundaries between different ideologies—and even within European party families, prominent disagreements on various fundamental issues arise fairly regularly. Hence, erring somewhat on the side of caution, the policy designs we have presented here should *not* strictly be seen as an attempt to 'predict' partisan proposals, let alone actual policies.

Considering these limitations, it is worth asking what precisely can be learned from the approach we have chosen. Despite all the caveats we have mentioned, our ideal-type analysis has a very specific practical use in that it sheds light on UBI and the debates associated with it. First, our analysis illustrates what fundamentally different EUBI proposals might look like. This is crucial as there is a tendency within UBI debates to simplify matters and ask whether a party, politician, or individual is straightforwardly 'for' or 'against' UBI, which suggests that what is at issue is a single, clearly defined, conceptually indivisible policy. We take the view that it is nearly pointless to discuss 'the' singular UBI. Rather, the question should be *what kind of* UBI someone is prepared to propose or oppose.

Second, our analysis illustrates how different dials in policy design can be adjusted to achieve different goals, which is relevant on both a theoretical and a practical level. From a theoretical perspective, it allows us to further develop our categorisations of 'UBI families' and makes more tangible what the various different dimensions of differentiation entail. Practically speaking, it provides concrete examples for how what is often an abstract idea could be pursued politically, and what kinds of factors or elements supporters of the policy would need to consider when doing so. A key takeaway here is that an EUBI's desirability from different perspectives is not only a matter of theoretical stances on UBI in general, but also of its particular policy details.

Third, our analysis provides a starting-point for figuring out where compromises can be made and where ideological ideal-types are irreconcilable. We elaborate on this in the following sections by going into detail on a concept we introduced at the beginning of this book: 'agenda coalitions'. To make this more concrete, we further sketch out examples for what such coalitions could look like based on the policy designs we presented in the previous chapters.

IN PURSUIT OF COMPROMISE

Given the current prevalence of parliamentary fragmentation and the far-reaching impact an EUBI would have on social policy, implementing one of the five ideological ideal-types we have outlined in practice would hardly be feasible, even if the relevant party committed to implementing it to the letter. This means that, in order to move the discussion of potential EUBI designs beyond these ideal-types requires adopting a perspective that bridges the ideological divides between them in some way. However, the empirical absence of an EUBI and national UBIs makes it difficult to discuss concrete political scenarios in anything other than a hypothetical way. Thus, what we attempt to offer below are some possible scenarios for policy compromises, viewed from a theoretical perspective.

Based on our previous summary of progressive ideologies as well as the ideal-types we have put forward, we discuss some possible coalitions that could be formed around specific elements of an EUBI. While an EUBI might seem a somewhat utopian proposition at first glance, it is one of the few social policies that unite the key ideals of all the various progressive ideologies in some permutation. Under the right circumstances, there could be far greater potential for implementing an EUBI than might be assumed. As cleavages around the policy run within ideologies rather than between them (De Wispelaere and Yemtsov 2019, 195), an EUBI could be a promising way to achieve meaningful social progress through building contingent 'agenda coalitions'—that is, coalitions of parties that join forces to push through EUBI as a stand-alone policy rather than settling on the larger roster of policies required to populate a fully-fledged coalition agreement. In specific circumstances, such coalitions might be necessary to achieve far-reaching change, as the parties that might be inclined to unite over a fully-fledged coalition agreement might—paradoxically—not be able to agree on policies as disruptive as an EUBI. Conversely, parties that would not usually consider working together in a governmental or oppositional 'bloc' capacity might be willing to rally around a few individual ideas such as an EUBI, which creates space for the option of otherwise unusual agenda coalitions.

The Concept of Compromise through Agenda Coalitions

The basic concept of 'agenda coalitions' is not new. It already exists in the literature on policy development, where the idea of 'policy coalitions' describes broader, strategic partnerships between diverse types of actors that strive for common goals. These actors are not only limited to political parties, but can also include NGOs, think tanks, individuals, organisations, or institutions (Ostrowski 2021; Warleigh 2000). One of the best-known formalisations of this interpretation consists in the concept of 'advocacy coalitions' (Mintrom and Vergari 1996). Crucially, such coalitions play a wider role in the policy process at large, meaning that they advocate for certain ideas not only in parliament but, for instance, also in the media or other parts of public discourse. In contrast to such approaches, we focus on intra-parliamentary 'agenda coalitions'—that is, coalitions of different members of parliament or parliamentary parties that push through a specific single policy or a specific set of conjoined and mutually supporting policies, without forming a formal government. In practice—though evidently outside the context of UBI—such cross-partisan cooperation on select policy issues has occasionally been observed in the United States (Evans 1994).

In theory, intra-parliamentary agenda coalitions can have several advantages. First and foremost, the concept addresses the problem of the ever-increasing complications involved in finding workable majorities. After all, an increasing atomisation of national parliaments could lead to ever more deadlocks regarding social policy development. Further, the concept of agenda coalitions addresses the fundamental problems faced by contemporary parties that fail to deliver on the purposes for which they were originally founded. If parties can push through policies they have agreed on only in a fully-fledged coalition agreement, this might stifle their ability to achieve far-reaching progress for marginalised groups in particular. For instance, social democrats and the far left may disagree on too many substantive issues to form complete government coalitions but might fare better if they restrict their efforts to merely agreeing on specific social policy programmes.

Intra-parliamentary agenda coalitions could also be a first step towards instituting a more deliberative form of democracy without sacrificing the representative character of the EU's democratic systems. This could take the form of incentivising members of parliament to deliberatively develop specific policy solutions while leaving the bulk of decisions to more traditional coalition agreements. At the same time, agenda coalitions could enable the formation of minority governments after elections with uncertain outcomes, focused on specific issues as the opposition may withdraw support in other areas. Thus, potentially short-term 'issue-specific coalitions' (Auel and Benz 2005, 377) could enable some vital reforms to be passed before new elections have to be called. However, if minority governments became the norm, this could undermine overall political stability. Ideally, intra-parliamentary agenda coalitions would thus combine the general stability and reliability of majority government coalitions with the occasionally necessary flexibility of minority governments, assuming that the coalition agreement to which the government coalition has committed itself does not explicitly rule out cooperation with opposition parties. To avoid undermining a government on a regular basis, a majority government may specify in their coalition agreement the areas where parties in the ruling coalition are allowed to 'break ranks' and join forces with opposition parties to achieve policy change.

Agenda Coalitions and EUBI

While many of these considerations around policy-specific agenda coalitions relate to democracy in general, the concept has particular relevance for policies such as an (E)UBI that might otherwise currently seem out of reach. Agenda coalitions could be an effective tool for achieving such policies if a compromise can be reached that delivers on the main goals that different ideologies aim for while avoiding infringing on any 'taboos' in concrete policy design. Finding such a common ground is anything but trivial and the comparison of ideologically rooted EUBI ideal-types above showed that there is no single clear agenda coalition that would agree on a single obvious policy design. Instead, there are many possible compromises that can take shape. While some elements of the EUBI designs we have presented here are irreconcilable between ideologies—for example, the funding approaches of the far left and liberals—many dimensions contain common denominators between ideologies.

The following sections outline agenda coalitions that can be formed around different visions of an EUBI that are particularly close to one another in specific ways. For each coalition, our working assumption is that its member parties would prioritise a specific element of an EUBI on which they can mostly agree. For instance, parties might share similar ideas regarding redistribution while disagreeing on some other dimensions of an EUBI. In such a case, the compromise they might come to would be designed in such a way that it delivers on redistribution while avoiding any excessively controversial choices in other elements of the policy. All the same, coalitions usually have points of contestation which they would need to resolve in order to achieve their common goal. After all, the complexity of an EUBI's policy design implies that it is unlikely for coalition members to be able to simply skip making decisions in some controversial areas, for instance on the role of the EU.

In theory, there are infinite possibilities for the different coalitions around an EUBI, given not only how many possible combinations of ideologies there are, but also how many qualitative goals they might pursue. What is more, many infinitesimally slight changes could be made to the policy design, increasing the number of possible coalitions even more. To simplify things, we have developed policy designs for potential coalitions based on the potential effects that an EUBI could have. We thus discuss potential coalitions based on the different fundamental goals they might agree on when pursuing an EUBI. That is, instead of discussing a social-democratic–green or liberal–Christian-democratic EUBI coalition, we explore a coalition dedicated to achieving a certain social goal—hence their construction as '*agenda* coalitions'. Again, these coalitions are only meant to serve as illustrations. To avoid repetition, we do not go over every single detail of policy design for each coalition. Since the earlier ideal-types already illustrate what directions policy designs might go down, we will only describe the coalitions' most important properties here.

We argue that there is a shortlist of likely goals and important social purposes around which agenda coalitions in support of an EUBI could form. First, coalitions might aim for poverty relief, in the hope that an EUBI would effectively eradicate at least the monetary dimension of poverty. Second, individual liberty could be a primary goal, as an EUBI theoretically has significant potential to emancipate individuals from various types of dependency. Third, an EUBI could aim for redistribution, acting as a simple tool for the state to control income. Fourth, a coalition might form around the reduction of bureaucracy, in the expectation that administratively burdensome systems such as means-testing could be partly or wholly eradicated. Fifth, the European dimension of an EUBI implies that actors might join forces for the cause of strengthening European unity.

Coalition for Poverty Relief

The agenda coalition for poverty relief aims for an ostensibly straightforward goal: putting an end to monetary poverty across the entire EU. In principle, this coalition would be open to all the ideologies we have discussed. After all, there is no progressive ideology that would reject poverty reduction in principle as such. However, given the differences in priorities and other fundamental goals, this does not mean that all ideologies would agree on the same scheme. For instance, mutually incompatible ideas around funding might prevent a coalition involving liberals and the far left from taking shape. In line with the considerations presented in the previous chapters, we argue that such decisive poverty reduction is of the highest priority to the far left and greens, followed by social democrats and Christian democrats, and finally liberals. While all these ideologies may in principle agree that nobody in Europe should live in monetary poverty, they would almost certainly clash on how to achieve this goal and whether it should trump other principles. For instance, some actors in this coalition might prefer needs-tested schemes over an EUBI. Nonetheless, the presence of intra-ideological cleavages around a UBI implies that they might eventually conclude that any needs-tested scheme runs the risk of (e.g.) low uptake rates or discriminatory decisions by caseworkers. At this point, priorities are key: if the actors involved find such drawbacks tolerable, they might be less prone to supporting an EUBI than actors who prioritise poverty reduction above all else. To foster compromises between some of the actors involved, mechanisms such as nonautomatic payouts for the rich could be used to mitigate potential conflicts around needs-testing, especially when involving social-democratic ideas of deservingness rooted in work.

Generally, an EUBI could be the basis for a cross-partisan agreement on how to get rid of poverty in contrast to more conditional schemes, as the latter are much more sensitive to conflicting ideas of justice. After all, the conditions that nonuniversal welfare schemes apply tend to amplify the principles associated with different ideologies such as contributory or needs-based ideas of justice. Such schemes might accept *some* individuals falling through the security net in order to push through a specific idea of justice *at large*. By contrast, an EUBI pursued by the coalition for poverty relief would emphasise the importance of nobody being left out. In its extreme form, an EUBI associated with this coalition would thus be paid out to every resident of the EU. Adding limitations based on citizenship requirements would run counter to the ideal-typical goal around which such a coalition would form, ensuring that *nobody* who lives in Europe faces severe poverty. Concerning implementation, an EU Directive would be a plausible compromise between guaranteeing the scheme's implementation on the one hand and not interfering with ideas of national sovereignty and subsidiarity held by liberals and Christian democrats on the other. Any nonbinding legislative instrument would again undermine the idea that nobody should be falling through the cracks, whereas more ambitious instruments would increase the thresholds for a coalition to form in the first place.

Payments provided through this EUBI would be monetary, ideally at the regional at-risk-of-poverty threshold of 60 percent of median income. Only then would the scheme fully deliver on its goal. However, if it was necessary to build electoral majorities for the scheme in a context where more ambitious goals seem unachievable, lower levels such as 40 percent of the median income might be more acceptable to the ideologies involved. After all, social democrats and greens, in particular, might prefer some basic poverty relief over no solution at all. Non-monetary payments, however, would only be acceptable as a last resort for this coalition, especially if liberals are involved. While vouchers might be considered an option to prevent absolute poverty, the ideas of individual freedom that the different parties involved are committed to mean that monetary payments are the common denominator that causes the least ideological tensions. While all parties might agree that monetary poverty relief is socially desirable, not all of them would necessarily do the same concerning vouchers. Relatively regular payouts would be preferable for this coalition, as they would minimise the risk of poverty occurring at any point. Furthermore, if this becomes necessary for fiscal reasons, automatic payouts could be tapered off as recipients' income increases, in line with the mechanism described under the social-democratic ideal-typical EUBI. However, this would only be tolerable to the coalition for poverty relief if the bureaucratic steps necessary to claim UBI actively are kept fairly simple. Otherwise, the risk that an individual who depends on UBI might unrightfully be excluded would be too high for them to countenance. Only if such scenarios can easily be remedied by finding ways for the excluded individual to claim their income would an EUBI minimise risks of poverty.

Coalition for Individual Liberty

Aside from eradicating poverty, an EUBI might instead revolve first and foremost around making the individual as independent as possible. There are two basic ways to interpret the resulting coalition for individual liberty. First, an emancipatory focus would chiefly appeal to social democrats, greens, and the far left. In contrast, a second more economically austere focus would primarily appeal to liberals, social democrats, and greens. As was already the case with the coalition for poverty relief, a coalition of liberals and the far left would hardly be viable due to their fundamental disagreements on matters of funding. The coalition for individual liberty would go far beyond poverty prevention. In principle, it would make no major distinction in priorities between the wealthiest and the most disadvantaged members of society. In this coalition, everyone should be able to make decisions in a fully unrestricted way, implying that the EUBI should be independent of wealth, income, previous decisions, or any other factor.

As this goal could be difficult to achieve due to the demanding implications for the generosity of the scheme, some compromises would be necessary. Such compromises could be made on issues like redistribution and the EU policy instruments deployed to implement it, but not regarding areas such as modality and adequacy. Part of the provision of individual liberty would be the goal of fostering a 'good life', including an appropriate work-life balance, rather than simply preventing (extreme) poverty. This point implies that the EUBI would need to be relatively high, to meet its aspirational social ambitions. The *lower* threshold of the payments involved would then be set at 60 percent of the respective regional median income, with higher amounts being entirely conceivable depending on how expansively the goal of individual independence is defined. Unlike the coalition for poverty relief, this EUBI would not be able to incorporate any limitations to automatic payouts. While the coalition for poverty relief would tolerate such limitations if this were financially absolutely necessary, it would fundamentally counteract the goals of the coalition for individual liberty. After all, this coalition specifically wants to sever the link between 'market performance' and individual freedom, which implies that it would find any conditionality of payouts unacceptable. Further, the associated EUBI would be paid out yearly or monthly in monetary units directly to individuals. Shorter payment intervals would limit individual flexibility without yielding the benefits that are central to this coalition.

The same basic logic applies to non-monetary payouts and intermediary recipients. As this EUBI would be very costly, its funding would likely be the biggest area of controversy between the coalition's members. Specific funding decisions would ultimately follow the preferences of the parties involved, depending on whether the coalition takes its emancipatory or its austere form. The former would likely be more open to redistributive approaches, such as taxation on high incomes and wealth while generally leveraging all sources of funding it could get. By contrast, the latter could focus on taxes on consumption, CO_2 emissions, financial transactions, or digital services, along with a heavy emphasis on the long-term yields from public investment strategies. However, given the high financial demands on both forms of this coalition, it is unlikely that the parties involved could afford to entirely do without any particular revenue sources, irrespective of their ideological preferences. Hence, the label 'austere' must be taken with something of a grain of salt.

Coalition for Redistribution

A third agenda coalition could revolve around redistribution. Members of this coalition would aim to redistribute financial means from the most privileged to the least well-off and to the lower middle class. Considering the deeply ingrained scepticism towards such goals among liberals and Christian democrats, this coalition is most likely to comprise (only) the far left, greens, and social democrats. While the previous coalitions—just as in many popular UBI debates—emphasise the dimension of UBI's outputs, the coalition for redistribution focuses on the role of funding as the main mechanism through which its goals can be achieved. This coalition would embrace high taxes in areas such as high incomes, wealth, inheritance, land value, financial transactions, corporate gains, and luxury goods. The logic here would be simple: collect money from revenue sources that predominantly affect the wealthier parts of society and pay it out to everyone equally. As a result, wealth is redistributed through regular income streams without the dangers of targeted payouts missing out those most in need. In its extreme form, an EUBI modelled after this agenda coalition would only secondarily be concerned with emancipating individuals financially. In the first instance, this EUBI would primarily be a simple tool designed to directly control the distribution of financial resources across society.

To maximise this function, the redistributive coalition might opt for further policy design tweaks. For instance, a fixed baseline EUBI might be optionally and temporarily topped-off with additional funds in case the parties involved find the idea of temporary increases in inequality unacceptable. This would mean that the EUBI would in principle be a permanent hands-off redistribution mechanism that can actively be 'turbo-charged' if and when inequality rises rapidly. Furthermore, nudges could be used to discourage the rich from taking up non-automatic payouts, in line with the earlier idea of tapering off automatic payouts. This EUBI would maintain the universal right to basic income, but also make it more cumbersome for wealthier individuals to claim this right. Furthermore, positive incentives such as drawing up publicly announced lists of EUBI 'donors' who waive their payouts could add to the redistributive capacities of the scheme. However, the coalition for redistribution is particularly prone to variation in ideological preferences regarding what counts as the 'right' degree of redistribution. Thus, compromises could be forged regarding aspects such as the EU policy instrument and even the level of the EUBI itself. After all, the latter is less central to this coalition than, for instance, for the coalition for poverty relief—and could even entirely be tied to fluctuating revenue levels. In practice, this may mean that EUBI payout levels could be near zero in months or years during which revenue sources are low. What is much more important to this particular agenda coalition is that all revenue sources for the EUBI are redistributive, in favour of the worst-off members of society. Accordingly, the complex and salient question of whether an EUBI can be funded is easily resolved for the coalition for redistribution, as payouts follow funds.

While conceptually intriguing, this coalition is particularly unlikely to form in practice. The ideologies involved could likely agree on needs-tested schemes much more easily, as these are likely to be even more strongly redistributive while avoiding complicated debates on needs-based justice and UBI. Should the potential members of this coalition secure a popular majority, there would be more immediate ways to achieve redistribution. One of the key elements that may make UBI relatively attractive in the logic of agenda coalitions is the fact that it could allow economically *laissez-faire* and economically interventionist ideologies to join forces over a major social policy reform. The coalition for redistribution, however, crowds out economically *laissez-faire* parties more-or-less by design. Thus, this agenda coalition is only likely to materialise if the majority on which it builds has been achieved in a context where the parties involved have previously embraced the promise of an EUBI in elections.

Coalition for Bureaucracy Reduction

In stark contrast to the coalition for redistribution, a fourth ideal-typical agenda coalition could revolve around a facet of UBI debates that is more concerned with administrative practices: bureaucracy reduction. This coalition would take shape over the general idea that an EUBI would be a way to simplify and streamline the welfare state, above all by reducing the bureaucratic apparatus involved in processes like means-testing. The coalition for bureaucracy reduction effectively forms a market-*laissez-faire* opposite to the state-interventionist coalition for redistribution. What sets an EUBI apart from a national UBI in this regard is the added potential for reducing the need for each EU member state to operate their own administrative structures for welfare provision. However, given that the prevailing consensus at the EU level still lies on leaving the integrity of national welfare states untouched by EU interference (EPP 2009, 2; PES 2019, 1), this goal is primarily a theoretical one. Thus, although a centralised EU-wide implementation would further reduce bureaucratic costs, the preferences of the parties involved would likely lead to national implementations—especially given the Christian-democratic emphasis on subsidiarity.

To approach this from a less intrusive perspective, an EUBI might be considered the least bureaucratic way of adding a palpable social layer to the EU. In this interpretation, the coalition for bureaucracy reduction would not aim to decrease existing national bureaucracy, but rather limit the degree to which new bureaucratic structures arise at the EU level. As this line of argument is still relatively negative—it builds on *avoiding* something *undesirable*—the facet of market-making can give it a more positive appeal. Among those parties that likely oppose bureaucracy, there tends to be support for the EU conceived primarily as a common market—which might lead to an EUBI being considered a tool for stabilising and legitimising economic integration. In this form, this coalition could comprise first and foremost liberals and Christian democrats. It may further appeal to integrationist greens, who generally represent a relatively broad platform of potential EUBI support.

The participation of the greens in this coalition would strongly moderate the degree to which bureaucracy is actually reduced, as greens would likely only embrace bureaucracy reduction as long as it does not come at the expense of a healthy layer of social protection. Either way, this coalition would likely produce a minimal EUBI that is primarily or purely funded through the savings the state makes from abolishing the bureaucratic structures linked to other welfare systems, such as the offices responsible for conducting needs-tests. Payments would take place in monetary form and comparatively rarely, in order to keep administrative costs low. Given that it is unlikely for social services and public goods to be easily replaceable through purely monetary means, this coalition might imply a net retrenchment of the welfare state—especially in the absence of a strong green party. The stronger economically anti-statist forces in this coalition would be, the more the idea of reducing bureaucracy might metastatise into shrinking the public sector in general. All things considered, this leads to three broad sub-scenarios for how this coalition would confront the introduction of EUBI: preventing additional bureaucracy while expanding the welfare state, reducing bureaucracy while keeping welfare-state generosity largely stable, and net welfare retrenchment.

Coalition for European Unity

While all the coalitions discussed so far could (partially) be mirrored at the national level, an EUBI would also include a crucial unique goal: to strengthen and further integrate the EU. One likely line of argument a coalition for European unity might pursue would revolve around the idea of a 'social Europe'. It might be hoped that an EUBI could give EU citizenship a tangible material dimension, making the EU more visible in Europeans' everyday lives, and reducing EU-wide inequalities, all the while providing the EU with an automatic stabiliser against crises.

Likely members of this coalition would be the greens, social democrats, liberals, and far left, albeit with the usual caveat that the far left and liberals would be highly unlikely to join such a coalition at the same time. Two ideologies, however, exhibit slightly complicated preferences here.

First, the far left has shown considerable Eurosceptic tendencies in recent decades—which somewhat undermines the idea that they would be interested in strengthening the EU. However, this Euroscepticism has often been rooted in rejecting the EU's focus on internal markets and its lack of a social dimension. In that context, an EUBI could be one concrete way for the far left to define their specific interpretation of a pro-European stance against the backdrop of a long history of internationalist and cosmopolitan preferences. The second ideology whose involvement in this coalition is harder to define is Christian democracy. Historically, Christian democrats have been at the forefront of pushing for greater European integration—as one half, opposite social democracy, of the 'right-left' bargain that gave rise to the first European Treaties after WW2. However, while in principle not averse to the EU, contemporary Christian democrats emphasise the idea of subsidiarity, here glossed as 'national autonomy', and on that basis have recently begun to explore ways of cooperating with decidedly anti-EU parties on the far right (Castaldi 2023). Generally, this policy profile would clash with the parties further to the left. Furthermore, it would undermine an EUBI's potential for EU integration, as it would likely make Christian democrats push vigorously towards national implementation. Social democrats and liberals might also struggle with the idea of delegating competences to the EU level, but this hesitancy is less strongly rooted in any of their core concepts than is the case for Christian democracy's relationship to subsidiarity. Thus, social democrats and liberals are, from a theoretical perspective, ultimately likelier to accept delegating competences in order to stabilise the EU.

The coalition for European unity would aim to shift as much concrete action as possible to the EU level—both as a political tool and as a goal in and of itself. As a political tool, the hope would be that a genuine EU-level social policy would be seen as more tangible if it comes directly 'from the EU' than taking a more indirect approach, thus strengthening the EU's social credibility. Procedurally, this would imply having to change the Treaties while requiring an overall strong mandate in order to achieve legitimacy across the EU. By implication, the coalition for European unity would have to rely on compromises in other areas. For instance, national welfare states could be left otherwise untouched, revenue sources could focus on the least controversial options, and the level of the EUBI itself could consequently be kept at a fairly moderate level. By implication, compromises between coalition members might partially undercut their ambitions regarding the adequacy of an EUBI. However, this might ultimately be an acceptable outcome for the actors involved, as *any* payment flowing directly from the EU to its citizens would give the EU a more tangible social face, irrespective of its exact amount. Viewed from this perspective, incrementalism regarding adequacy might be a price worth paying for fundamental institutional change in the eyes of the actors involved. Crucially, this argument only holds as long as this adequacy is sufficiently high to warrant increased support for the EU. If payments are so low that the public perceives them as purely symbolic, the scheme would lose its primary benefit.

EUBI COALITIONS IN PRACTICE

As we suggested at the start, the coalitions presented here are not intended as detailed blueprints for future governments, but rather as overarching illustrations of the theoretical options at stake. This is the sense in which they represent ideal-typical ways of thinking about the otherwise rather generic idea of an EUBI. This is important to note, not only because of the empirical hesitancy of European parties to embrace UBI in general, let alone an EUBI, but also because of the underlying theoretical nature of our approach. As we have engaged with ideologies from a theoretical perspective rather than with actually existing parties, we have treated matters in a simplified way, and cannot necessarily account for considerations that would be key in empirical political analyses. If an agenda coalition around an EUBI was imminently about to form in practice, the parties involved would not unitarily be representing the ideal-typical priorities expressed by their underlying ideologies. Rather, they would be pursuing complex, context-specific sets of internally diverse preferences. For instance, a party would be unlikely to exclusively prioritise poverty reduction, but might, for example, also simultaneously aim for a sizeable measure of redistribution and European integration. Thus, the potential and actual compromises between parties and their priorities would be much less starkly delimited in practice.

Consequently, it is likely that some elements of these five ideal-typical proposals would be dropped rather quickly or might not even be negotiated in the first place. These are optional mechanisms designed to maximise an EUBI's capacity to deliver on a single ideology's principles. For instance, non-monetary modalities like sustainability vouchers or extreme funding choices like collectivising the financial sector might be plausible ways of making an EUBI conform closely to the ideals of green or far left ideology respectively on paper. However, they are hardly suited to fostering compromise, even while they are also less crucial for these ideologies than other elements of the policy.

Generally, a healthy measure of caution is advisable when formulating specific policy expectations based on the considerations we have presented here. Within the dominant logic of the EU, the most feasible scenario for an EUBI to actually be implemented would be some form of lowest common denominator. Due to institutional hurdles like the Treaties and member states' veto rights in the Council of the EU, as well as (perceived) national interests, intra- and inter-partisan disagreements, and legitimacy issues, an EUBI has a series of major hurdles to overcome. By implication, the most realistic scenario whereby at least *some* of the ideas presented here might be translated into reality might be a Recommendation. The EU could ask member states to voluntarily implement nationally designed UBIs that are fully tied to the available funding based on uncontroversial choices around taxation and investment revenue. However, such a scheme would have limited impact, and would abandon most of the key elements of an actual EUBI.

Yet the potential and actual cleavages around an (E)UBI that underpin the challenges the policy faces in reality are also precisely the reason why political actors might want to engage with the policy idea in the first place. After all, parties of all ideological stripes have to confront the risk within UBI debates that schemes with little impact and policy designs that fundamentally contradict an ideology's basic priorities are the ones that are ultimately proposed and eventually implemented. Considering the salience of the idea of UBI in general (Laenen, Van Hootegem, and Rossetti 2023, 849; Parolin and Siöland 2020, 5), this risk is liable to increase rather than decrease in the future. Thus, it might be a strategically beneficial approach for parties to get started on developing their own concrete conceptualisations of an EUBI sooner rather than later, and to mobilise on their behalf in order to win the prerogative to interpret UBI in political discourse for the whole of society.

Chapter 9

Conclusion

We began this book by describing a dilemma for contemporary Europe: even as an increasingly global permacrisis is raising demands for swift, bold, and unified action, the current constellation of diversified electoral interests and atomised party systems make it exceedingly difficult to agree on meaningful reforms. This is particularly pressing in the realm of social policy. The COVID-19 pandemic and the war in Ukraine have triggered a new wave of unemployment and precarity, as well as enhanced health risks, and have caused millions of people to seek refuge wherever they can find it across Europe. Inflation rates have reached record highs, and extremist, often virulently Eurosceptic parties have won elections in an EU still shaken by the fallout of the Eurozone crisis, an unexpected increase in migration (especially across the EU's Mediterranean border), and Brexit.

These developments have undoubtedly fuelled demands for better social protection across Europe. In the past, global crises have often triggered substantial public policy reforms intended to address increasing demands for state intervention, such as the expansion of unemployment insurance schemes after WW1 and WW2 (Obinger and Schmitt 2020). However, such disruptive policy reforms are difficult, if not strictly impossible, to achieve in what have become increasingly common forms of eclectic multiparty coalition governments driven by the lowest common denominator.

To address this issue, we have argued in this book that parliamentary democracies may increasingly need to turn to policy-specific 'agenda coalitions'. Parties that agree on a specific policy but have disagreements in other areas that prevent them from forming a fully-fledged government coalition can temporarily join forces in parliament to push through a specific policy reform. Beyond such individual cases, more stable coalition governments could remain the norm. As far as the policy domain of 'social Europe' is concerned, we suggest that UBI would be one promising policy for such 'agenda coalitions', on the grounds that its support and opposition both cut across ideological lines.

In practice, however, such 'agenda coalitions' around UBI have yet to materialise. Instead, UBI is caught in a frankly puzzling tension between its public popularity and a persistent lack of representation at the institutional political tier. On the one hand, UBI has become a salient proposal to address multiple pressing issues such as poverty relief, effective redistribution, and strengthening the EU. On the other, the policy has been met with scepticism by politicians and parties and thus lacks a dedicated reserve of political support. UBI is often considered a threat to the *status quo* by liberals and conservatives, while at the same time it is dismissed as not radical enough by the ideologies of the left. The idea thus exists in an unusual limbo between intrigued curiosity and resolute aversion, between hope and fear, and between support and rejection within almost all the major political ideologies. Against this background, agenda coalitions over UBI likewise seem simultaneously just within reach and utterly unattainable.

Examining this situation through a theoretical lens, we have taken the view that conceptual ambiguity is a key driver of this political limbo in which the idea of UBI finds itself. When engaging with the idea, many supporters and opponents alike speak of UBI as if it were one coherent proposal—all the while using it to refer to a potentially dizzying array of fundamentally different things. This discourse over UBI obscures the crucial role that policy design plays for the likely outcomes of a UBI scheme. In this book, we have set ourselves against this tendency by taking the position that, for UBI as much as if not more than for any other social policy, the devil will be in the detail. UBI may take any number of different shapes, some of which would have diametrically opposing effects and implications. Different UBI designs could support competing political goals, eliminating some potential risks at the cost of inviting varying other respective drawbacks. Hence, as long as the discourse on UBI remains ambiguous concerning the question of policy design, the policy will retain its inherent tension between potential promise and potential pitfalls that makes it in equal parts politically attractive and politically risky.

In this context, we suggest that agenda coalitions around UBI could in practice be formed only if the parties involved make explicit what kind of UBI they would prefer if the policy were to be implemented. What exactly the empirical preferences of all of Europe's parties would be on this front lies well beyond the scope of realistic prediction. Instead, we have used theoretical ideal-types as proxies: building on granular conceptions of five political ideologies, we have illustrated how concretely different UBI policy designs could be adjusted to maximise different ideological goals.

Addressing and developing the idea of a progressive coalition over an EUBI, we looked at the idea of basic income and its multiple possible shapes based on the dimensions of universality, individuality, conditionality, uniformity, frequency, duration, modality, adequacy, fuzziness of policy design, funding, and ways of implementation. Conceptually, we have engaged with different UBI policy designs at the EU rather than the national or local level. The political ideologies we considered for different EUBI designs are those that fit under a broad parsing of the 'progressive' label: social democracy, green ideology, the ideologies of the far left, liberalism, and—residually—Christian democracy.

From the perspective of social democracy, the ideal-typical EUBI proposal would follow a middle-of-the-road design that covers the basic economic, social, and cultural needs of individual members of society, while also preserving national welfare states and the value of earning income through work. The ideal-typical green EUBI proposal, by contrast, would be less concerned with the role of labour and national welfare states, but would emphasise the importance of local communities and sustainability. From the perspective of the far left, state planning would remain the key approach, while the policy design would be strongly redistributive and lean towards more radical choices in terms of funding. Meanwhile, an ideal-typical liberal EUBI would reduce the prominence of the state and partly replace existing welfare arrangements, leaving as many decisions up to the individual as possible. Finally, the ideal-typical Christian-democratic EUBI proposal would be the least disruptive among all the policy designs, strengthening conservative welfare schemes but remaining committed to individual social stability.

While these ideal-typical policy designs offer EUBI supporters rather different starting points, they leave some room for compromise to achieve common political goals. We have discussed five proposals for potential agenda coalitions between different political ideologies, oriented towards different goals: for poverty relief, for political liberty, for redistribution, for bureaucracy reduction, and for European unity. For each coalition, we have assumed that the member parties or movements would prioritise a specific aspect of EUBI on which they can largely agree.

The EUBI coalition for poverty relief would have the central political goal of eradicating monetary poverty across the entire EU. This goal may resonate with all ideologies but would be most appealing to the far left, greens, and social democrats. Although this might well be a plausible political goal for all the potential coalition members, incompatible ideas around funding may prevent a coalition between the far left and liberals. Another potential hurdle to this coalition derives from the fact that some ideologies may prefer needs-tested schemes over an EUBI. However, this issue could be addressed via policy design, for instance through ensuring nonautomatic payouts for the rich.

Another option for a cross-partisan coalition over an EUBI could be built around the political goal of enhancing individual liberty. Considering again the potential conflict between liberals and the far left around funding, two potential policy designs might be pursued. One would have an emancipatory focus that could unite social democrats, greens, and the far left. By contrast, the other would have a more economically 'austere' focus that would primarily appeal to liberals as a potential replacement of the far left as a coalition partner for social democrats and greens. Going beyond the political goal of eradicating poverty, such a coalition would imply a policy design in which relatively high UBI payouts are independent of the level of income, wealth, previous decisions, or any other similar factors.

The third potential coalition we have discussed could develop around the political goal of redistributing financial means from the wealthier to the more disadvantaged classes. While this may be less appealing to the political agenda of Christian democrats and liberals, such a coalition may unite political actors located closer to the left end of the political spectrum, that is, greens, social democrats, and the far left. Embracing progressive tax mechanisms in areas such as high income, wealth, inheritance, land value, financial transactions, corporate gains, and luxury goods, this coalition would focus on the role of funding as the main mechanism through which redistribution may be achieved, rather than on social policy outputs alone.

Another political goal that may prompt the formation of a cross-party coalition over EUBI is the evergreen aim to reduce superfluous bureaucracy. Since UBI may take the form of automatic payments to all citizens without any additional paperwork, the policy could plausibly be among the least bureaucratic ways to add a palpable social layer to the EU. Such an EUBI would not necessarily aim to decrease existing national bureaucracy—although some elements of existing means-tested policies may lose their relevance after such a scheme has been implemented. Rather, the policy would aim to limit the accumulation of new bureaucratic apparatus at the EU level when constructing the structures and processes for a social Europe. Thus, this coalition would be most appealing to liberals, as well as to Christian democrats and greens.

Finally, common political goals may motivate different parties to form a coalition with the aim of stabilising the EU. While all potential members may be interested in strengthening the EU to varying degrees, forming such a coalition in practice would almost certainly encounter multiple challenges. First of all, again, the far left and liberals are unlikely to agree on the issue of funding. In addition, Christian democrats' emphasis on subsidiarity and their potential orientation towards national implementation may clash with the internationalist preferences—insofar as they are expressed—of parties further to the left.

THE WAY FORWARD FOR A EUROPEAN UBI

Agenda coalitions could prove crucial in future political debates when it comes to decontesting the idea of an EUBI—that is, winning the discursive prerogative to interpret what an EUBI actually means. Certainly, the actors involved can also simply choose not to engage with the idea of a UBI in the first place. However, a major risk to progressive democrats of ignoring UBI is that its salience might create the necessary space for the idea of basic income to be, in turn, decontested and leveraged by those who aim for goals that are antithetical and detrimental to progressive ideals. The ideal-typical policy designs we have proposed throughout this book illustrate this issue from different perspectives. For instance, a UBI forced through in the interests of dismantling the welfare state would be a real political danger for actors in favour of emancipatory redistribution. In more extreme forms, anti-democratic and nationalist actors might use the popular appeal of UBI to mobilise voters and subsequently erode EU institutions or the rule of law while appealing to protecting 'our basic income' against 'outside threats'. However, UBI is not just a risk for progressive democrats, as it also carries the potential to address new challenges and strengthen the foundations of a more 'social' settlement for Europe.

Our arguments should not be read as suggesting that there are currently cross-partisan *majorities* in favour of UBI, or that the coalitions we have presented here are set to materialise imminently. UBI remains a controversial proposal with multiple potential cleavages. Nonetheless, its potential to act as a complementary policy in addressing pressing social challenges at the EU level while appealing to various political ideologies creates the theoretical grounds for several possible cross-party coalitions. Our work is intended to illustrate how an EUBI could ideal-typically be designed to maximise specific aspects of its prodigious overall social potential—either from the perspective of single ideologies, or of shared cross-ideological goals. In this vein, our arguments matter for UBI debates in three closely intertwined ways: theory, policy, and politics.

From the theoretical angle, our work explores the complexities of UBI from various perspectives. It maps out the relationships between UBI and five political ideologies that share a number of broadly progressive characteristics. It also proposes one approach for how political theory—here concerning political ideologies—could be linked to policy research in a productive way. This link is all too often relegated to the sidelines of research, as political theorists and policy analysts focus on their own respective fields. By applying the analytical tool of ideal-types to popular policy ideas, political scientists and analysts can derive concrete policy designs from political theory, which can then serve as a basis for democratic processes to negotiate actual policies.

By implication, theory is closely linked to practice, both in the areas of policymaking and politics more generally. For the first of these, our findings can inform progressive stakeholders about how the abstract idea of UBI can be put into practice while avoiding some of its potential pitfalls. This is key in current policy debates, as UBI is often misleadingly discussed as if it were one coherent, fixed measure rather than an umbrella term that captures countless possible approaches. We do not mean to suggest that our policy designs are intended to function as finished blueprints. If they were to be pursued in practice, they would all need to be carefully adjusted to the respective political context. Further, we are not normatively claiming that any particular one of our proposals *should* be implemented ahead of any of the others. Rather, starting from the premise of an overarching positive disposition towards UBI in its outline form, this book is intended to provide a conceptual platform to help political actors with different preferences exposit and expand their own ideas of UBI. The practical policy dimension of our book is therefore meant to serve as a source of inspiration for all those interested in UBI from a progressive perspective.

Furthermore, if not more importantly, this book should act as a reminder to proponents and opponents of UBI alike that the validity of their respective arguments is almost always relative. It is largely contingent on the specific interplay between ideological perspectives and policy design. This 'relativity of arguments' around UBI is twofold. On the one hand, the normative desirability of UBI's potential effects hinges on the ideological preferences of the individual who happens to be judging the policy. On the other hand, the plausibility of whether or not these policy effects will actually materialise empirically depends largely on policy design. However, neither the normative desirability of specific effects, nor the associated decisions regarding policy design can be judged as 'right' or 'wrong' from any individual perspective in a straightforwardly generalisable way. UBI—and by implication an EUBI—is neither 'good' or 'bad' *per se*, nor is it universally a 'solution' or a 'problem'. Thus, while policy practice can be *informed* by theory, it can only legitimately be negotiated through democratic processes. Again, the dimensions of theory, policy, and politics are closely intertwined.

Finally, the dimension of politics builds directly on this 'relativity of arguments' in policymaking space. The more an EUBI policy design addresses the concerns of one ideology, the less attractive it might be to another. Yet this is an issue that is hardwired into democratic political space in general: the very existence of contrasting ideologies hinges in large part on their mutual differences and distinctions, and thus forms the basis for functional democratic competition. If this were not the case, contrasting political views within a *demos* could hardly be effectively represented in parliament. Thus, compromises and constructive policy discourses are vital for democracies to produce timely solutions without sacrificing the operations of proper democratic processes. Here, too, UBI is not fundamentally different from policies that have already been established, in the sense that it requires a healthy injection of political compromise. Given UBI's potential ability to address increased demand for a social *acquis* of the EU at a time of pressing challenges, diversified electorates, and partisan deadlocks, political parties might quickly find themselves in debates over how to best implement (elements of) an EUBI. As our overview of potential agenda coalitions has shown, the politics that would unfold in such a scenario do not necessarily need to produce deadlocks but could yield pragmatic policy designs centred around different goals. On that basis, our analysis has not only explored potential conflicts and agreements in the politics of UBI, but also fleshed out their meaning in the form of concrete EUBI proposals.

All of this culminates in a picture that fundamentally clashes with one of the most common ways in which UBI is perceived. Many consider UBI—often without much reflection—as an exceptional idea that captivates the masses due to its sheer simplicity. By contrast, our argument ultimately leads to a sobering conclusion: once put into practice, most people may find that UBI looks surprisingly boring and mundane. If it were to be implemented, UBI would be a technical, complex policy with countless dials that could—and would have to—be adjusted to match the preferences of almost any political ideology with (residual) progressive traits. In the concrete case of Europe, an EUBI could foster a proto-socialist utopia, act as a social-democratic tool to empower workers, offer a liberal way of providing unconditional freedom, introduce an ecological lever for making the green transition work, or insert a new avenue through which Christian democrats could stabilise the broader *status quo*. The salience of the idea of a UBI implies that all of these scenarios are simultaneously latent opportunities and risks for the different ideologies we discussed. Thus, if and when democratic coalitions become mobilised on behalf of a UBI, the scheme would most likely not deliver on all the ideal-typical preferences for any single ideology. Rather, if it ever materialises, UBI can be expected to be a radical bargain. Whether and how political parties decide to become proactive in European UBI debates remains to be seen. Either way, they will not only have to answer *if* they want to embrace UBI, but perhaps even more crucially: Which one?

Bibliography

Aerts, Elise, Ive Marx, and Gerlinde Verbist. 2023. *Not that Basic: How Level, Design and Context Matter for the Redistributive Outcomes of Universal Basic Income*. Bonn: IZA, Institute of Labor Economics.

Afscharian, Dominic. 2023. "Konstanz durch Wandel—Ein Grundeinkommen als Stabilisator der EU?" In *Grundeinkommen braucht Europa: Europa braucht Grundeinkommen*, edited by Otto Lüdemann, Bernhard Neumärker, and Ulrich Schachtschneider, 23–38. Münster: LIT Verlag.

Afscharian, Dominic, Cecilia Bruzelius, and Martin Seeleib-Kaiser. 2024. "Agency, Institutions, and Welfare Chauvinism: Tracing the Exclusion of EU Migrant Citizens from Social Assistance in Germany." *Journal of European Social Policy*.

Afscharian, Dominic, Viktoriia Muliavka, Marius Ostrowski, and Lukáš Siegel. 2021. *The European Basic Income—Delivering on Social Europe*. Brussels: Foundation for European Progressive Studies.

———. 2022a. "Into the Unknown: Empirical UBI Trials as Social Europe's Risk Insurance." *European Journal of Social Security* 24 (3): 257–75.

———. 2022b. "The State of the UBI Debate: Mapping the Arguments for and Against UBI." *Basic Income Studies* 17 (2): 213–37.

Afscharian, Dominic, and Marius Ostrowski. 2022. *Building Resilient Democracies—Challenges and Solutions Across the Globe*. Brussels: Foundation for European Progressive Studies.

Alexander, James. 2015. "The Major Ideologies of Liberalism, Socialism and Conservatism." *Political Studies* 63 (5): 980–94.

Allegri, Giuseppe, and Renato Foschi. 2020. "Universal Basic Income as a Promoter of Real Freedom in a Digital Future." *World Futures* 77 (1): 1–22.

Almond, Gabriel A. 1948. "The Political Ideas of Christian Democracy." *The Journal of Politics* 10 (4): 734–63.

Atkinson, Antony B. 2015. *Inequality: What Can Be Done?* Cambridge, MA: Harvard University Press.

Auel, Katrin, and Arthur Benz. 2005. "The Politics of Adaptation: The Europeanisation of National Parliamentary Systems." *The Journal of Legislative Studies* 11 (3–4): 372–93. doi: 10.1080/13572330500273570.

Avnon, Dan, and Avner de-Shalit. 1999. "Introduction." In *Liberalism and Its Practice*, edited by Dan Avnon and Avner de-Shalit, 1–13. London: Routledge.

Bandau, Frank. 2023. "Social Democracy." In *Elgar Encyclopedia of Political Sociology*, edited by Maria Grasso and Marco Guigni. Cheltenham: Edward Elgar.

Bartha, Dániel, Tamás Boros, Maria Freitas, Gergely Laki, and Meghan Stringer. 2020. *What Is the European Dream? Survey on European Dreams for the Future of Europe*. Brussels: FEPS and Policy Solutions.

Basic Income Earth Network. 2021. "About Basic Income." Accessed 27.10.2021, https://basicincome.org/about-basic-income/.

Bauböck, Rainer. 2009. "Global Justice, Freedom of Movement and Democratic Citizenship." *European Journal of Sociology* 50 (1): 1–31.

Baute, Sharon, and Bart Meuleman. 2020. "Public Attitudes Towards a European Minimum Income Benefit: How (Perceived) Welfare State Performance and Expectations Shape Popular Support." *Journal of European Social Policy* 30 (4): 404–20. doi: 10.1177/0958928720904320.

Belgium, Germany, France, Italy, Luxembourg, and Netherlands. 1957. *The Treaty of Rome*. Rome: European Economic Community.

Bellamy, Richard. 1993. "Liberalism." In *Contemporary Political Ideologies*, edited by John Eatwell, 23–49. New York: Routledge.

Berman, Sheri. 2002. "The Roots and Rationale of Social Democracy." *Social Philosophy and Policy* 20 (1): 113–44.

———. 2006. *The Primacy of Politics. Social Democracy and the Making of Europe's Twentieth Century*. New York: Cambridge University Press.

Bernstein, Eduard. 1922. *Der Sozialismus einst und jetzt: Streitfragen des Sozialismus in Vergangenheit und Gegenwart*. Berlin: J. H. W. Dietz.

Bick, Alexander, Nicola Fuchs-Schündeln, and David Lagakos. 2018. "How Do Hours Worked Vary with Income? Cross-Country Evidence and Implications." *American Economic Review* 108 (1): 170–99.

Birnbaum, Simon. 2010a. "Introduction: Basic Income, Sustainability and Post-Productivism." *Basic Income Studies* 4 (2). doi: 10.2202/1932-0183.1178.

———. 2010b. "Radical Liberalism, Rawls and the Welfare State: Justifying the Politics of Basic Income." *Critical Review of International Social and Political Philosophy* 13 (4): 495–516. doi: 10.1080/09692290.2010.517968.

Biskamp, Floris. 2019. "A Great Variety of Transformations—and Populisms." *Culture, Practice & Europeanization* 4 (1): 92–102.

Blaschke, Ronald, Adeline Otto, and Norbert Schepers, eds. 2010. *Grundeinkommen—Von der Idee zu einer europäischen politischen Bewegung*. Hamburg: VSA Verlag.

Boggs, Carl. 1986. "Review: The Green Alternative and the Struggle for a Post-Marxist Discourse." *Theory and Society* 15 (6): 869–99.

Boswell, Terry, and William J. Dixon. 1993. "Marx's Theory of Rebellion: A Cross-National Analysis of Class Exploitation, Economic Development, and Violent Revolt." *American Sociological Review* 58 (5): 681–702.

Brandal, Nik, Øivind Bratberg, and Dag Einar Thorsen. 2013. *The Nordic Model of Social Democracy*. London: Palgrave Macmillan.

Bregman, Rutger. 2016. *Utopia for Realists: The Case for a Universal Basic Income, Open Borders, and a 15-hour Workweek*. Amsterdam: The Correspondent.

Cabrera, Miguel A. 2023. "From Liberal Organicism to Social Citizenship." *Journal of Iberian and Latin American Studies* 29 (1): 5–19. doi: 10.1080/14701847.2023.2184010.

Callaghan, John. 2002. "Social Democracy and Globalisation: The Limits of Social Democracy in Historical Perspective." *The British Journal of Politics and International Relations* 4 (3): 429–51.

Cappelen, Alexander W., and Ole Frithjof Norheim. 2005. "Responsibility in Health Care: A Liberal Egalitarian Approach." *Journal of Medical Ethics* 31 (8): 476–80.

Carrel, Paul. 2017. "Merkel Tells Voters: 'Don't Experiment' With the Left." Accessed 19.11.2023, https://www.reuters.com/article/uk-germany-election-merkel/merkel-tells-voters-dont-experiment-with-the-left-idUKKCN1BH2PL/.

Carrese, Paul O. 2016. *Democracy in Moderation: Montesquieu, Tocqueville, and Sustainable Liberalism*. New York: Cambridge University Press.

Cassel-Piccot. 2013. "The Liberal Democrats and the Green Cause: From Yellow to Green." In *Environmental Issues in Political Discourse in Britain and Ireland*, edited by Gilles Leydier and Alexia Martin, 105–23. Newcastle upon Tyne: Cambridge Scholars Publishing.

Castaldi, Roberto. 2023. "EU Liberals Seek to Drag EPP Away From Meloni's 'Extreme Right'." Accessed 14.08.2023, https://www.euractiv.com/section/politics/news/eu-liberals-seek-to-drag-epp-away-from-melonis-extreme-right/.

CDU. 2020. *Unsere Haltung zu Linkspartei und AfD*. Berlin: CDU.

Charney, Evan. 2014. "Political Liberalism, Deliberative Democracy, and the Public Sphere." *American Political Science Review* 92 (1): 97–110.

Chase-Dunn, Christopher K. 1980. "Socialist States in the Capitalist World-Economy." *Social Problems* 27 (5): 505–25.

Chattopadhyay, Paresh. 2021. *Socialism in Marx's Capital: Towards a Dealienated World*. Cham: Palgrave Macmillan.

Chiapello, Eve. 2013. "Capitalism and Its Criticisms." In *New Spirits of Capitalism? Crises, Justifications, and Dynamics*, edited by Paul du Gay and Glenn Morgan, 60–81. Oxford: Oxford University Press.

Christman, John. 1991. "Liberalism and Individual Positive Freedom." *Ethics* 101 (2): 343–59.

Cieplinski, André, Simone D'Alessandro, Tiziano Distefano, and Pietro Guarnieri. 2021. "Coupling Environmental Transition and Social Prosperity: A Scenario-Analysis of the Italian Case." *Structural Change and Economic Dynamics* 57: 265–78.

Clemens, Clayton Marc. 2013. "Beyond Christian Democracy? Welfare State Politics and Policy in a Changing CDU." *German Politics* 22 (1–2): 191–211. doi: 10.1080/09644008.2013.787595.

Cockshott, Paul, Allin Cottrell, Pat Devine, and David Laibman. 2002. "The Relation between Economic and Political Instances in the Communist Mode of Production." *Science & Society* 66 (1): 50–71.

Condruz-Băcescu, Monica. 2014. "Euroscepticism Across Europe: Drivers and Challenges." *European Journal of Interdisciplinary Studies* 6 (2): 52–59.

Coote, Anna, and Edanur Yaziki. 2019. *Universal Basic Income—A Union Perspective*. Ferney-Voltaire: Public Services International.

Crouch, Colin. 2017. "Neoliberalism and Social Democracy." In *Alternatives to Neoliberalism—Towards Equality and Democracy*, edited by Bryn Jones and Mike O'Donnell, 195–208. Bristol: Policy Press.

Dahrendorf, Ralf. 1991. "Liberalism." In *The World of Economics*, edited by John Eatwell, Murray Milgate, and Peter Newman, 385–89. London: Palgrave Macmillan.

Dancygier, Rafaela, and Stefanie Walter. 2015. "Globalization, Labor Market Risks, and Class Cleavages." In *The Politics of Advanced Capitalism*, edited by Pablo Beramendi, Silja Häusermann, Herbert Kitschelt, and Hanspeter Kriesi, 133–56. Cambridge: Cambridge University Press.

de Cabanes, Antoine. 2017. *The Front National and the 2017 Electoral Cycle: Mixed Fortunes*. Brussels: transform! europe.

De Wispelaere, Jurgen, and Lindsay Stirton. 2004. "The Many Faces of Universal Basic Income." *The Political Quarterly* 75 (3): 266–74.

De Wispelaere, Jurgen, and Ruslan Yemtsov. 2019. "The Political Economy of Universal Basic Income." In *Exploring Universal Basic Income: A Guide to Navigating Concepts, Evidence, and Practices*, edited by Ugo Gentilini, Margaret Grosh, Jamele Rigolini, and Ruslan Yemtsov, 183–215. Washington, DC: World Bank Group.

Denuit, François. 2019. *Fighting Poverty in the European Union: An Assessment of the Prospects for a European Universal Basic Income (EUBI)*. Brussels: Université Libre de Bruxelles.

Dewey, John. 1935. "The Future of Liberalism." *The Journal of Philosophy* 32 (9): 225–30.

Dickens, Peter. 1992. *Society and Nature: Towards a Green Social Theory*. Philadelphia: Temple University Press.

Draper, Hal. 1987. *The 'Dictatorship of the Proletariat' from Marx to Lenin*. New York: Monthly Review Press.

Dullien, Sebastian. 2013. *A Euro-Area Wide Unemployment Insurance as an Automatic Stabilizer: Who Benefits and Who Pays?* Brussels: European Commission.

Ellis, Evelyn, and Philippa Watson. 2012. *Equality in Social Security*. Oxford: Oxford University Press.

Ellis, Nan S., and Cheryl M. Miller. 2000. "Welfare Waiting Periods: A Public Policy Analysis of Saenz v. Roe." *Stanford Law & Policy Review* 11 (2): 343–67.

Ellman, Michael. 2014. *Socialist Planning*. Cambridge: Cambridge University Press.

Engels, Friedrich. 2013 (1892–1893). *Über historischen Materialismus*. Berlin: Hofenberg.

EPP. 2009. *Strong for the People: EPP Election Document 2009*. Warsaw: European People's Party.

Esping-Andersen, Gøsta. 1990. *The Three Worlds of Welfare Capitalism*. Princeton, NJ: Princeton University Press.

European Greens. 2018. *Time to Renew the Promise of Europe*. Berlin: European Green Party.

European Parliament. 2014. *The Open Method of Coordination*. Brussels: European Parliament.

———. 2019. "2019 European Parliament Election Results." Accessed 05.03.2021, https://www.europarl.europa.eu/election-results-2019/en/european-results/2019-2024/.

European Union. 2022. "EU Motto." Accessed 28.11.2022, https://european-union.europa.eu/principles-countries-history/symbols/eu-motto_en.

Evans, Diana. 1994. "Policy and Pork: The Use of Pork Barrel Projects to Build Policy Coalitions in the House of Representatives." *American Journal of Political Science* 38 (4): 894. doi: 10.2307/2111726.

Evrard, Aurélien. 2012. "Political Parties and Policy Change: Explaining the Impact of French and German Greens on Energy Policy." *Journal of Comparative Policy Analysis: Research and Practice* 14 (4): 275–91. doi: 10.1080/13876988.2012.698582.

Fanning, Bryan. 2021. *Three Roads to the Welfare State: Liberalism, Social Democracy and Christian Democracy*. Bristol: Policy Press.

Festenstein, Matthew, and Michael Kenny. 2005. *Political Ideologies: A Reader and Guide*. Oxford: Oxford University Press.

Fitzpatrick, Tony. 2010. "Basic Income, Post-Productivism and Liberalism." *Basic Income Studies* 4 (2).

Flanigan, Jessica. 2017. "Rethinking Freedom of Contract." *Philosophical Studies* 174 (2): 443–63. doi: 10.1007/s11098-016-0691-6.

Fosse, Elisabeth. 2009. "Norwegian Public Health Policy: Revitalization of the Social Democratic Welfare State?" *International Journal of Health Services* 39 (2): 287–300.

Freeden, Michael. 1976. "Biological and Evolutionary Roots of the New Liberalism in England." *Political Theory* 4 (4): 471–90.

———. 1996. *Ideologies and Political Theory: A Conceptual Approach*. Oxford: Clarendon Press.

———. 2003. *Ideology: A Very Short Introduction*. Oxford: Oxford University Press.

Freeden, Michael, Lyman Tower Sargent, and Marc Stears, eds. 2013. *The Oxford Handbook of Political Ideologies*. Oxford: Oxford University Press.

Friedman, Milton. 1987. "Free Markets and Free Speech." *Harvard Journal of Law & Public Policy* 10 (1): 1–10.

Froese, Katrin. 2001. "Beyond Liberalism: The Moral Community of Rousseau's Social Contract." *Canadian Journal of Political Science* 34 (3): 579–600.

Gabor, Alexandru. 2012. "Christian Democracy and Welfare." *European Journal of Science and Theology* 8 (1): 313–20.

Galetti, Nino, Karsten Grabow, Manfred Agethen, Rudolf Uertz, Reinhard Willig, Matthias Schäfer, David Jonathan Grunwald, Christine Henry-Huthmacher, Tim Kallweit, Christopher Beckmann, Patrick Keller, Anna Wirtz, Helmut Reifeld, and Wolfgang Stock. 2011. *Christian Democracy: Principles and Policy-Making*. Berlin: Konrad-Adenauer-Stiftung.

Gaus, Gerald F. 1994. "Property, Rights, and Freedom." *Social Philosophy and Policy* 11 (2): 209–40. doi: 10.1017/s0265052500004490.

Geoghegan, Vincent. 2014. "Socialism." In *Political Ideologies: An Introduction*, edited by Vincent Geoghegan and Rick Wilford, 71–98. London: Routledge.

Gerhards, Jürgen, Holger Lengfeld, Zsófia S. Ignácz, Florian K. Kley, and Maximilian Priem. 2020. *European Solidarity in Times of Crisis: Insights from a Thirteen-Country Survey, Routledge Advances in Sociology*. London: Routledge.

Giugliano, Ferdinando. 2019. "Italy Starts Handing Out Free Money." Accessed 25.11.2023, https://www.bloomberg.com/view/articles/2019-01-28/italy-s-populists-hand-out-some-free-money#xj4y7vzkg.

Giulietti, Corrado. 2014. *The Welfare Magnet Hypothesis and the Welfare Take-up of Migrants: Welfare Benefits are not a Key Determinant of Migration*. Bonn: IZA.

Goodhart, Michael. 2008. "A Democratic Defense of Universal Basic Income." In *Illusion of Consent: Engaging with Carole Pateman*, edited by Daniel I. O'Neill, Mary Lyndon Shanley, and Iris Marion Young, 139–64. Pennsylvania: Penn State University Press.

Gottfried, Paul. 2007. "The Rise and Fall of Christian Democracy in Europe." *Orbis* 51 (4): 711–23.

Graeber, David. 2018. *Bullshit Jobs: A Theory*. New York: Simon & Schuster.

Gray, Phillip W. 2019. *Vanguardism: Ideology and Organization in Totalitarian Politics*. New York: Routledge.

Greenberg, Udi. 2015. "The Origins of Christian Democracy: Politics and Confession in Modern Germany." *Politics, Religion & Ideology* 16 (2–3): 326–29. doi: 10.1080/21567689.2015.1081468.

Greenwell, Megan. 2022. "Universal Basic Income Has Been Tested Repeatedly. It Works. Will America Ever Embrace It?" Accessed 08.08.2023, https://www.washingtonpost.com/magazine/2022/10/24/universal-basic-income/.

Gunder, Michael. 2020. "Visionary Idealism in Environmental Planning." In *The Routledge Companion to Environmental Planning*, edited by Simin Davoudi, Richard Cowell, Iain White, and Hilda Blanco, 43–51. London: Routledge.

Haagh, Louise. 2011. "Basic Income, Social Democracy and Control Over Time." *Policy & Politics* 39 (1): 43–66.

Hall, Peter. 1993. "Policy Paradigms, Social Learning, and the State: The Case of Economic Policymaking in Britain." *Comparative Politics* 25 (3): 275–96.

Hamilton, Leah, and Stacia Martin-West. 2019. "Universal Basic Income, Poverty, and Social Justice: A Moral and Economic Imperative for Social Workers." *Social Work* 64 (4): 321–28. doi: 10.1093/sw/swz028.

Hanley, David. 1994. "The European People's Party: Towards a New Party Form?" In *Christian Democracy in Europe: A Comparative Perspective,* edited by David Hanley, 185–201. London: Pinter.

Hardin, Russell. 1999. *Liberalism, Constitutionalism, and Democracy*. Oxford: Oxford University Press.

Hay, Colin. 1999. "Marxism and the State." In *Marxism and Social Science*, edited by Andrew Gamble, David Marsh, and Tony Tant, 152–74. London: Red Globe Press.

Healy, Kieran. 2017. "Fuck Nuance." *Sociological Theory* 35 (2): 118–27.

Helbling, Marc, and Céline Teney. 2015. "The Cosmopolitan Elite in Germany: Transnationalism and Postmaterialism." *Global Networks* 15 (4): 446–68. doi: 10.1111/glob.12073.

Held, David. 2002. "Culture and Political Community: National. Global and Cosmopolitan." In *Conceiving Cosmopolitanism: Theory, Context and Practice,* edited by Steven Vertovec and Robin Cohen. Oxford: Oxfird University Press.

Heller, Agnes, and Ferenc Fehér. 1991. *The Grandeur and Twilight of Radical Universalism*. London: Transaction.

Henderson, Troy, and John Quiggin. 2019. "Trade Unions and Basic Income." In *The Palgrave International Handbook of Basic Income*, edited by Malcolm Torry, 493–505. London: Palgrave Macmillan.

Heywood, Andrew. 2021. *Political Ideologies: An Introduction*. London: Red Globe Press.

Hobhouse, Leonard Trelawney. 1911. *Liberalism*. London: Williams and Norgate.

Hodgson, Ann, and Ken Spours. 2016. "The Evolution of Social Ecosystem Thinking: Its Relevance for Education, Economic Development and Localities." A Stimulus Paper for the Ecosystem Seminar, June 22, 2016. Organised by the Centre for Post-14 Education and Work, UCL Institute of Education London: UCL Institute of Education.

Imlay, Talbot C. 2018. *The Practice of Socialist Internationalism: European Socialist and International Politics, 1914–1960*. Oxford: Oxford University Press.

in't Veld, Jan, Martin Larch, and Marieke Vandeweyer. 2012. Automatic Fiscal Stabilisers: What They Are and What They Do. In *European Economy: Economic Papers*. Brussels: European Commission.

Inazu, John D. 2012. *Liberty's Refuge: The Forgotten Freedom of Assembly*. New Haven: Yale University Press.

Inglehart, Ronald F. 1977. *The Silent Revolution: Changing Values and Political Styles among Western Publics*. Princeton, NJ: Princeton University Press.

———. 1990. *Culture Shift in Advanced Industrial Society*. Princeton, NJ: Princeton University Press.

———. 2018. *Cultural Evolution: People's Motivations are Changing, and Reshaping the World*. Cambridge: Cambridge University Press.

Invernizzi Accetti, Carlo. 2019. *What is Christian Democracy? Politics, Religion and Ideology*. Cambridge: Cambridge University Press.

Jackson, Ben. 2013. "Social Democracy." In *The Oxford Handbook of Political Ideologies*, edited by Michael Freeden, Lyman Tower Sargent, and Marc Stears, 348–63. Oxford: Oxford University Press.

Joerges, Christian, and Florian Rödl. 2004. "'Social Market Economy' as Europe's Social Model?" In *A European Social Citizenship? Preconditions for Future Policies from a Historical Perspective*, edited by Lars Magnusson and Bo Stråth, 125–58. Brussels: P.I.E.-Peter Lang.

Joseph Rowntree Foundation. 2021. "Is Universal Basic Income a Good Idea?" Accessed 08.08.2023, https://www.jrf.org.uk/report/universal-basic-income-good-idea.

Jud, Stefano, and Dan Reiter. 2023. "Populism, Party Ideology, and Economic Expropriations." *International Interactions* Online: 1–31. doi: 10.1080/03050629.2023.2264464.

Kaarsholm, Preben. 2020. "Marx, Globalisation and the Reserve Army of Labour." In *What's Left of Marxism: Historiography and the Possibilities of Thinking with Marxian Themes and Concepts*, edited by Benjamin Zachariah, Lutz Raphael, and Brigitta Bernet, 309–22. Oldenbourg: De Gruyter.

Kahan, Alan S. 2003. *Liberalism in Nineteenth Century Europe: The Political Culture of Limited Suffrage*. London: Palgrave Macmillan.

Kalyvas, Stathis N. 1999. "The Decay and Breakdown of Communist One-Party Systems." *Annual Review of Political Science* 2: 323–43.

Kalyvas, Stathis N., and Kees van Kersbergen. 2010. "Christian Democracy." *Annual Review of Political Science* 13: 183–209.

Kaminski, Bartlomiej. 1996. "The Legacy of Communism." In *East-Central European Economies in Transition*, edited by John P. Hardt and Richard F. Kaufman. New York: Routledge.

Kastning, Thomas. 2013. *Basics on Social Democracy*. Accra: Friedrich-Ebert-Stiftung.

Kautz, Steven. 1993. "Liberalism and the Idea of Toleration." *American Journal of Political Science* 37 (2): 610–32.

Kearney, Melissa, and Magne Mogstad. 2019. "The Math is Clear: Universal Basic Income is a Terrible Idea." Business Insider. Accessed 11.12.2020, https://www.businessinsider.de/international/yang-warren-universal-basic-income-idea-bad-2019-11/?r=US&IR=T.

Kelly, John. 1999. "Social Democracy and Anti-Communism: Allan Flanders and British Industrial Relations in the Early Post-War Period." In *British Trade Unions and Industrial Politics: The High Tide of Trade Unionism, 1964–79*, edited by John McIlroy, Nina Fishman, and Alan Campbell, 192–221. London: Routledge.

Keman, Hans. 2010. "Third Ways and Social Democracy: The Right Way to Go?" *British Journal of Political Science* 41 (3): 671–80.

Kenworthy, Lane. 2019. *Social Democratic Capitalism*. Oxford: Oxford University Press.

Kitschelt, Herbert. 2010. *The Transformation of European Social Democracy*. Cambridge: Cambridge University Press.

Kleingeld, Pauline. 1997. "Kants politischer Kosmopolitismus." *Jahrbuch für Recht und Ethik* 5: 333–48.

Klitgaard, Michael Baggesen. 2007. "Why Are They Doing It? Social Democracy and Market-Oriented Welfare State Reforms." *West European Politics* 30 (1): 172–94. doi: 10.1080/01402380601019753.

Korpi, Walter. 2008. "Origins of Welfare States: Changing Class Structures, Social Democracy, and Christian Democracy." RC19, Stockholm.

Kraynak, Robert. 2004. "The Illusion of Christian Democracy." *Catholic Social Science Review* 9: 87–95. doi: 10.5840/cssr2004912.

Kriesi, Hanspeter, Edgar Grande, Romain Lachat, Martin Dolezal, Simon Bornschier, and Timotheos Frey. 2008. *West European Politics in the Age of Globalization*. Cambridge: Cambridge University Press.

Kuhn, Theresa, Hector Solaz, and Erika J. van Elsas. 2018. "Practising What You Preach: How Cosmopolitanism Promotes Willingness to Redistribute Across the European Union." *Journal of European Public Policy* 25 (12): 1759–778.

Kuisma, Mikko. 2007. "Social Democratic Internationalism and the Welfare State After the 'Golden Age'." *Cooperation and Conflict* 42 (1): 9–26.

Kuivalainen, Susan, and Kenneth Nelson. 2010. *The Nordic Welfare Model in a European Perspective*. Stockholm: Institute for Futures Studies.

Kurasawa, Fuyuki. 2011. "Cosmopolitanism's Theoretical and Substantive Dimensions." In *Routledge International Handbook of Contemporary Social and Political Theory*, edited by Gerard Delanty and Stephen P. Turner, 301–11. New York: Routledge.

Kymlicka, Will. 1989. *Liberalism, Community, and Culture*. Oxford: Clarendon Press.

Lacewell, Onawa Promise, and Wolfgang Merkel. 2013. "Value Shifts in European Societies: Clashes Between Cosmopolitanism and Communitarianism." In *Progressive Politics After the Crash: Governing from the Left*, edited by Olaf Cramme, Patrick Diamond, and Michael McTernan, 77–95. London: I. B. Tauris.

Laenen, Tijs. 2023. *The Popularity of Basic Income: Evidence from the Polls*. Cham: Palgrave Macmillan.

Laenen, Tijs, Arno Van Hootegem, and Federica Rossetti. 2023. "The Multidimensionality of Public Support for Basic Income: A Vignette Experiment in Belgium." *Journal of European Public Policy* 30 (5): 849–72. doi: 10.1080/13501763.2022.2055112.

Langlois, Anthony J. 2007. "Human Rights and Cosmopolitan Liberalism." *Critical Review of International Social and Political Philosophy* 10 (1): 29–45. doi: 10.1080/13698230601122396.

Langridge, Nicholas, Milena Buchs, and Neil Howard. 2023. "An Ecological Basic Income? Examining the Ecological Credentials of Basic Income Through a Review of Selected Pilot Interventions." *Basic Income Studies* 18 (1): 47–87. doi: 10.1515/bis-2021-0044.

Lawhon, Mary, and Tyler McCreary. 2020. "Beyond Jobs vs Environment: On the Potential of Universal Basic Income to Reconfigure Environmental Politics." *Antipode* 52 (2): 452–74. doi: 10.1111/anti.12604.

Lombardi, Michele, Kaname Miyagishima, and Roberto Veneziani. 2016. "Liberal Egalitarianism and the Harm Principle." *The Economic Journal* 126 (597): 2173–196. doi: 10.1111/ecoj.12298.

Lombardozzi, Lorena, and Frederick Harry Pitts. 2020. "Social Form, Social Reproduction and Social Policy: Basic Income, Basic Services, Basic Infrastructure." *Capital & Class* 44 (4): 573–94. doi: 10.1177/0309816819873323.

Lu, Catherine. 2000. "The One and Many Faces of Cosmopolitanism." *Journal of Political Philosophy* 8 (2): 244–67. doi: 10.1111/1467-9760.00101.

Lubarda, Balsa. 2020. "'Homeland Farming' or 'Rural Emancipation'? The Discursive Overlap Between Populist and Green Parties in Hungary." *Sociologia Ruralis* 60 (4): 810–32. doi: 10.1111/soru.12289.

Luterman, Sara. 2019. "Andrew Yang Wants to Sell You Universal Basic Income. Beware if You Have Disabilities." Vox. Accessed 27.09.2023, https://www.vox.com/first-person/2019/12/19/21026925/andrew-yang-disability-policy.

Lyman, Eric J. 2019. "Andrew Yang's Universal Basic Income Plan Has Already Gotten a Test Run—In Italy." Accessed 25.11.2023, https://fortune.com/2019/09/22/andrew-yang-universal-basic-income-italy-ubi/.

MacMillan, John. 2007. "Liberal Internationalism." In *International Relations Theory for the Twenty-First Century: An Introduction*, edited by Martin Griffiths. London: Routledge.

Mahoney, Jon. 2008. "Liberalism and the Moral Basis for Human Rights." *Law and Philosophy* 27 (2): 151–91.

March, Luke. 2009. "Contemporary Far Left Parties in Europe: From Marxism to the Mainstream?" *Internationale Politik und Gesellschaft* (1): 126–43.

Marks, Gary, and Carole J. Wilson. 2000. "The Past in the Present: A Cleavage Theory of Party Response to European Integration." *British Journal of Political Science* 30 (3): 433–59. doi: 10.1017/s0007123400000181.

Marshall, Thomas Humphrey. 1950. *Citizenship and Social Class. And Other Essays.* Cambridge: Cambridge University Press.

Martinsen, Dorte Sindbjerg, and Benjamin Werner. 2019. "No Welfare Magnets—Free Movement and Cross-Border Welfare in Germany and Denmark Compared." *Journal of European Public Policy* 26 (5): 637–55. doi: 10.1080/13501763.2018.1481136.

Marx, Karl. 2019 (1932). *Ökonomisch-philosophische Manuskripte aus dem Jahre 1844*. Berlin: Henricus.

Marx, Karl, and Friedrich Engels. 1978 (1845–1846). *Werke, Band 3*. Berlin: Dietz Verlag.

Mathers, Alex. 2020. "Universal Basic Income and Cognitive Capitalism: A Post-Work Dystopia in the Making?" *Capital & Class* 44 (3): 325–43.

Mays, Jenni. 2019. "Social Effects of Basic Income." In *The Palgrave International Handbook of Basic Income*, edited by Malcolm Torry, 73–90. Cham: Palgrave Macmillan.

McManus, Matthew. 2020. *A Critical Legal Examination of Liberalism and Liberal Rights*. Cham: Palgrave Macmillan.

Mehrer, Hannes, ed. 2021. *European Green Perspectives on Basic Income*. Brussels: Green European Foundation.

Merkel, Wolfgang, Christoph Egle, Christian Henkes, Tobias Ostheim, and Alexander Petring. 2006. *Die Reformfähigkeit der Sozialdemokratie: Herausforderungen und Bilanz der Regierungspolitik in Westeuropa*. Wiesbaden: VS Verlag für Sozialwissenschaften.

Merkel, Wolfgang, and Alexander Petring. 2007. "Social Democracy in Power: Explaining the Capacity to Reform." *Zeitschrift für vergleichende Politikwissenschaft* (1): 125–45.

Meyer, Henning. 2012. "The Challenge of European Social Democracy: Communitarianism and Cosmopolitanism United." In *The Future of European Social Democracy*, edited by Henning Meyer and Jonathan Rutherford, 152–65. London: Palgrave Macmillan.

Meyer, Max. 2020. *Liberal Democracy: Prosperity through Freedom*. Cham: Springer International Publishing.

Meyer, Thomas, and Lewis Hinchman. 2007. *The Theory of Social Democracy.* New York: John Wiley & Sons.

Midões, Catarina. 2019. "Universal Basic Income and the Finnish Experiment." Bruegel. Accessed 08.12.2020, https://www.bruegel.org/2019/02/universal-basic-income-and-the-finnish-experiment/?utm_content=buffer2a243&utm_medium=social&utm_source=twitter.com&utm_campaign=buffer+(bruegel).

Milbradt, Georg. 2016. "History of the Constitutional Debt Limits in Germany and the New 'Debt Brake': Experiences and Critique." In *Multi-Level Finance and the Euro Crisis: Causes and Effects*, edited by Ehtisham Ahmad, Massimo Bordignon, and Giorgio Brosio, 66–82. Cheltenham: Edward Elgar.

Milevska, Tanja. 2014. "EU 'Has the Power' to Put in Place a Universal Basic Income." Accessed 24.09.2020, https://www.euractiv.com/section/social-europe-jobs/news/eu-has-the-power-to-put-in-place-a-universal-basic-income/.

Miller, David. 2013. *Justice for Earthlings: Essays in Political Philosophy*. Cambridge: Cambridge University Press.

Millward, Peter, and Shaminder Takhar. 2019. "Social Movements, Collective Action and Activism." *Sociology* 53 (3).

Mintrom, Michael, and Sandra Vergari. 1996. "Advocacy Coalitions, Policy Entrepreneurs, and Policy Change." *Policy Studies Journal* 24 (3): 420–34.

Obinger, Herbert, and Carina Schmitt. 2019. "Total War and the Emergence of Unemployment Insurance in Western Countries." *Journal of European Public Policy* 27 (12): 1879–901.

Ostrowski, Marius S. 2020. *Left Unity: Manifesto for a Progressive Alliance*. London: Rowman & Littlefield International.

———. 2021. "How (not) to form a progressive alliance: Lessons from the history of left cooperation." *Political Quarterly* 92(1): 23–31.

———. 2022a. *Ideology*. Cambridge: Polity Press.

———. 2022b. "Forward-Looking: Building a Better World One Step at a Time." In *Enduring Values: How Progressives Across Europe Can Win*, edited by Kate Murray and Ania Skrzypek, 76–81. Brussels/London: Foundation of European Progressive Studies/Fabian Society.

———. 2023a. "The Ideological Morphology of Left–Centre–Right." *Journal of Political Ideologies* 28(1): 1–15.

———. 2023b. "Europeanism: A Historical View." *Contemporary European History* 32(2): 287–304.

———. 2024. "Ideology and the Individual." *Journal of Political Ideologies* 29(1): 1–25.

Oudenampsen, Merijn. 2022. "Neoliberal Sermons: European Christian Democracy and Neoliberal Governmentality." *Economy and Society* 51 (2): 330–52. doi: 10.1080/03085147.2022.1987743.

Pabst, Adrian. 2013. "Liberalism." In *Handbook on the Economics of Reciprocity and Social Enterprise*, edited by Luigino Bruni and Stefano Zamagni, 217–26. London: Edward Elgar.

Paine, Thomas. 1877 (1794). *The Age of Reason; Being an Investigation of True and Fabulous Theology*. New York: D. M. Bennett.

Palmer, Bryan D. 2021. *James P. Cannon and the Emergence of Trotskyism in the United States, 1928–38*. Leiden: Brill.

Parolin, Zachary, and Linus Siöland. 2020. "Support for a Universal Basic Income: A Demand-Capacity Paradox?" *Journal of European Social Policy* 30 (1): 5–19. doi: 10.1177/0958928719886525.

Paster, Thomas. 2008. "The Renewability of Social Democracy." *European Political Science* 7 (4): 507–12.

Pateman, Carole. 2004. "Democratizing Citizenship: Some Advantages of a Basic Income." *Politics & Society* 32 (1): 89–105.

Pearson, Mitya, and Wolfgang Rüdig. 2020. "The Greens in the 2019 European Elections." *Environmental Politics* 29 (2): 336–43.

Pepper, David. 1993. *Eco-Socialism: From Deep Ecology to Social Justice*. London: Routledge.

PES. 2019. A New Social Contract for Europe—PES Manifesto 2019. Madrid: Party of European Socialists.

Piketty, Thomas. 2014. *Capital in the Twenty-First Century*. Harvard: Harvard University Press.

———. 2020. *Capital and Ideology*. Cambridge: MA: Belknap Press.

Pitts, Frederick Harry, Lorena Lombardozzi, and Neil Warner. 2017. *Beyond Basic Income: Overcoming the Crisis of Social Democracy?* Brussels: Foundation for European Progressive Studies.

Pombeni, Paolo. 2013. "Christian Democracy." In *The Oxford Handbook of Political Ideologies*, edited by Michael Freeden and Marc Stears, 312–28. Oxford: Oxford University Press.

Prandini, Riccardo. 2018. "Themed Section: The Person-Centred Turn in Welfare Policies: Bad Wine in New Bottles or a True Social Innovation?" *International Review of Sociology* 28 (1): 1–19. doi: 10.1080/03906701.2017.1422888.

Przeworski, Adam. 1985. *Capitalism and Social Democracy*. Paris: Cambridge University Press.

Rawls, John. 1971. *A Theory of Justice*. Cambridge: Harvard University Press.

Raworth, Kate. 2017. *Doughnut Economics: Seven Ways to Think Like a 21st Century Economist*. White River Junction: Chelsea Green Publishing.

Read, Jason. 2022. *The Production of Subjectivity: Marx and Philosophy*. Leiden: Brill.

Reid-Henry, Simon. 2013. "Humanitarianism as Liberal Diagnostic: Humanitarian Reason and the Political Rationalities of the Liberal Will-To-Care." *Transactions of the Institute of British Geographers* 39 (3): 418–31. doi: 10.1111/tran.12029.

Rhodes, Martin. 2013. "Labour Markets, Welfare States and the Dilemmas of European Social Democracy." In *The Crisis of Social Democracy in Europe*, edited by Michael Keating and David McCrone, 140–55. Edinburgh: Edinburgh University Press.

Roosma, Femke, and Wim Van Oorschot. 2020. "Public Opinion on Basic Income: Mapping European Support for a Radical Alternative for Welfare Provision." *Journal of European Social Policy* 30 (2): 190–205. doi: 10.1177/0958928719882827.

Ryan, Alan. 2017. "Liberalism." In *A Companion to Contemporary Political Philosophy*, edited by Robert E. Goodin, Philip Pettit, and Thomas W. Pogge, 360–82. Hoboken: Blackwell Publishing.

Sargeant, Jack, Luke Fletcher, Joel James, and Buffy Williams. 2022. *A UBI Pilot for Wales*. Swansea: Petitions Committee of the Welsh Parliament.

Sayers, Sean. 2011. *Marx and Alienation: Essays on Hegelian Themes*. London: Palgrave Macmillan.

Schmidt, James. 1999. "Liberalism and Enlightenment in Eighteenth-Century Germany." *Critical Review: A Journal of Politics and Society* 13 (1–2): 31–53.

Schmidt, Manfred G. 2016. "Richard Rose, Do Parties Make a Difference?" In *The Oxford Handbook of Classics in Public Policy and Administration*, edited by Martin Lodge, Edward C. Page, and Steven J. Balla, 405–16. Oxford: Oxford University Press.

Schmidt, Susanne K. 2019. "Ein Kampf der Staatsgewalten? Die schwierige soziale Absicherung des europäischen Freizügigkeitsregimes." *Zeitschrift für Sozialreform* 65 (1): 29–57. doi: 10.1515/zsr-2019-0002.

Schmitt, Étienne. 2021. "Socialism. Two Centuries of Social Progress." In *Political Ideologies and Worldviews: An Introduction*, edited by Valérie Vézina, 73–92. Online: KPU Open Education.

Selinger, William. 2019. *Parliamentarism: From Burke to Weber*. Cambridge Cambridge University Press.

Sharlamanov, Kire. 2023. *The Left Libertarianism of the Greens*. Cham: Palgrave Macmillan.

Singer, Peter. 1999. *A Darwinian Left: Politics, Evolution and Cooperation*. New Haven: Yale University Press.

Skevik Grødem, Anne. 2014. "A Review of Family Demographics and Family Policies in the Nordic Countries." *Baltic Journal of Political Science* (3): 50–66.

Smith, Nicholas H. 2021. "Basic Income, Social Freedom and the Fabric of Justice." *Critical Review of International Social and Political Philosophy* 24 (6): 845–65.

Spath, Nathalie Julia. 2016. *Automatic Stabilizers for the Euro Area: What Is on the Table? Promises and Problems of Three Proposals for Cyclical Stabilization*. Berlin: Jacques Delors Institut.

Stavrakakis, Yannis. 1997. "Green Ideology: A Discursive Reading." *Journal of Political Ideologies* 2 (3): 259–79.

Straubhaar, Thomas. 2017. "On the Economics of a Universal Basic Income." *Intereconomics* 52 (2): 74–80.

———. 2018. *Universal Basic Income: New Answer to New Questions for the German Welfare State in the 21st Century*. Munich: ifo Institut.

Strengmann-Kuhn, Wolfgang. 2023. "Ein Europäisches Basis-Kindergeld gegen Kinderarmut und für mehr sozialen Zusammenhalt in der Europäischen Union." In *Grundeinkommen braucht Europa, Europa braucht Grundeinkommen*, edited by Otto Lüddemann and Ulrich Schachtschneider. Münster: LIT Verlag.

Strom, Kaare. 1990. "A Behavioral Theory of Competitive Political Parties." *American Journal of Political Science* 34 (2): 565–98.

Swank, Duane. 1998. "Funding the Welfare State: Globalization and the Taxation of Business in Advanced Market Economies." *Political Studies* 46 (4): 671–92.

Talshir, Gayil. 2002. *The Political Ideology of Green Parties: From the Politics of Nature to Redefining the Nature of Politics*. London: Palgrave Macmillan.

Thorsen, Dag Einar. 2021. "Introduction: Social Democracy in the 21st Century." In *Social Democracy in the 21st Century*, edited by Nik Brandal, Øivind Bratberg, and Dag Einar Thorsen, 1–14. Bingley: Emerald Publishing Limited.

Thorwarth, Katja. 2022. "Lindner gegen Neuberechnung der Grundsicherung: 'Reine Erhöhung nicht fair.'" Accessed 07.08.2023, https://www.fr.de/politik/hartz-4-buergergeld-fdp-christian-lindner-neuberechnung-buergergeld-sanktionen-heil-spd-91682635.html.

Tilton, Tim. 1991. *The Political Theory of Swedish Social Democracy: Through the Welfare State to Socialism*. Oxford: Clarendon Press.

Torgerson, Douglas. 2008. "Constituting Green Democracy: A Political Project." *The Good Society* 17 (2): 18–24.

Tucker, David F. B. 1994. *Essays on Liberalism*. Dordrecht: Springer.

Van Gerven, Minna, and Marinus Ossewaarde. 2012. "The Welfare State's Making of Cosmopolitan Europe." *European Societies* 14 (1): 35–55. doi: 10.1080/14616696.2011.624188.

van Kersbergen, Kees. 1994. "The Distinctiveness of Christian Democracy." In *Christian Democracy in Europe: A Comparative Perspective*, edited by David Hanley, 31–50. London: Pinter.

van Kersbergen, Kees, and Barbara Vis. 2015. "Three Worlds' Typology: Moving Beyond Normal Science?" *Journal of European Social Policy* 25 (1): 111–23.

van Oorschot, Wim. 2000. "Who Should Get What, and Why? On Deservingness Criteria and the Conditionality of Solidarity among the Public." *Policy and Politics: Studies of Local Government and its Services* 28 (1): 33–48.

———. 2006. "Making the Difference in Social Europe: Deservingness Perceptions among Citizens of European Welfare States." *Journal of European Social Policy* 16 (1): 23–42. doi: 10.1177/0958928706059829.

Van Parijs, Philippe. 2004. "Basic Income: A Simple and Powerful Idea for the Twenty-First Century." *Politics & Society* 32 (1): 7–39.

———. 2016. "Basic Income and Social Democracy." Accessed 07.08.2023, https://www.socialeurope.eu/44878.

Van Parijs, Philippe, and Yannick Vanderborght. 2015. "Basic Income in a Globalized Economy." In *Inclusive Growth, Development and Welfare Policy: A Critical Assessment*, edited by Reza Hasmath, 241–60. New York: Routledge.

———. 2017. *Basic Income: A Radical Proposal for a Free Society and a Sane Economy*. Cambridge, MA: Harvard University Press.

Vandenbroucke, Frank. 2015. "The Case for a European Social Union: From Muddling through to a Sense of Common Purpose." In *The Future of Welfare in a Global Europe*, edited by Bernd Marin, 489–520. London: Routledge.

Vanderborght, Yannick. 2006. "Why Trade Unions Oppose Basic Income." *Basic Income Studies* 1 (1). doi: 10.2202/1932-0183.1002.

Vertovec, Steven, and Robin Cohen. 2002. "Introduction: Conceiving Cosmopolitanism." In *Conceiving Cosmopolitanism: Theory, Context and Practice*, edited by Steven Vertovec and Robin Cohen, 1–22. Oxford: Oxford University Press.

von Beyme, Klaus. 1985. *Political Parties in Western Democracies*. New York: St Martin's Press.

———. 2014. "A Comparative View of Democratic Centralism." *Government and Opposition* 10 (3): 259–77.

Wagner, Peter, and Bénédicte Zimmermann. 2004. "Citizenship and Collective Responsibility—On the Political Philosophy of the Nation-Based Welfare State and Beyond." In *A European Social Citizenship? Preconditions for Future Policies from a Historical Perspective*, edited by Lars Magnusson and Bo Stråth. Brussels: P.I.E.-Peter Lang.

Walker, Ignacio. 1991. "Democratic Socialism in Comparative Perspective." *Comparative Politics* 23 (4): 439–58.

Walter, André. 2019. "A Race to the Middle: The Politics of Interstate Cost Distribution and Welfare State Expansion." *Journal of Politics* 81 (3): 952–67. doi: 10.1086/703132.

Walter, Stefanie. 2010. "Globalization and the Welfare State: Testing the Microfoundations of the Compensation Hypothesis." *International Studies Quarterly* 54 (2): 403–426.

Wang, Peng, and Altanbulag Altanbulag. 2022. "A Concern for Eco-Social Sustainability: Background, Concept, Values, and Perspectives of Eco-Social Work." *Cogent Social Sciences* 8 (1). doi: 10.1080/23311886.2022.2093035.

Warleigh, Alex. 2000. "The Hustle: Citizenship Practice, NGOs and 'Policy Coalitions' in the European Union—The Cases of Auto Oil, Drinking Water and Unit Pricing." *Journal of European Public Policy* 7 (2): 229–43. doi: 10.1080/135017600343179.

Warren, Samuel D., and Louis D. Brandeis. 1890. "The Right to Privacy." *Harvard Law Review* 4 (5): 193–220.

White, Stuart. 1997. "Liberal Equality, Exploitation, and the Case for an Unconditional Basic Income." *International Political Science Review* 45 (2): 312–26.

Widerquist, Karl. 2019. "Three Waves of Basic Income Support." In *The Palgrave International Handbook of Basic Income*, edited by Malcolm Torry, 31–44. Cham: Palgrave Macmillan.

Williams, Christopher, and John Ishiyama. 2018. "Responding to the Left: The Effect of Far-Left Parties on Mainstream Party Euroskepticism." *Journal of Elections, Public Opinion and Parties* 28 (4): 443–66. doi: 10.1080/17457289.2018.1434783.

Williams, David. 2018. "Liberalism, Colonialism and Liberal Imperialism." *East Central Europe* 45 (1): 94–118.

Wissenburg, Marcel. 2006. "Liberalism." In *Political Theory and the Ecological Challenge*, edited by Andrew Dobson and Robyn Eckersley, 20–34. Cambridge: Cambridge University Press.

Wolkenstein, Fabio. 2020. "The Social Democratic Case Against the EU." *Journal of European Public Policy* 27 (9): 1349–367.

———. 2023. "Christian Europe Redux." *JCMS: Journal of Common Market Studies* 61 (3): 636–52. doi: 10.1111/jcms.13400.

Yang, Andrew. 2018. *The War on Normal People: The Truth about America's Disappearing Jobs and Why Universal Basic Income Is Our Future*. New York: Hachette.

Ypi, Lea. 2014. "On Revolution in Kant and Marx." *Political Theory* 42 (3): 262–87.

Zeit Online. 2013. "CSU plant härteren Kurs gegenüber Armutsmigranten." Accessed 19.11.2023, https://www.zeit.de/politik/deutschland/2013-12/csu-einwanderer-bulgarien-eu.

Zelleke, Almaz. 2008. "Institutionalizing the Universal Caretaker Through a Basic Income?" *Basic Income Studies* 3 (3). doi: 10.2202/1932-0183.1133.

Zielonka, Jan. 2023. "Social Democracy Versus the Nativist Right." Accessed 14.11.2023, https://www.socialeurope.eu/social-democracy-versus-the-nativist-right.

Zimmerman, Michael E. 2003. "On Reconciling Progressivism and Environmentalism." In *Explorations in Environmental Political Theory: Thinking About What We Value*, edited by Joel Jay Kassiola, 149–77. New York: Routledge.

Zohlnhöfer, Reimut. 2015. "Globalisierung." In *Handbuch Policy-Forschung*, edited by Georg Wenzelburger and Reimut Zohlnhöfer, 199–224. Wiesbaden: Springer VS.

Zürn, Michael, and Pieter De Wilde. 2016. "Debating Globalization: Cosmopolitanism and Communitarianism as Political Ideologies." In *Journal of Political Ideologies*: Routledge.

Zutlevics, Tamara L. 2001. "Libertarianism and Personal Autonomy." *The Southern Journal of Philosophy* 39 (3): 461–71.

Index

For most concepts, this index lists all pages on which they occur. For some concepts that are ubiquitous throughout all parts of the book (e.g., ideologies, UBI), only key pages (e.g., definitions or dedicated discussions) are referenced. Page references for figures are italicised.